For Ely Calil
who thought this book must be written

A HOUSE OF MANY MANSIONS

The History of Lebanon
Reconsidered

KAMAL SALIBI

University of California Press
Berkeley   Los Angeles   London

Published by
University of California Press
Berkeley and Los Angeles, California
University of California Press, Ltd.
London, England

Library of Congress Cataloguing in Publication Data.

Salibi, Kamal S. (Kamal Suleiman), 1929–
  A house of many mansions.

  Bibliography: p.
  Includes index.
  1. Lebanon—History. I. Title.
DS80.9.S26   1988   956.92   88-20679
ISBN 0-520-07196-4 (alk. paper)

  3   4   5   6   7   8   9   10

Printed in the United States.

The paper used in this publication meets the minimum
requirements of American National Standard for Information
Sciences—Permanence of Paper for Printed Library Materials,
ANSI Z39.48–1984. ∞

Contents

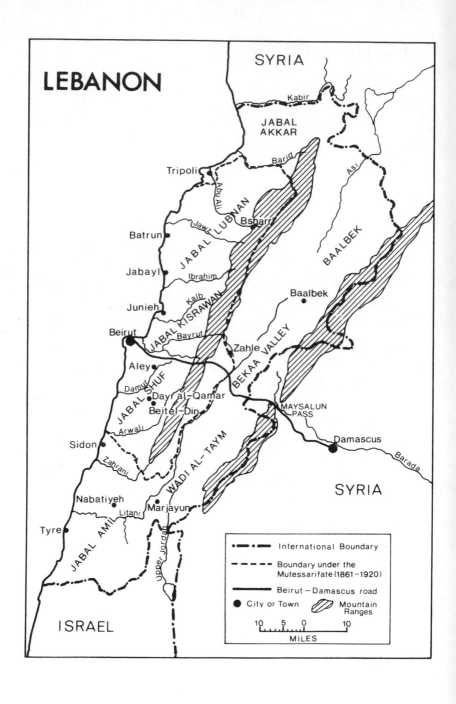

Acknowledgements

This book was written under the auspices of the Lebanese Studies Foundation, as part of a series of studies geared towards the reconstruction of Lebanon. The work on it was made possible by the generous support of Ely Calil, who took a sustained interest in the research and read and commented on most of the chapters in first draft as they were completed.

Ihsan Abbas, Ralph Crow, Mustafa Hiyari, Abbas Kelidar, Wolfgang Koehler and Abdul-Rahim Abu Husayn also went through various chapters of the the first draft critically, and made valuable suggestions. Albert Hourani read the whole of the completed work, and recommended important revisions. The Centre for Lebanese Studies enabled me to be in England while the book was in the process of publication. Josephine Zananiri edited the text of the different chapters more than once, and she and Jonathan Livingstone were extremely helpful in preparing the book to go to press.

While I naturally hold myself alone responsible for everything that is said in this book, I owe all these friends and colleagues a debt of gratitude which I feel honoured to acknowledge.

Kamal Salibi

February 1988

Introduction

Since 1975, Lebanon has stood out in the world as a supreme example of political and social disorganization. Yet its people boast of being the most highly motivated and advanced among the Arabs; indeed, there are many Arabs and non-Arabs who would agree that they are so. Lebanese society, moreover, once enjoyed the reputation for liberalism and tolerance, being traditional rather than zealous or fanatical in its attitude towards religion and political ideology, and more interested in the enjoyable and practical aspects of life. Yet, beginning in 1975, the Christian and Muslim Lebanese have been locked in an armed conflict in which each side has decimated the other; repeated clashes have occurred even between the different sects and political parties on each side; and general destruction and impoverishment has befallen the country as a result of the continuing strife.

Officially, the Lebanese Republic still exists within its internationally recognized borders, and so does the state, with its governmental machinery intact. The state, however, has long ceased to exercise sovereign control over its national territory. There remains an administrative bureaucracy which continues to provide a cover of legitimacy to public and private transactions, as well as a minimum of public services of steadily deteriorating quality. Otherwise, particularly where security is concerned, citizens are left to fend for themselves. In different parts of the country, different Christian or Muslim gangs are in control, some organized and efficient enough to assume the more important functions of the state and maintain the minimum level of public order; others so inefficient, divided and disorganized that they remain a terror, most of all, to the very constituencies whose vital interests they claim to represent.

In all but name, Lebanon today is a non-country. Yet, paradoxically, there has not been a time when the Muslims and Christians of Lebanon have exhibited, on the whole, a keener consciousness of common identity, albeit with somewhat different nuances. They did not in 1920, when the country was first established as a state under French mandate, enthusiastically accepted by the Christians, but adamantly rejected by the Muslims; nor did they really in 1943, when the Lebanese Republic gained its independence on the basis of a polite fiction of national unity among its people. In 1958, the Muslim and Christian Lebanese were at each other's throats for six months over the issue of pan-Arab unity under the leadership of President Nasser of Egypt, who was at the time president of the short-lived United Arab Republic of Egypt and Syria (1958–61). The deep rift between the two groups, whereby the Christians identified themselves in terms of Lebanese particularism and the Muslims with pan-Arabism, continued during the years that followed, breaking out into open conflict again over yet another crucial issue: the refusal or acceptance of the free right of the Palestinian revolution to operate in Lebanon and from Lebanon, as a state within the state. Compounded by a host of other thorny issues, it was this last conflict that ultimately led to the outbreak of the civil war in the country – a war which continues today.

The people of Lebanon remain as divided as ever; the differences among them have come to be reflected geographically by the effective cantonization of their country, and by massive population movements between the Christian and Muslim areas which have hardened the lines of division.

In the continuing national quarrel, however, the central issue is no longer the question of the Lebanese national allegiance, but the terms of the political settlement which all the sides to the conflict, certainly at the popular level, generally desire. Disgraced and abandoned by the world, it is possible that the Lebanese are finally beginning to discover themselves. There is a noticeable consensus among all but the more committed extremists today that all are Lebanese, sharing the same national identity, regardless of other, secondary, group affiliations and loyalties. Yet, before this emerging consciousness of common identity can be translated into a new national order, there are countless hurdles to be overcome. What are these hurdles, real or imagined, and how can they best be approached?

With this broad question in the background, the present book will address itself to a particular aspect of the Lebanese problem. Since the emergence of Lebanon as a state in 1920, the Christian and Muslim Lebanese have been in fundamental disagreement over the historicity of their country: the Christians by and large affirming it, and the Muslims denying it. Because the Christians, in the Lebanese state, have been at the helm from the very start, it fell to them to come forward with historical visions of Lebanon which provide a theoretical basis for a generally acceptable concept of Lebanese nationality. However, none of their attempts have had much success. From the Muslim side, there has been an insistence that whatever history Lebanon can claim for itself is in reality part of a broader Arab history. Yet the notion of what really constitutes Arab history remains confused by the fundamental historical association between Arabism and Islam. In the chapters that follow, the diametrically opposed Christian and Muslim theories of Lebanese history underlying the ongoing political conflict in the country will be critically assessed to determine why none have yet managed to gain general acceptance.

The present book, in short, is not a history of Lebanon, but a critical study of different views of Lebanese history. For this reason, the chronological order of the historical events and developments which form the substance of the subject cannot be strictly observed. Backward and forward leaps between periods which can be centuries apart are bound to be involved, and this may occasionally confuse the reader. Therefore, a preliminary survey of the historical background of the emergence of modern Lebanon, marking the main stages for subsequent reference, is included at this point.

First, however, something must be said about the geography of Lebanon (for more detail regarding the general historical geography of the area, see chapter 3). The country today comprises a territory of just over 10,000 square kilometres, extending about 200 kilometres along the eastern Mediterranean coast and bordered from the north and east by Syria, and from the south by Israel. Apart from the coastal cities (including the capital, Beirut) and some narrow stretches of coastal plain, the Lebanese territory consists mostly of mountain and hill country: the Lebanon; the western flanks of the Anti-Lebanon; and the highlands of upper Galilee which are commonly called Jabal Amil. Between the ranges of the Lebanon and the Anti-Lebanon lies the alluvial valley of the Bekaa (*al-Biqa'*) and, in the south, the adjoining valley of Wadi al-Taym. The Lebanese population is composed of different religious communities, some Christian (mainly Maronite, Greek Orthodox, and Greek Catholic), others Islamic (Sunnite Muslim, Shiite Muslim and Druze). Apart from the Armenians of Lebanon, who are relative newcomers to the country, all the Lebanese communities – Christian and Muslim – have historically spoken Arabic, and shared at the traditional level in what may be described in common language as an Arab way of life.

In antiquity, a seafaring people called the Phoenicians established a number of flourishing city-states along the stretch of the eastern Mediterranean coast between the towns of Latakia and Acre, mostly in the areas which are today Lebanese territory. The Phoenicians, in their time, spoke a dialect of a Semitic language called Canaanite, not unlike Biblical Hebrew, which they wrote in alphabetical script. However, they wrote very little about themselves. Because of the paucity of records, the history of the Phoenician city-states cannot be properly reconstructed. Their independence, however, is known to have ended in the sixth century BC with the Persian conquest of geographical Syria. Two centuries later came the destruction of the Persian empire by Alexander the Great; and after the death of Alexander and the division of his empire among his generals, the territory of present-day Lebanon became part of the Hellenistic Seleucid kingdom which comprised most of Syria and had its capital at Antioch (today in Turkey). In the first century BC came the Roman conquest, and the present Lebanese territory became part of the Roman province of Syria, in a Roman empire which comprised the whole Mediterranean world. Roman rule in Syria continued until the Arab conquest of the seventh century AD. After the fourth century, however, the capital of the Roman empire was transferred from Rome to Byzantium, or Constantinople (today Istanbul), on the Bosphorus, sometimes called New Rome. In Italy, Old Rome was subsequently re-established as the capital of a western Roman empire which was conquered and destroyed by the Ostrogoths in AD 476, leaving only the eastern Roman empire of Byzantium to survive. For this reason, historians frequently refer to the late Roman empire as being Byzantine, the two terms for the period being synonymous.

Apart from the fact that the early Roman empire had its capital in Rome, while the late Roman or Byzantine empire was centred in Constantinople, the Byzantine empire, unlike the pagan early Roman empire, was Christian from the very beginning. Moreover, Byzantium made a point of dictating exactly what constituted correct, or 'orthodox' Christian belief. This Byzantine (and hence Roman) definition of Christian orthodoxy was first advanced by the Council of Nicea (the First Ecumenical Council) in 325, then further redefined by subsequent councils. While the confession of Christian faith formulated at Nicea (called the Nicene Creed) did manage in time to gain general

Christian acceptance, none of the subsequent redefinitions of Christian orthodoxy pleased everybody. In 451, for example, the Fourth Council (that of Chalcedon) ruled that Chistians must confess two Natures in Christ: one divine; the other human. The Copts of Egypt, the Gregorians of Armenia and the Jacobites in Syria (so called after Jacob Baradeus, who first organized them as a church) preferred to regard Christ as being essentially God, and both Rome and Byzantium came to regard them as Monophysite, or 'One Nature' heretics. In 680, the Sixth Council (the Third of Constantinople) proceeded further to assert that Christ had not only two natures, but also two energies and two wills. Those who refused to accept this ruling were condemned as Monothelite, or 'One Will' heresiarchs. The outcome was that Christianity, in Byzantine Syria, came to consist of different sects: some followed Byzantine orthodoxy and were called Melchites (usually taken to mean the 'king's men', with reference to the Byzantine emperor); while others adhered to the Monophysite, Monothelite or other 'heterodox' confessions of the Christian faith.

Syria was still under Roman – or Byzantine – rule when the Prophet Muhammad began to preach Islam in AD 610 in Mecca, in the west Arabian land of the Hijaz. During his lifetime, Muhammad unified the tribes of Arabia under his command beneath the banner of Islam. Two years following his death in 632, the conquest of Syria commenced under the caliphs of Medina who were his immediate successors, and the last Byzantine forces withdrew across the Taurus mountains into Anatolia in 641. From that time, and until 1918, Syria, including today's Lebanon, formed part of the territory of a succession of Islamic empires ruled by caliphs or by sultans, except for the period between 1098 and 1291 – that of the Crusades – when the coastal and northern parts of the Syrian territory fell under 'Frankish' or 'Latin' (i.e. Western Christian) domination. Also, prior to the Crusades, the Byzantines in 969 reconquered Antioch, in northern Syria, on the lower course of the Orontes river, which they held until 1085, maintaining from there sporadic control over other parts of the Orontes valley from 976 until about 1070.

Beginning with the seventh century, the Islamic empires which controlled or claimed control of the whole of geographical Syria, or different parts of it, were the following:

1 The Umayyad caliphate (661–750), which had its capital in Damascus, and whose empire grew to extend from the borders of India and Central Asia, across North Africa, to the shores of the Atlantic, and to the inclusion of the Iberian Peninsula (today Spain and Portugal).

2 The Abbasid caliphate (750–1258), which established its capital in Baghdad, and whose empire, at its greatest extent, included the whole of the former Umayyad empire except Spain and Morocco. After 820, and more so after 861, the Abbasid empire began to disintegrate, as the central authority of the caliphs in Baghdad weakened, sometimes almost to the point of extinction. This resulted in different principalities and kingdoms sprouting throughout its territory. Among these were the so-called Tulunid and Ikhshidid states which were successively established in Egypt and controlled the southern parts of Syria between 868 and 969, and the Hamdanid and Mirdasid principalities which succeeded one another in the control of the northern parts of Syria between 845 and 1070.

3 The Fatimid caliphate (909–1171), which originally established its capital at Mahdiyya in Tunisia, before moving it to Cairo in 973, shortly after the Fatimid conquest of Egypt and their defeat of the Ikhshidids (969). While the Abbasid caliphate in Baghdad stood for Sunnite, or orthodox Islam (see below), the Fatimid stood for a heterodox interpretation of Islam – that of the Shiite sect of the Ismailis, headed at the present time by the Agha Khans. The Fatimids conquered Egypt in 969, where they founded the city of Cairo as their capital. Having moved to Cairo in 973, they extended their control over Syria, including present-day Lebanon, and the Mirdasids of

Aleppo, certainly after 1015, recognized their overlordship.

4 The Seljuk sultanate (1058–1157), with its capital in the Persian city of Isfahan. The Seljuks were originally the chiefs of the Turkish Oghuz tribes of Transoxania, who conquered Persia between 1037 and 1044 and established for themselves a kingdom there, with Ispahan as their capital. As Sunnite Muslims, they came to the assistance of the Abbasid caliph of Baghdad in 1055, then again in 1058, when he was facing serious difficulties in his capital. In return, the caliph recognized the Seljuk ruler in Ispahan as sultan (literally, 'sovereign') of the universal State of Islam, handing over to him the temporal authority which, in theory, had resided until then with the caliphs. In 1070, Turkish tribal leaders conquered Syria and wrested its territory from the Fatimids; the Seljuks occupied Syria in 1086, and a Seljuk viceroy established himself in Aleppo. After the death of this viceroy in 1095, his two sons divided Syria between them, one establishing himself in Aleppo, the other in Damascus. In Damascus, as in Aleppo, what followed was the rule of different dynasties of atabegs (roughly, the equivalent of the mayors of the palace in the Frankish kingdom of the Merovingians), who paid lip service to the Seljuk sultan in Ispahan.

5 The Ayyubid sultanate (1183–1250), with its capital in Cairo. The founder of this sultanate was Saladin (Salah al-Din ibn Ayyub), a Kurdish army officer who was sent by the ruler of Damascus in 1169 to Egypt, where he overthrew the last Fatimid caliph two years later and replaced him in power. In 1174, Saladin occupied Damascus, then proceeded to take over Aleppo in 1183, after which he was generally recognized as sultan. Subsequently, Saladin distinguished himself as the paramount hero of the Islamic holy war against the Crusaders in Syria. After his death in 1193, in Damascus, his sons and successors quarrelled among themselves; but his brother al-Adil (to the Crusaders, Saphadin) finally managed to succeed him as sultan in Cairo in 1200, where the rule of his descendants continued until 1250. Meanwhile, in Syria, different members of the Ayyubid family ruled different regions, while recognizing

the suzerainty of the Ayyubid sultan in Cairo. After the death of the last of these sultans, Ayyubid rule in Syria continued in its different branches until 1259.

6 The Mamluk sultanate (1261–1517), with its capital also in Cairo. The Mamluks who first took over power in Egypt in 1250 were originally Turkish slaves whom the last Ayyubid sultan had purchased and trained as soldiers to form the crack regiment of his army. After the death of this sultan in 1250, one of his leading Mamluks replaced him in power. Meanwhile, in 1258, the Mongols, who had shortly before established a state for themselves in Persia, conquered Baghdad, where they disestablished the Abbasid caliphate; they immediately swept through the Muslim-held parts of Syria, where they put an end to Ayyubid rule. In 1260, the Mamluks arrived from Egypt to defeat the Mongols in Syria, putting them to flight and establishing their own rule. In the following year, an Abbasid caliphate with nominal powers was re-established in Cairo, and the Mamluk rulers, in theory as the associates of this new line of Abbasid caliphs, began to call themselves sultans. One of them, Qalawun (1279–90), became the founder of a Mamluk dynasty which lasted until 1382. He also started the practice of recruiting Circassians from the Caucasus region, rather than Turks, as Mamluks. In 1382, one of these Circassian Mamluks, Barquq (1382–99), overthrew the last of Qalawun's descendants and became the first of a succession of Circassian Mamluk sultans who continued to rule Syria until 1516, and Egypt until 1517.

7 The Ottoman sultanate (1379–1922) established its capital first in Edirne (or Adrianople), then after 1453 in Istanbul. From small beginnings as a Turkish principality in western Anatolia, the Ottoman state (named after its founder) embarked on a phenomenal career of territorial expansion, first at the expense of the Byzantine and Serbian states in the Balkans, then at the expense of other Turkish principalities in Anatolia. In 1379, following their conquest of the Serbian kingdom, the rulers of the Ottoman dynasty assumed the title of sultan. In 1516 they turned southwards to conquer Syria from the Mamluks; then they

conquered Egypt, ending the Mamluk sultanate in Cairo in 1517. At the height of their power, the Ottoman sultans, in the Arab world, controlled Iraq and large parts of Arabia as well as Syria and Egypt, and their suzerainty was also recognized in all of North Africa except Morocco. Twice, in 1524, then again in 1683, their triumphant forces stood at the gates of Vienna. Having conquered Egypt, the Ottomans put an end to the Abbasid caliphate in Cairo and carried away its insignia (which included the Prophet's mantle) to Istanbul. This gave them a claim to the caliphate which they sometimes chose to emphasize. In 1918, the Ottoman state, which had sided with the Central Powers in the first world war, was defeated by the Allies and lost its Arab lands. Subsequently, the Ottoman sultanate in Istanbul was abolished by the Kemalist revolution, which transformed the Turkish remnants of the Ottoman empire into the Turkish Republic. A member of the Ottoman dynasty remained in Istanbul as caliph of Islam until 1924, when the institution of the caliphate was also abolished.

Just as Christianity, under the Byzantines, had come to exist in Syria in different sects, so did Islam. Since the death of the Prophet there had been a quarrel as to who could legitimately be the Imam, or paramount leader, of the Muslim community. Those who insisted that the Imamate must be restricted to the Prophet's family (Arabic *al al-bayt*) – namely his cousin Ali, who was married to his daughter Fatima, and their descendants – were called Shiites (Arabic *shi'ah*, literally 'party', or 'faction'). Ali was actually elected as caliph, or 'successor' to the Prophet (656–61), but only after three other caliphs had held office before him. Moreover, neither of Ali's two sons, Hasan and Husayn, were elected to succeed him. After his murder in 661, the caliphate became the preserve of two successive dynasties, the Umayyads and the Abbasids: the first unrelated to the Prophet, but merely belonging to the same Arab tribe; and the second claiming descent from the Prophet's uncle Abbas. The Shiites recognized neither the Umayyad caliphs, nor the Abbasids, as legitimate Imams.

Instead, they recognized different descendants of Ali as Imams, and therefore became divided into as many Shiite sects.

In Syria, the most important of these sects, historically, were two. Firstly, the Sevener or Ismaili Shiites, who regarded the Imamate as the preserve of the descendants of Ali's son Husayn, and the seventh Imam as being a descendant of Husayn's called Ismail. They maintained that this Ismail went into *satr*, or 'hiding', so that his identity remained known to only a select group of his followers. Other 'hidden' Imams succeeded Ismail, according to this sect, until one of them, called Ubaydallah, emerged from his 'hiding' in Tunisia and openly proclaimed himself to be *al-Mahdi*, the 'divinely guided' one. He became the founder of the Fatimid caliphate in Tunisia; and all his successors, who later moved their capital to Egypt, ruled as Ismaili Imams. All Ismailis regarded their Imams as infallible, and as having attributes of divinity which set them apart from ordinary humanity. One of the Fatimid caliphs, al-Hakim (996–1121), was regarded by some Ismailis to be an Imam with a unique attribute: the ultimate human manifestation of the unity of God. This special Ismaili preaching was only successful in Syria, where its followers came to be known as the Druzes.

The second Shiite sect of historical importance in Syria was that of the Twelver or Imami Shiites, who recognized a succession of twelve Imams: Ali, his two sons Hasan and Husayn in succession, followed by nine who were descendants of Husayn. According to the ·Twelver Shiites, the seventh Imam was not Ismail, but his younger brother Musa, as Ismail had died before his father, the sixth Imam, and had not gone into 'hiding', as his followers believed. The Twelver Shiites, moreover, maintained that the twelfth Imam, Muhammad al-Mahdi, went in 874 or 879 into a cosmic *ghaybah*, or 'absence', from which he would ultimately return to fill the world with justice in place of the prevailing iniquity. While the Ismailis believed it to be their duty, when their Imams happened to be in hiding, to prepare the way for their re-emergence into the open by political activism, the Twelver Shiites maintained that nothing could be humanly done to hasten the return of the twelfth Imam from his *ghaybah*, except hope and prayer. As long as the Imam remained 'absent', no true justice in the world was possible, and all Islamic rule was illegitimate. The distinction, however, could be made between relative and absolute injustice. The first could be tolerated; only the second had to be actively opposed.

Apart from the Ismailis, the Twelver Shiites, and the Druzes who were originally Ismailis, another Shiite sect whose following, historically, has been mainly limited to Syria is that of the Nusayris, also called the Alouites (following the French spelling). About the origins of this particular sect, however, which holds Ali in special veneration, nothing is known for certain.

As these and other Shiite sects were proliferating in the Islamic world, the Abbasid caliphate in Baghdad established the principles of what it considered Islamic orthodoxy, starting with the reign of the caliph al-Mutawakkil (847–61). Islam being a juridical religion, four existing schools of Islamic jurisprudence – the Hanifite, the Shafiite, the Malikite and the Hanbalite – were recognized, alone, as being valid. Those who accepted the state ruling of what was Islamically orthodox came to be called the Sunnites, meaning followers of the *Sunnah*, or the tradition of the Prophet and his immediate successors. Other Muslims were regarded as *firaq*, or 'sects' – all of them reprehensible, albeit to varying degrees.

It is against this background of general Islamic history that one can trace the broad lines of the developments which culminated in the emergence of modern Lebanon. One can begin to discern these lines in the eleventh century, when Syria was mostly under Fatimid rule, while the Byzantines, from their Syrian base in Antioch, maintained a presence in the valley of the Orontes. It was at that time that the Druzes first emerged as a special sect in different parts of Syria – among others, in the southern parts of Mount Lebanon and some adjacent regions, such as Wadi al-Taym, in the southern parts of the Bekaa valley.

Meanwhile, the Syrian Christian sect of the Maronites became principally concentrated in northern Lebanon. Originally, most of these Maronites had inhabited the valley of the Orontes, but they had always been on poor terms with the Byzantine church and its Syrian followers, the Melchites. Their Christian and Muslim contemporaries considered them to be Monothelites – a charge which their own historians, since the fifteenth century, have consistently denied. The available evidence indicates that the final exodus of the Maronites into Mount Lebanon occurred at some point between the tenth and eleventh centuries. This was the time when the Byzantines, from their base in Antioch, maintained sporadic control over the Orontes valley, the original Maronite homeland.

When the Crusaders arrived in Syria at the end of the eleventh century, the main body of the Maronites in northern Mount Lebanon rallied around them; later, in about 1180, the Maronite church entered into a formal union with Rome which continues to the present time. Meanwhile, in southern Mount Lebanon, the Druzes of the Gharb region, which overlooks Beirut, rallied around the Sunnite Muslim atabegs of Damascus. For this period, and also for the Mamluk period that followed, the history of the Druzes is far better documented than that of the Maronites. Under the Mamluks, the Druze chieftains of the Gharb called the Buhturs, or the Tanukhs, were enrolled as cavalry officers in a special regiment of the Mamluk army, and continued to serve the Mamluk state to the very end. Occasionally, members of this family were appointed to govern Beirut, sometimes along with Sidon. After 1291 the winter residence of the Buhturs was established in Beirut, while different branches of the family maintained summer residence in different villages of the Gharb – notably in Abey, Ainab and Aramun. In Abey, the ruins of the old Buhturid palace, and of other houses that belonged to the family, can still be seen.

Between the Maronite and Druze territory in Mount Lebanon, in the region of Kisrawan, the population consisted mainly of Twelver Shiites. Muslims of the same sect also inhabited the Baalbek region, in the Bekaa valley, and the highlands of upper Galilee (Jabal Amil), south of Mount Lebanon. But it was the presence of the Twelver Shiites in the strategic mountain region of Kisrawan, overlooking the coastal highway north of Beirut, which worried the staunchly Sunnite Mamluks. Between 1291 and 1305 three Mamluk expeditions were sent to subdue the Shiites in that area, the last of which was successful. Subsequently, the Mamluks brought Turkoman clans and settled them in the lower parts of Kisrawan to keep watch over the region and the coastal highway, and also to secure the mountain roads leading inland to Damascus. After 1382, the Turkomans of Kisrawan fell afoul of the Circassian Mamluk regime in Egypt, and regressed for a time into obscurity.

The coming of the Ottomans in 1516 changed the situation. In Kisrawan, the Turkomans re-emerged to local importance under a dynasty of chiefs called the Assafs (1516–93), who established themselves in the town of Ghazir. These Assafs, who were Sunnite Muslims, favoured the Maronites and appointed members of a Maronite Hubaysh family as their chief political agents. With the encouragement of the Assafs and their Hubaysh stewards, Maronites from the northern regions of Mount Lebanon began to settle in Kisrawan. Among them were notables of a family called the Khazins who arrived in 1545 to settle in Balluna; others from a family called Gemayel, arrived the same year to settle in Bekfaya. Of these two families, the Khazins were to play the leading Maronite role in the politics of Mount Lebanon during the seventeenth and eighteenth centuries, maintaining a considerable import-ance thereafter. The Gemayels, on the other hand, only rose to political prominence in the present century, mainly in connection with the career of Pierre Gemayel – the founder of the Kataeb party in the Lebanese Republic, which leads the Christian side in the present civil war.

While the Assafs were governing Kisrawan, the utmost confusion reigned in the Druze country to the south, where the coming of the Ottomans had spelt the end of the hegemony of the house of Buhtur. Repeated Ottoman military expeditions were sent between 1523 and 1586 to the rugged region of the Shuf, to suppress local rebellions which were led by chieftains of the house of Maan. In about 1590, after the success of the last of these expeditions, a member of this family called Fakhr al-Din was accorded recognition as the local Ottoman governor. (Of the career of Fakhr al-Din Maan and his changing relations with the Ottomans, which ended in 1633 with his downfall, more will be said in due course.) Later, in 1667, a grandnephew of his, Ahmad Maan, was appointed to govern the Druze country with Kisrawan. Both Maanids, Fakhr al-Din as well as Ahmad, favoured the Maronites and encouraged them to immigrate into the Druze districts. After the death of Ahmad Maan in 1697, the government of the Druze country and Kisrawan passed to his Sunnite relatives, the Shihabs, who came from the Wadi al-Taym. The Shihabs, as a family, retained the government of these regions until 1841, by which time they were also governing the Maronite districts north of Kisrawan. The residence of the Maans and early Shihabs can still be seen in the Shuf, in the town of Dayr al-Qamar, while the magnificent palace of the second last of the Shihabs (Bashir II, 1788–1840), periodically restored, remains a tourist attraction in nearby Beit el-Din. From the last decades of the eighteenth century, the ruling branch of the Shihabs converted from Sunnite Islam to Christianity and became Maronites.

Relations between the Maronites and Druzes, which were already showing signs of deterioration under the later Shihabs, broke into open conflict in 1840, bringing about the downfall of the Shihab regime in Mount Lebanon the following year. An attempt to replace it with direct Ottoman rule met with no success. Thereupon, from 1843, the mountain was divided into two administrative units called kaymakamates: one for the Maronites; the other for the Druzes. But this system again did not work: in the Druze kaymakamate, for example, the majority of the population was Christian, and mostly Maronite, which gave rise to endless complications. Moreover, the nineteenth

century, particularly after 1840, was the period when
Mount Lebanon, along with the rest of Syria, was first
exposed to disturbing modern influences from the West; not
least among these was the invasion of the Syrian markets
by the industrial products of Europe, which played havoc
with the traditional economy of the country and led to
serious social tensions. These social tensions contributed to
a worsening of the situation in Mount Lebanon, where
outbreaks of warfare between Maronites and Druzes
gained in frequency, culminating in the events of 1860. In
that year, the Druzes in the Shuf and Wadi al-Taym,
reinforced by co-religionists from the Hawran region in
Syria, fell upon the local Christians and massacred large
numbers of them, the accepted estimate being about
11,000. This triggered off a wave of persecutions in other
parts of Syria, including the massacre of about 12,000
Christians in Damascus in one day. These disturbances
attracted the attention of the European powers, in particular
France, which as a leading Roman Catholic power had for a
long time considered itself the protector of the Maronites as
fellow Roman Catholics. The troubles in the Druze country
and in Damascus were hardly over when French forces
landed in Beirut, and entered the Shuf. Meanwhile, a
conference of representatives of the European powers that
had signed the Treaty of Paris following the Crimean War
(1856) – among them the Ottoman state, now a member of
the so-called Concert of Europe – was convened in Beirut
by French initiative to consider the reorganization of
Mount Lebanon. The outcome, the *Règlement Organique* of
1861 (revised in 1864), established Mount Lebanon as a
mutesarrifate, or privileged sanjak (administrative region)
of the Ottoman empire, internationally guaranteed, under
an Ottoman Christian governor called a Mutesarrif who
was appointed and sent from Istanbul with the approval of
the guaranteeing European powers.

The Mutesarrifate remained operative in Mount Lebanon
until 1915, shortly after the outbreak of the first world war
(1914–1918). It provided the mountain with orderly government, under which considerable advances were made in

social development. In the mountain, and more so in Beirut, this was the period of the Arabic cultural awakening, of which more will be said later. It was also the period when the first important migrations began from the Lebanese country-side to Beirut and other towns of the coast – migrations which were to accelerate and assume greater importance later on, accounting for much of the social and political character of present-day Lebanon (chapter 10).

After the collapse of the Ottoman empire in 1918 following its defeat in the war, the British and the French divided the Syrian provinces as mandates between them, with the present territory of Lebanon being part of the French mandate. In response to pressure from their Maronite friends, in 1920 the French annexed different parts of the former vilayets (or Ottoman provinces) of Beirut and Damascus to the territory of the old Lebanese Mutesarrifate, and so created the State of Greater Lebanon within the present frontiers. In 1926, the State of Greater Lebanon was reconstituted as the Lebanese Republic. In 1943, during the second world war, the French mandate over Lebanon was terminated, and the country became independent, and a founding member of the League of Arab States and the United Nations shortly after.

Having marked the main stages in the history relating to the emergence of modern Lebanon, against the back-ground of the general history of the Arab and Islamic world, we are in a better position to examine the various interpretations that have been given to this history by different Lebanese parties at different times. As will be observed in the last two chapters of this book, the present civil war in Lebanon is being fought between Lebanese groups flying different historical banners: the Lebanese particularist and Christian on one side; the Arab nationalist and Islamic – not to speak of the Sunnite, Shiite and Druze – on the other. If the various factions are to lay down their arms and live in peace and full co-operation as citizens of one country, the Lebanese will first have to reach a consensus on what makes of them a nation or political community, and this can only be achieved if they manage to agree on a common vision of their past.

Before the different theories of Lebanese history can be investigated, however, there are other matters to consider. How did Lebanon emerge as a state? What have been the endemic Lebanese problems, and why did they arise? What really are the Maronites, who came to wield such an influence on French decision making with respect to the creation of Greater Lebanon after the first world war? Why did some Lebanese communities support their policies, while others – most vehemently, the Muslims – opposed them? The first five chapters of this book will address themselves mainly to these questions, to provide proper perspective for the consideration of the problems relating to the historical interpretation of Lebanon in the later chapters.

1 How it all began

To create a country is one thing; to create a nationality is another. In the wake of the first world war, which ended with the destruction of the German, Austro-Hungarian, Russian and Ottoman empires, it was possible for the victorious Allies to redraw the political map of much of the world. In Europe, Germany and Austria-Hungary, defeated in the war, re-emerged as the German, Austrian and Hungarian republics. Meanwhile, the Bolshevik revolution was already beginning to transform the Russian empire into the Union of Soviet Socialist Republics. From European territories formerly German, Austro-Hungarian or Russian, new European states emerged. The overseas colonies of Germany, in Africa and elsewhere, were divided between Britain and France as mandates under licence from the newly organized League of Nations.

Meanwhile, the Ottoman empire, as a result of its defeat in the war, had virtually ceased to exist. The Turkish heartlands, successfully reclaimed from Allied occupation by the Kemalist revolution, were ultimately reconstituted as the Turkish Republic; but the Arab provinces in historical Mesopotamia and Syria were irretrievably lost, and subsequently divided between Britain and France, again as mandated territory, with the provision that they must be prepared as soon as possible for independence.

Here, as in Central and Eastern Europe, new states were formed, but with an important difference. In Europe, where nationalist thinking was already a firmly established tradition, the sense of separate nationality among the former subject peoples of the German, Austro-Hungarian and Russian empires was already in existence, and in most cases such clear and well-defined expectations were to be heeded in the formation of the new states. This was not the case with the Arab subjects of the Ottoman empire, where national consciousness, to the extent that it existed, was blurred and confounded by traditional loyalties of other kinds which were often in conflict with one another. The Allies felt they could ignore such rudimentary and confused national sentiments among the Arabs of their newly mandated territories as they set out to reorganize them into states, redrawing the political map of the Arab world in the manner which they thought suited them best.

By the spring of 1920 agreement had been reached between Britain and France at San Remo on how the former Arab territories of the defunct Ottoman empire would be divided between them. The principal considerations taken into account were oil and communications. During the course of the war, the British had gone to considerable trouble to occupy Mesopotamia. The onset of the war had brought home the supreme strategic importance of oil; the British already had command over the vast oil resources of Iran, and they were determined to prevent the Germans, who were major shareholders in the Turkish Petroleum Company, from gaining access to the proven Mesopotamian oil resources of Kirkuk. In 1916, an agreement negotiated between Mark Sykes on behalf of Britain, and François Georges-Picot on behalf of France (the so-called Sykes–Picot Agreement), had assigned the Vilayet (Ottoman province) of Mosul, in northern Mesopotamia, to the French, and the vilayets of Baghdad and Basra, in central and southern Mesopotamia, to the British. In Syria, France was to get the Vilayet of Aleppo and the northern parts of the Vilayets of Beirut and Damascus, leaving the southern parts of these two vilayets essentially to Britain, with the understanding that the Holy Land of Palestine would have an international status. During the last months of the war however the British, who already occupied much of Mesopotamia, took occupation of Palestine. Now, at San Remo, the wartime Sykes–Picot Agreement between the two sides was scrapped.

By the terms of the new agreement, France gave up her claim to the Vilayet of Mosul in return for a major share in the Turkish Petroleum Company, which had been confiscated by the Allies and reorganized as the Iraq Petroleum Company (IPC). Moreover, the older agreement had specified that France would have direct control over the coastal parts of the Vilayet of Aleppo and its share of the Vilayet of Beirut, but only a sphere of influence in inland Syria where an Arab state or states of independent status would be established. Under the new agreement, the French were to have a free hand in the whole area which they were to hold as a mandate under the League of Nations – a continuous stretch of territory extending from the Euphrates river to the Mediterranean coast. On the other hand, the British, in addition to keeping the whole of Mesopotamia as a mandate, were also to have the mandate over all the southern parts of the vilayets of Damascus and Beirut – a territory which they first called the Palestine east and west of the Jordan; then, more simply, Transjordan and Palestine. In effect, Britain came to control a stretch of north Arabian desert territory which secured the required contiguity between its Mesopotamian and Palestinian mandates, and an uninterrupted overland route all the way from the borders of Iran to the Mediterranean.

Apart from its agreement with France over the partition of the Arab provinces of the Ottoman empire, Britain had made promises during the war to other parties concerning the same area. In central Arabia, there was a standing British alliance with Abdul-Aziz Ibn Saud, the Wahhabi Emir of Riyad who was subsequently to become the founder of the kingdom of Saudi Arabia. Wahhabism was a movement of militant Islamic religious revival which had appeared in central Arabia in the middle decades of the eighteenth century, and the house of Saud had been politically associated with it since that time. In conflict with this British–Saudi alliance was the wartime alliance reached between Britain and Sharif Husayn, the Emir of Mecca, who enjoyed a special Arab and Islamic prestige as a recognized descendant of the Prophet, and whose family were called the Hashemites.

In return for leading an Arab revolt against the Ottomans, the Sharif had been promised recognition as the head of an Arab kingdom the exact nature of which was left undefined. The Sharif, however, was led to understand that it would include all of Mesopotamia; all but a negotiable strip of coastal Syria; and the whole of peninsular Arabia, except for the parts which were already established as British protectorates. While the British relations with Ibn Saud were maintained by the British government of India, those with the Sharif were initiated and pursued by the British Arab Bureau in Cairo. Meanwhile, the British Foreign Office, in close touch with the World Zionist Organization, had by 1917 formally committed itself to viewing with favour the establishment of a Jewish National Home in Palestine.

Naturally, it was impossible for Britain after the war to honour simultaneously all these conflicting commitments fully. The need to reach a settlement with France over the area was most pressing, and this was taken care of by the San Remo agreement. During the last months of the war, as the British drove the Ottoman forces out of Syria, with the forces of Sharif Husayn's Arab Revolt protecting their right flank, the Sharif's third and most popular son, Faysal, was allowed to enter Damascus and establish an Arab government on behalf of his father in that ancient Arab capital. As the Allies met at San Remo to redraw the map of the Arab world, Sharif Faysal was proclaimed King of Syria, with a view to place Britain and France before an accomplished fact. Once the San Remo agreement had been concluded, however, the French, already in occupation of Beirut, made a show of trying to reach an accommodation with King Faysal; they then crushed his forces at

Maysalun, outside Damascus, forcing him to abandon his short-lived Syrian kingdom. To compensate their gallant wartime ally for his loss, the British created another Arab kingdom for him out of the old Ottoman vilayets of Mesopotamia, which now became the kingdom of Iraq.

The British wartime commitment to facilitate the establishment of a Jewish National Home in the Palestine west of the Jordan, which again received high priority, was formalized in 1920 and included as a special article in the statutes of the British mandate for Palestine, as registered in the League of Nations. For the Palestine east of the Jordan, or Transjordan, a special administrative arrangement was soon made. In 1916, when Sharif Husayn solemnly declared the start of the Arab Revolt against the Turks in Mecca, he also proclaimed himself king of the Arabs, and the British actually recognized him as king of the Hijaz, which was the furthest they felt they could go at the time. After the war, however, Ibn Saud, with his Wahhabi forces, began to attack the Hijaz, and completed its conquest by putting an end to Sharifian rule there in 1925.

In the earlier stages of the Saudi–Sharifian conflict, the Sharifian forces, led by the Sharif's second son Abdallah, suffered a serious defeat in battle. Sharif Abdullah thereupon left the Hijaz in 1921 and arrived in Transjordan, where the British soon recognized him as the sovereign emir. With British military help, Abdullah succeeded in repelling Wahhabi attempts to extend the Saudi domain northwards in the direction of Syria, thereby securing the extension of Transjordan eastwards continuously to the border of Iraq. In the south, Abdullah's Transjordanian emirate extended beyond the borders of the old Ottoman Vilayet of Damascus to reach the Red Sea at the strategic Gulf of Aqaba, and so include the northernmost parts of what had formerly been the Ottoman Vilayet of the Hijaz. In the east, the border of the emirate, in the Jordan valley, set the limits beyond which the projected Jewish National Home in Palestine could not extend.

The British at the time knew what they wanted, and

they got it: control over the oilfields of Iraq; unimpeded access from there to the Mediterranean; control of the Red Sea and the Persian Gulf (which were the two vital maritime highways leading to the Indian Ocean). To secure their interests, they naturally preferred to deal with parties in the area, or concerned with the area, who also knew what they wanted, and who were willing to make realistic accommodations to achieve their ends. During the war, the British had made a point of encouraging Arab nationalist activity in Syria against the Ottomans; and it was partly through British intermediaries that the Arab nationalists in Syria were put in touch with Sharif Husayn and his sons, which subsequently gave the Sharifian revolt in the Hijaz the extra dimension it needed to gain recognition as a true Arab Revolt. After the war, however, it became clear to the British that the claims of Arab nationalism were most urgently pressed either by romantic dreamers who were unwilling to be taught that politics was the art of the possible, or by unprincipled schemers who were out to secure personal rather than national interests. In either case, the nationalist claims, it was felt, where they threatened to embarrass British interests, could be discounted at negligible cost.

However, there remained Britain's wartime Arab allies to deal with. In the Hijaz, King Husayn was demanding more than the British were prepared to give. He wanted to be recognized as king of all the Arabs; considered himself the rightful claimant of the caliphate of Islam; and was unwilling to recognize the arrangements which the Allies were determined to introduce to the area in accordance with the San Remo agreement. More than that, he was adamant in refusing to recognize the Jewish claims in Palestine, as approved by the British. His two sons, Abdullah and Faysal, took the more realistic view; so did his great rival in Arabia, Ibn Saud. Those were practical men who were willing to give and take, and settle for what was ultimately achievable in given circumstances. In the arrangements which the British made in the parts of the area allotted to them, or where they already wielded dominant influence, all three were readily accommodated.

In their own mandated territories, which they called the Levant, the French took the same attitude as the British: they were willing to attend to reasoned and concrete demands by parties who knew what they wanted, but had no patience for the claims and clamours of those who did not. In Mount Lebanon and the adjacent parts of the old Vilayet of Beirut, the Maronites – a Christian communion with a long tradition of union with the Roman Catholic church in Europe – were one party whose demands the French were prepared to listen to. Of all the Arabs, barring only individuals or politically experienced princely dynasties, they appeared to be the only people who knew precisely what they wanted: in their case, as they put it, a 'Greater Lebanon' under their paramount control, separate, distinct and independent from the rest of Syria. Behind them, the Maronites had a rich and eventful past which will be reviewed as a separate story in due course.

In 1861, with the help of France, they had already secured a special political status for their historical homeland of Mount Lebanon as a mutesarrifate, or privileged sanjak (administrative region), within the Ottoman system, under an international guaranty. Since the turn of the century, however, the Maronites had pressed for the extension of this small Lebanese territory to what they argued were its natural and historical boundaries: it would then include the coastal towns of Tripoli, Beirut, Sidon and Tyre and their respective hinterlands, which belonged to the Vilayet of Beirut; and the fertile valley of the Bekaa (the four Kazas, or administrtative districts, of Baalbek, the Bekaa, Rashayya and Hasbayya), which belonged to the Vilayet of Damascus. According to the Maronite argument, this 'Greater Lebanon' had always had a special social and historical character, different from that of its surroundings, which made it necessary and indeed imperative for France to help establish it as an independent state.

While France had strong sympathies for the Maronites, the French government did not support their demands without reserve. In Mount Lebanon, the Maronites had formed a clear majority of the population. In a 'Greater Lebanon', they were bound to be outnumbered by the Muslims of the coastal towns and their hinterlands, and by those of the Bekaa valley; and all the Christian communities together, in a 'Greater Lebanon', could at best amount to a bare majority. The Maronites, however, were insistent in their demands. Their secular and clerical leaders had pressed for them during the war years among the Allied powers, not excluding the United States. After the war, the same leaders, headed by the Maronite patriarch Elias Hoyek in person, pursued this course at the Paris Peace Conference; and in the end the French yielded. On 1 September 1920 – barely four months after the conclusion of the San Remo agreement; barely two months after the flight of King Faysal and his Arab government from Damascus – General Henri Gouraud, from the porch of his official residence as French High Commissioner in Beirut, proclaimed the birth of the State of Greater Lebanon, with Beirut as its capital. The flag of this new Lebanon was to be none other than the French tricolour itself, with a cedar tree - now hailed as the glorious symbol of the ancient country since Biblical times – featuring on the central white.

Following the establishment of the State of Greater Lebanon, the French turned to deal with the rest of their mandated territory in the Levant, where they were at a loss what to do. In the case of Lebanon, the Maronites had indicated precisely what they wanted. Elsewhere, no community seemed willing to speak its mind unequivocally, which left the French to their own devices. To begin with, in addition to Lebanon, they established four Syrian states: two of them regional, which were the State of Aleppo and the State of Damascus; and two of them ethno-religious, which were the State of the Alouites and the State of Jebel Druze. In response to strong nationalist demands, the states of Aleppo and Damascus were subsequently merged to form the State of Syria, later reconstituted as the Syrian Republic, to which Jebel Druze and the Alouite country were ultimately annexed. Meanwhile, on 23 May 1926, the State of Greater Lebanon received a Constitution which transformed it into the Lebanese Republic.

Thus the two sister republics came into being, Lebanon and Syria; both under French mandate, sharing the same currency and customs services, but flying different flags, and run by separate native administrations under one French High Commissioner residing in Beirut. Before long, each of the two sister countries had its own national anthem. But are administrative bureaucracies, flags and national anthems sufficient to make a true nation-state out of a given territory and the people who inhabit it? What about the question of nationality?

To the Maronites and many other Christians in Lebanon, there were no doubts about the matter. The Lebanese were Lebanese, and the Syrians were Syrians, just as the Iraqis were Iraqi, the Palestinians Palestinian, and the Transjordanians Transjordanian. If the Syrians, Iraqis, Palestinians or Transjordanians preferred to identify themselves as something else, such as Arabs united by one nationality, they were free to do so; but the Lebanese remained Lebanese, regardless of the extent to which the outside world might choose to classify them as Arabs, because their language happened to be Arabic. Theirs, it was claimed, was the heritage of ancient Phoenicia, which antedated the heritage they had come to share with the Arabs by thousands of years. Theirs, it was further claimed, was the broader Mediterranean heritage which they had once shared with Greece and Rome, and which they now shared with Western Europe. They also had a long tradition of proud mountain freedom and independence which was exclusively theirs, none of their neighbours ever having had the historical experience.

Unfortunately for the Maronites, however, not everybody in Lebanon thought or felt as they did. There were even many Maronites who dissented and freely expressed their divergent views. After all, who could reasonably deny that Lebanon, as a political entity, was a new country, just as the other Arab countries under French or British mandate were? Certainly, Lebanon was as much a new country as the others, but with an important difference: it had been willed into existence by a community of its own people, albeit one community among others. Moreover, those among its people who had willed it into existence were fully satisfied with what they got, and wanted the country to remain forever exactly as it had been finally constituted, without any territory added or subtracted.

The Syrian Republic, it is true, had also been finally put together in response to nationalist demand; in fact, following a nationalist uprising which lasted more than two years (1925–7), provoking a French bombardment of Damascus. In Syria, however, the nationalists were only partly satisfied with what they got, and continued to aspire for much more. They knew what they did not want rather than what they wanted, and what they were opposed to more than what they were in favour of. For a brief term, they had had an Arab kingdom, with its capital in historical Damascus, once the seat of the great Umayyad caliphs and the capital of the first Arab empire. The French had destroyed their kingdom and established statelets on its territory, among them Lebanon. The Maronites, they argued, were perhaps entitled to continue to enjoy the sort of autonomy they had enjoyed since the 1860s in the Ottoman Sanjak of Mount Lebanon, although they had no real reason to feel any different from other Syrians or Arabs. On the other hand, they had no right securing for their Greater Lebanon Syrian territory which had formerly belonged to the vilayets of Beirut or Damascus, and which had never formed part of their claimed historical homeland.

From the Arab nationalist point of view, it was not permissible to accord the French-created Lebanese Republic recognition as a nation-state separate and distinct from Syria. Moreover, from the same point of view, the Syrian Republic itself was not acceptable as the final and immutable achievement of the aspirations of its people. The Syrians, after all, were Arabs, and their territory, historically, which had always included Palestine and

Transjordan along with Lebanon, was not a national
territory on its own, but part of a greater Arab homeland: a
homeland whose ancient heartlands were Syria, Iraq and
Arabia, but which, since Islam, had also come to include
Egypt and the countries of North Africa all the way to the
Atlantic. During the war years, the Allies had cheated the
Arabs. The British had promised them national independ-
ence on their historical homelands, but they had failed to
honour their promises. Instead, they had partitioned this
Arab territory with the French, and committed themselves
to hand over a particularly precious part of it, namely
Palestine, to the Jews.

To accept all this, or any part of it, would be nothing less
than high treason. Equally unacceptable in principle,
though admittedly problems of a less pressing nature, were
the continuing British control of Egypt; the Italian
colonization of Libya; and the French and Spanish imperial
presence in the remaining parts of North Africa. This
concept of one indivisible Arab national homeland extending
all the way from the Indian Ocean to the Atlantic was
expressed by the Damascene nationalist and man of letters,
Fakhri al-Barudi, in a song which enjoyed wide circulation:

> The countries of the Arabs are my homelands:
> From Damascus to Baghdad;
> From Syria to the Yemen,
> to Egypt, and all the way to Tetuan.

Significantly, the Syrian national anthem written by
another Damascene nationalist, Khalil Mardam, did not
sing the virtues of Syria as a nation-state standing by
itself, but as the 'lion's den of Arabism', its glorious
historical 'throne', and its sacred 'shrine'. By contrast the
Lebanese national anthem, written by the Maronite poet
Rashid Nakhleh, sang of the old men of Lebanon and the
young, in the mountains and the plains, responding to the
call of the historical fatherland and rallying around the
'eternal' cedar flag to defend 'Lebanon forever'.

Clearly, in the case of the Syrian Republic, the French

had put together a state but failed to create a special nationality to go with it. The same, in a way, applied to Lebanon where, contrary to the claims of the national anthem, the concept of a natural and historical Lebanese nationality was meaningful to some people in the country, but not to others. The case was no different in the countries created by the British in their own mandated Arab territories.

In Palestine, which was assembled from what was formerly the Sanjak of Jerusalem and the southern parts of the Vilayet of Beirut, the British had deliberately attempted to recreate the Biblical Land of Israel, 'from Dan to Beersheba', where the Jews were to have their national homeland. The immigrant Jews actually called the country Eretz Israel, and looked forward to the day when it would be transformed into a Jewish state. To them, Palestine as a country was meaningful, but only as a prelude to something else: the Zionist concept of a Jewish nationality, reconstituted on what was conceived to be its historical home grounds. To its native Arab population, however, Palestine was no more of a natural country than Lebanon, Syria, Transjordan or Iraq, and might as well have been given another shape or size.

Transjordan, formed essentially out of the southern parts of the old Vilayet of Damascus, but with bits of Arabia added, was certainly not a natural country. Apart from a few towns and small clusters of villages scattered along the highlands east of the Jordan valley, and some pastoral areas and grainlands here and there, this Arab emirate consisted mostly of open desert. Even its founder, Emir Abdullah, did not regard it as a real country. To him it was no more than historical Arab territory salvaged for the cause of the Great Arab Revolt, to serve one day as a base for the re-establishment of a Greater Arab Syria. Significantly, Emir Abdullah called his army not the Transjordanian, but the Arab Legion. To the British and others, Abdullah's emirate may have appeared as a recreation of the Biblical territory of Edom and Moab, or of the Roman province of Arabia; but such concepts, certainly at the time, were meaningless to the Transjordanians and did not readily contribute to a sense of separate historical nationality among them.

The British had hoped that Abdullah's younger brother Faysal, who was widely regarded in 1920 as the pre-eminent Arab national hero, would be a man of sufficient stature to make a real country out of Iraq, made up of the former Ottoman vilayets of Mosul, Baghdad, Basra and Shahrazor. Faysal's territory was declared politically independent almost immediately after its organization as a kingdom. Separated from other Arab countries by desert, and having the potential of enjoying a rich revenue from oil, Iraq could become a country on its own more easily than the others, as it had indeed been in ancient times, in the days of the Assyrians and the Babylonians. Internally, however, the Iraqis, apart from the Christian and Jewish minorities among them, were divided between Sunnites and Shiites, Arabs and Kurds. As King of Iraq, Faysal was surrounded by veterans of the Arab Revolt who had followed him to Baghdad in the flight from Damascus, and he himself never forgot his lost Syrian kingdom. His regime was more Arab nationalist than specifically Iraqi in character, dominated by the Sunnite Arab element and resented by the Shiite Arab element as well as by the Kurds. Much was indeed done under Faysal and his successors to assuage these resentments. Nevertheless, to the extent that it did develop, the sense of special nationality among the people of Iraq remained rudimentary and confused.

This was a new beginning in the history of the area: five countries formed out of Arab territory which had formerly been Ottoman, and none of them with a true or unarguable concept of special nationality to go with it. All things considered, all five of these countries were artificial creations established and given their initial organization by foreign imperial powers. Of the five, however, common Arab opinion singled out Lebanon as being an artificial creation of foreign imperialism in a special way. No one denied that the other four countries were equally artificial;

the point lay elsewhere. Among the Syrians, Iraqis, Transjordanians and Palestinian Arabs, no one seriously advanced a thesis in support of the national validity of the given country. Among the Lebanese, however, there were those who did, which amounted to a serious aberration, and one which could not be allowed to pass. By refusing to accept the national validity of their given countries as a matter of Arab nationalist principle, the other Arabs, paradoxically, did manage in time to secure an accepted legitimacy for these countries as states. By the ready enthusiasm with which many Lebanese – but not all – accepted the validity of their country and the new nationality that went with it, what was immediately achieved was the exact reverse. The legitimacy of Lebanon alone as a state, for the Arabs in general and also among the Lebanese, remained in full question.

By willing not only a separate country but also a separate Lebanese nationality into existence, against the wishes of their neighbours and without the consent of people who were forced to become their compatriots, the Maronites and their overwhelmingly Christian supporters in Lebanon had broken the Arab consensus – more particularly, the Syrian Arab concensus – and they had to pay the price. This price was to be significantly heavier as the Maronites had actively solicited the help of France to achieve their ends; even more so, because they had knowingly exhibited a marked insensitivity to Arab frustrations around them. In October 1918, when French forces landed in Beirut to put an end to the short-lived Arab government of Sharif Faysal there, Maronites and other Christians waving French flags had cheered their arrival at the port, hailing France as the 'tender, loving mother' (Arabic, *al-umm al-hanun*) who was to be their saviour. Among the Muslims of Beirut, who had watched the arrival of the French with grave apprehension, this was not a matter to be easily forgotten. Between 1918 and 1920, while these same urbane Muslims of Beirut stood sullenly by, or kept to their homes, rough and fierce-looking Maronite mountaineers had descended from their villages to demonstrate in the streets of the city which they already took to be their own, clamouring for an 'independent' Greater Lebanon, and threatening to migrate to Europe in a body if they did not get it. Going beyond their demand of Lebanese 'independence', by which they meant independence from Syria, not from the French mandate, the Maronites at the time had not hesitated to express their continuing hostility to the Arab regime which was still established in Damascus. Before they could attain their Greater Lebanon, France had first to actualize its control over the rest of its Syrian territorial claim, and the Arab regime in Damascus had to be destroyed. At the battle of the Maysalun Pass, in the Anti-Lebanon, the French did crush the forces of King Faysal in July 1920, which finally opened the way for their occupation of Damascus. Maronite volunteers reportedly fought with the French in the battle, and there were open Maronite celebrations of the French victory, or rather of the Arab defeat. This was not to be forgotten in Damascus.

The creation of the new Arab state system had hardly been completed by the late 1920s and early 1930s when political inertia and vested interests began to give it a reality. As men of political ambition began to compete for power and position in the different countries, and as each of these countries came to have its own ruling establishment and administrative bureaucracy, the lines of demarcation between them, hardly any of which was a natural or historical frontier, began to harden. Everywhere, circumspect rulers and career politicians who actually worked for the consolidation of the system, as their interests dictated, made a point of denying its immutable validity, and never missed an opportunity to denounce it as an imperialist partition of the single Arab homeland. Palestine in one way, and Lebanon in another, stood out as exceptions. In Palestine, Arabs who aspired for leadership could only make their mark by yielding to popular nationalist pressure, because of the Jewish threat. This forced them to obstruct repeated attempts by the British mandatory authorities to provide the country with a political government, because in any such government the Jews, with the international influence they wielded, were bound to be greatly over-represented. Thus, the politically ambitious among the Palestinian Arabs had to compete for the leadership of the nationalist opposition, not for power and position in an actual ruling establishment. In Lebanon, while the Christian political establishment dominated by the Maronites was fully determined to make a success of the state, there was a Muslim opposition which was equally determined to make of it a failure. Here the Christian ruling establishment, secure with the backing of France, spoke its mind freely and acted accordingly, while the opposition, with the moral backing of the prevailing nationalist sentiment in Syria and other Arab countries, did the same.

It was not only the Christian political establishment, but also France who wanted to make of Lebanon a success; and France was fully alert to the country's fundamental problem: unless the Christians managed to sell the idea of Lebanon to their Muslim compatriots, Lebanon as a state could not gain the required minimum of legitimacy it needed, politically, to be truly viable. France, as the historical friend of the Maronites, was willing to do for them and their fellow Christians all it could do. It had already established for them the Greater Lebanon they wanted, to some extent against its better judgement. It now helped them to organize their state, and for the time being provided it with the needed power protection. More than that France could only give advice, because one day they would be on their own: the advice was given, and even pressed. Maronite leaders who accepted it, and began to show prudence in speech and action, were given all the necessary backing to reach office. Those who did not accept the advice received no support; and when they happened to be in office, they were left in political isolation, and their wiser opponents were helped to bring them down.

Originally, the Maronites had wanted Lebanon, politic-ally, for themselves. When the country received its Constitution and became a parliamentary republic, the

French saw to it that a Greek Orthodox Christian rather than a Maronite became its first president, with a Sunnite Muslim as a speaker of its parliament; but the Maronites nevertheless managed to secure for themselves all other key positions in the government and the administration, and ultimately the presidency of the republic as well. What made this possible, at the initial stages, was the effective boycott of the state by all but a handful of the Sunnite Muslims, who were the only community in the country who could have stopped the Maronites from achieving their virtual monopoly of power at the time. Stage by stage, however, the French saw to it that the effectiveness of this Muslim boycott of the state was eroded, and pressed on the Maronite leaderships the vital necessity of giving the Muslims enough stake in the country to encourage them to help maintain the state. To many Maronites, this appeared as an outright French betrayal of their cause. Others were willing to learn, though not always as much as needed.

In Lebanon, however, the Christians on the whole had an advantage over the Muslims. By and large, in rank and file, they were socially far more developed or, more correctly, far more familiar with the ways of the modern world. This placed them in a position to provide the country, for a long time, with most of the needed infrastructure. It also enabled them to provide a social gloss which covered the fragile and faulty structure of the state and the social tension which lay underneath, mainly due to the glaringly uneven development of the different Lebanese communities and regions. Outside Lebanon, except for Egypt, this kind of gloss at the time, on the required scale, was not to be found elsewhere in the Arab world. It certainly existed in Palestine, even more so than in Lebanon; but there it was provided largely by the European Jewish settlers rather than by the Palestinian Arabs, among whom development was limited to a small middle and upper class.

What further helped to cover up the faults of Lebanon was the stunning natural beauty of the country, coupled with its pleasant Mediterranean climate. Lebanon, moreover, was relatively green, and could appear lush green – a veritable paradise – by contrast with the desert which began as one crossed the eastern borders from the Bekaa valley into Syria. Where else, in the Arab world, could one see majestic peaks capped with snow for much of the year, rising hoary above terraced mountain slopes dotted with the red roof-tops of countless villages nestled among orchards or vineyards, set against a stark blue sky, and directly overlooking the sparkling waters of the Mediterranean? Yet another initial advantage of the country was its geographic location, which could make of it the ideal gateway from the West to the Arab world. In addition to all this, there was the experienced mercantile initiative and exceptional adaptability of the people, and the cultural tolerance which they generally exhibited, most notably in the coastal cities, and most of all in cosmopolitan Beirut.

All that Lebanon needed to be a success was political accord and an even social development among the different communities which had come to form its population and in the different regions it had come to comprise. However, for two reasons, it was exactly these conditions that proved hard to reach. First, the Maronites in Lebanon were determined to maintain their own paramount control of the state, and were fundamentally unwilling to have Christians and Muslims share in the country as political equals; their argument was that the Muslims were naturally susceptible to the strong influence of their co-religionists in other Arab countries, and could therefore not be trusted with the more sensitive political and administrative positions in Lebanon, such as those which involved national security and ultimate decision making. Second, the prevalent nationalist mood in the Arab world, especially in Syria, was against Lebanon achieving political success; and within the country, the Muslim sector of the population could easily be swayed by external Arab nationalist influence, and could be used by other Arab countries as political leverage to keep the Lebanese state perennially unstable. For the duration of the French mandate in the Levant, Lebanon was adequately protected against such destabilizing Arab interventions in its affairs. The real problems of the country, however, were to come blatantly into the open as soon as the French mandate came to an end, leaving an independent Lebanon at the mercy of external and internal forces acting in the name of Arab nationalism with which the Lebanese state, in the long run, was unable to come to reasonable terms.

Thus in Lebanon, from the very beginning, a force called Arabism, acting from outside and inside the country, stood face to face with another exclusively parochial social force called Lebanism; and the two forces collided on every fundamental issue, impeding the normal development of the state and keeping its political legitimacy and ultimate viability continuously in question. Each force, at the internal level, claimed to represent a principle and ideal involving a special concept of nationality; yet in each case one had to look behind the articulated argument to discover the real nature of the quarrel. True, there were individuals in Lebanon who sincerely believed in the historical and political validity of Lebanism, and others who were committed to Arabism with equal sincerity. But it was certainly no accident that the original proponents of Lebanism in the country were almost exclusively Christians, and for the most part Maronites, while the most unbending proponents of Arabism, as a community, were the Muslims. Clearly, in both cases, what was actually said by way of argument on the surface covered something else underneath: the source of the problems. What was this underlying element in each case, which made the declared positions of the two sides so irreconcilable as to keep the question of Lebanon, interminably, an outstanding one?

2 The confidence game

In the formulation of social and political ideals, it is essential to take realities fully into account. This, commonly, does not occur in societies which have still not found their bearings. In such cases, unless a given ideal is implemented by force, or by the charisma of truly convinced and determined leadership, it can easily be eroded by the existing realities that contradict it. If the ideal is pressed hard, but not to the extent of effecting the desired change, society finds ways and means to circumvent it, and a social hypocrisy develops. Set patterns of behaviour can then remain in operation, functioning in one way or another in the name of the ideal or under its cover. Thus the ideal, whose original purpose was the remodelling of a given society according to new precepts or a new vision, with a view to the common good, is transformed into a false witness to the obstinate persistence of that society in traditional ways. Should it happen to have the required minimum of popular appeal, the ideal then can also become the stock-in-trade of political opportunists and demagogues who make use of it to achieve devious ends.

In the new Arab world emerging from the ruins of the Ottoman empire after the first world war, Arabism was a contemporary ideal which came to enjoy wide popularity. Essentially, however, Arabism then was little more than a romantic notion whose full implications had not been carefully worked out. It conceived of the Arabs, more particularly those of the Arab heartlands of Syria, Iraq and Arabia, as a people who had lost consciousness of their nationhood through the vicissitudes of history, but whose natural right and destiny was to unite and become a great historical nation again. The destruction of the Ottoman empire had provided them, for a brief while, with the needed opportunity for a genuine and indeed glorious national revival; but French and British imperialism had wished matters differently. To prevent the Arabs, at that propitious moment, from actualizing their nationhood through political unity, the colonizers had divided the Arab national territory into diverse countries against the natural wishes of the people. In two instances, they had proceeded even further. In Lebanon, the French had found among the Maronites perfidious or deluded native Arabs who were willing and in fact eager to help the colonizers achieve their ends. In Palestine, the British had committed themselves to the encouragement of foreign Jewish settlement, with a view to transforming that integral part of the Arab national homeland into a country for the Jews.

From the Arab nationalist perspective, what had actually come to be was unacceptable at every level. However, certain matters came first. To begin with, there was to be no compromise over the question of Palestine under any condition. In Lebanon, the Maronites could not be allowed to get away with the role they had played in the dismemberment of Syria. They had either to be persuaded to join the Arab national ranks again, or somehow coerced to do so. More than that, for the moment, Arab nationalism had little to say. It was simply believed that once the Arabs were left alone to become independent, they would naturally unite, and all for them would be well.

Historically, the Arabs had always been a people distinguishable by their language and traditional culture, and inhabiting territories which Arab nationalism regarded as their rightful homelands. They had existed in Syria and Iraq as well as in Arabia long before Islam. The coming of

Islam, in the seventh century AD, then provided them with the impetus to make their lasting mark in history as the founders of a great empire. However, the leadership of this empire, which they established in the name of Islam, subsequently passed into the hands of other Islamic peoples, Persians or Turks.

In pre-Islamic times, the history of the Arabs had been one of tribes and regional principalities, more often than not in conflict with one another where they happened to be neighbours. After Islam, Arab history continued at two levels, the Islamic and the Arab, and the lines of demarcation between the two were never clear. As one Islamic people among others, the Arabs, in theory, were supposed to owe their prime loyalty to what was conceived of as the supreme and universal State of Islam, whatever its actual condition; whoever happened to be its rulers; and wherever the capital of its caliphs or sultans happened to be located. Under the Ottoman Turkish sultans, the capital of the Islamic state was actually located in Istanbul, outside the Arab world. At the same time, however, the Arabs in Islamic times continued to have a parochial history all to themselves, either as tribes or as the inhabitants of various regions, much as had been the case before Islam, but with an important difference. Unless the Arabs now, as Muslims, could justify how they actually behaved politically in Islamic terms, they could not claim for their different tribal and regional autonomies any legitimacy, because Islam as a universal religion and state did not recognize any claim that would give race, tribe or region a special political standing.

Therefore, wherever Arabs chose to be autonomous or independent of the universal Islamic rule without appearing to be rebels, they had to justify their political dissidence by opting for sectarian interpretations of Islam – Kharijite or Shiite – which challenged the established Sunnite, or orthodox interpretation represented by the universal State of Islam. Thus, for example, the tribes of Oman justified their frequently achieved independence from the established Islamic state by becoming Ibadi Kharijites, while those of the northern Yemen highlands did the same by becoming Shiites of the Zaydi sect. Both the Ibadis of Oman and the Zaydis of the Yemen regarded the caliphs and sultans of the Sunnite, or orthodox Islamic state as usurpers, and claimed universal Islamic legitimacy for their own respective Imams instead. Meanwhile, there were tribes and local communities in Syria and the Yemen which rebelled or conspired against the established Sunnite caliphs or sultans in the name of Ismaili Shiism; while others in Syria, Iraq and eastern Arabia articulated their political disaffections in terms of what was known as Imami, or Twelver Shiism. In the Syrian mountains, there were disaffected tribes and peasant communities which made even greater esoteric departures from Islamic orthodoxy by becoming Nusayris (also called Alouites) or Druzes, warding off the wrath of orthodox Islam against them when the need arose by dissimulation.

The Arabs under Islam did not only come to be organized in different Islamic sects; there were many among them who never became Muslims, including the two historical Christian Arab communities of Syria, the Melchites and the Maronites. Of these two Syrian Christian communities, the Melchites, who followed the Byzantine Greek rite and ultimately came to be divided between Greek Orthodox and Greek Catholic communions, were by far the more numerous. With their greater social solidarity, however, and their geographic concentration in a rugged and limited mountain territory, the Maronites were the more forceful, and politically, with time, the more important.

The Maronites actually behaved more as a tribe or tribal confederation with a special church than as a purely religious community, such as the Melchites were. What held them together was mainly their strong sense of group solidarity, rather than their devotion to particular religious beliefs and practices. In this respect, they were not unlike their Druze neighbours to the south, or their Nusayri neighbours to the north, except that, being non-Muslims, they did not need to practice dissimulation. As Christians, they were under no obligation to make any apology for their community particularism, and felt no guilt about making contacts or developing regular relations with foreign Christian powers regardless of the status of such powers as friends or enemies of the Islamic state. This gave the Maronites a distinct advantage over dissident Muslim Arab communities who behaved similarly – most notably their Druze neighbours, with whom they came to be politically associated in Mount Lebanon during the formative years of the Ottoman period. The Druzes therefore became resentful of the Maronites in a specific manner. The Melchites, however, were no less resentful of the Maronites as fellow Arab Christians, envying their uncanny ability to manipulate the Islamic rule even at its most rigorous.

It was actually among the Christian Arabs of Syria – not the Maronites, but the Melchites of Aleppo – that a rudimentary consciousness of Arabism first developed in modern times. As Christians, the Melchites followed the Greek rite. Under the Ottomans, their church in Syria had come to be controlled by a Greek upper clergy, under the influence of the Phanariot Greeks of Istanbul who were close to the centre of political power. Though following the same rite as the Greeks, and paying special regard to the Phanariot Patriarch of Constantinople as the head of the ecumenical Orthodox church, the Melchites were strictly an indigenous Syrian church whose head was the titular Patriarch of Antioch residing in Damascus. There was also the Melchite church of Jerusalem, headed by its own patriarch. By tradition, however, both patriarchs, and also most of the bishops who served under them, were Greeks. Few Arab clergymen in either church, under these conditions, could aspire to be anything more than priests. By the late seventeenth century there were many Melchites in the church of Antioch who were beginning to find the situation intolerable.

Starting from the early years of that same century, the city of Aleppo, in northern Syria, had been rising to importance as a leading centre for European commerce with the East. English, Dutch, French and other European trading companies began to set up offices there; and Roman Catholic missionaries also gained access to the city, including the Jesuits who were already active among the Maronites in Mount Lebanon. With time, European commercial activity in Aleppo brought it a special prosperity. A number of resident Melchite families consequently became rich and influential and began to show impatience with the Greek dominance over their church, and the Jesuits encouraged them. Under the influence of these Jesuits, increasing numbers of the local Melchites were attracted to the idea of union with Rome, whereby they would become a Uniate Roman Catholic communion as the Maronites already were, with a church organization all to themselves.

Matters came to a head in 1683 when a Melchite cleric of Aleppo, Euthymius Sayfi, newly appointed Archbishop of Tyre, recognized the supremacy of the Roman pope, which had the immediate effect of splitting the Melchites of Syria into what came to be called the Greek Catholics and the Greek Orthodox. In 1724, when the Melchite see of Antioch fell vacant, the Uniate Melchites, or Greek Catholics, elected their own patriarch, who was naturally a native Syrian Arab, and the organization of their church, with an entirely native Arab clergy, became complete.

The Greek Catholics in the seventeenth and eighteenth centuries were certainly not aware that their split from the mother Melchite church was prompted by a new national consciousness among them. It was on purely ecclesiastical and religious grounds that they defended their union with Rome, which ended with their emergence as a separate church. There can be no doubt, however, that what lay behind their movement was a growing resentment among well-to-do Melchites in Syria of the dominance of their church by Greeks. Without giving any articulation to their Arabism, these Melchites had actually pitted their Arab ethnicity, at the ecclesiastical level, against that of the Greeks. It was not until the end of the nineteenth century that their former fellow Melchites, the Greek Orthodox, following their example, secured the election of an Arab patriarch instead of a Greek to the see of Antioch, and began pressing for the election of Arabs to the see of Jerusalem, where the patriarchs remain Greek to this day. Moreover, as learned Greek Catholics began to write in defence of their new communion, they did so in Arabic, and using for the first time in the Arab world an Arabic press. Not surprisingly, by the nineteenth century, members of the Greek Catholic church were among the leading figures of the Arabic literary revival of the period. Significantly, in the late nineteenth century, it was a Greek Catholic poet and man of letters from Mount Lebanon, Ibrahim al-Yaziji, who first gave poetic expression to the concept of an Arab national 'awakening'.

That Arab nationalism should have been so especially meaningful to Ibrahim al-Yaziji was only natural. His father, Nasif al-Yaziji, earlier in the century, had been a leading pioneer in the rediscovery of the Arabic literary heritage, recognized as such by Muslim and Christian Arabs alike. Both the father and the son had close associations with the American and British Protestant missionaries in Beirut, who had started their activity in the 1820s. In the early history of the Arab national movement, the influence of these missionaries was particularly important. The local converts to Protestantism were Maronite or Greek Catholic in some cases, but Greek Orthodox in most others. The majority of these converts became Protestant because they went to the excellent schools which the British and American missionaries were establishing in Beirut and elsewhere. Starting in 1866, conversion to Protestantism received a new boost with the establishment of the Syrian Protestant College, which was later renamed the American University of Beirut. The Protestant missionaries in general encouraged national feeling among their followers, and taught them to think of themselves as Syrians, or as Arabs: essentially, as Syrian Arabs. The American missionaries, in particular, encouraged interest in the Arabic language and cultural heritage, and some among them – notably Eli Smith and Cornelius Van Dyck – were in fact competent Arabists. Among their achievements was the translation of the Bible from the original languages into a simplified modern Arabic – a task which was actually executed by a team of local scholars, Christian and Muslim, working in Beirut under American supervision. It was one of these scholars, Butrus al-Bustani – a Maronite convert to Protestantism – who first made a point of articulating the idea of a secular Arab nationality, which he called Syrian, within the Ottoman political context. At least, his is the first clear articulation of the idea on record.

One can easily understand why Christian rather than Muslim Arabs should have been the first to exhibit and articulate a sense of Arab nationality, under whatever name; also, why this should have occurred in Beirut, and among Christians from Mount Lebanon. After all, it was in Beirut and Mount Lebanon that Roman Catholic and Protestant missionaries in Syria were mainly active; and it was the Christians rather than the Muslims who went to their schools, or consorted with European resident traders and political or consular agents, and consequently became exposed to modern Western ideas, including the idea of nationalism. There were also other important factors to consider in this connection. The Muslim Arabs, because they were Muslims, regarded themselves as the social and political equals of the Muslim Turks who were actually their rulers, and therefore had no problem living under a Turkish empire which, to them as to the Turks, represented the State of Islam. The Christian Arabs could not take the same attitude, because they were Arabs but not Muslims. As Arabs, however, these same Christians could legitimately consider themselves the equals of the Muslim Arabs among whom they actually lived, and hope to be accepted by them as such.

That it was the Christian Arabs of Syria rather than those of Iraq or Egypt who became the first advocates of Arab nationality is also understandable. The Copts of Egypt, who spoke Arabic but were not ethnically Arab by origin, could easily consider themselves Egyptian, but not as easily Arab. The same applied to the Nestorian

Christians of Iraq, many of whom spoke Syriac rather than Arabic. Among the Syrian Christians, the Jacobites, who also spoke Syriac, could not easily identify themselves as Arabs; only the Maronites and the Melchites who were actually Arab in ethnicity and language could. Furthermore, it was mainly because the Christian Arabs, who initially identified themselves in terms of nationality, were Syrian that they confused Arabism with Syrianism. Had there been Christians elsewhere in the Arab world who could as readily identify themselves as Arabs, the question of Syrianism among the Arabs of Syria might not have arisen.

The first Muslim Arabs to gain consciousness of their Arabism were again Syrian; and this was partly, but not entirely, under the influence of their Christian compatriots. In the nineteenth century the idea of nationalism was in the air, but in the Ottoman empire it made headway more readily among the Christian than the Muslim subjects of the sultan. First the Greek, then other Balkan Christians, rose in revolt against Ottoman rule and gained their independence. In Asia Minor, nationalist agitation among the Armenians brought about their first massacre in 1894.

From the Islamic point of view, all these peoples were Christians revolting against the legitimate Islamic state, which made the Muslims of the empire react and rally strongly around Ottoman rule. In the middle decades of the century, between 1839 and 1876, the Ottoman state made a determined attempt to modernize its institutions by a series of reforms called the *Tanzimat*, and the idea of a secular Ottoman nationality was promoted to give the empire a greater internal cohesion. This idea, however, was too subtle to be understood for what it was by the common run of Muslims, who continued to regard the Ottoman state as the State of Islam; and it was naturally rejected by the common run of Christians as an Islamic ploy. After 1876, the official promotion of the idea was dropped, and the Islamic nature of the Ottoman state was again emphasized. In these circumstances, there was no particular reason for the Muslim Arabs of the empire to begin thinking of themselves as a separate nationality, and the idea of Arab nationalism among them, to the extent that it did develop, remained a matter of individual idiosyncrasy.

As a result of the Tanzimat, however, the Ottoman state had tightened its grip over its Arab provinces by its policy of centralization as at no time before; this came to be most felt in Syria and Iraq. Meanwhile, the Ottoman bureaucratic classes in Istanbul had become increasingly conscious of their Turkishness, and the same consciousness of Turkish nationality had also begun to permeate the European-trained officer class of the Ottoman army. By the turn of the century, this new Turkish nationalism emanating from the Ottoman capital was beginning to cause some concern to Muslim Arabs in Syria; but this concern was allayed because the policy of the state, under Sultan Abdul-Hamid II (1876–1909), remained Islamic. It was only when the so-called Young Turks seized power in Istanbul in 1908, during the last year of Abdul-Hamid's reign – more so, when these Young Turks proceeded to transform the Ottoman state into a Turkish military dictatorship in 1913 – that their new Turkish nationalism began to alienate Muslim Arabs and force them to develop a nationalism of their own in reaction. Why this occurred in Syria rather than elsewhere may be attributed to two causes. In Syria there was the example of the Christians which the Muslims could now follow. Moreover, leading Syrian cities such as Beirut, Damascus and Aleppo already had the prerequisite degree of social development to encourage the growth of nationalism, as well as an evolving and politically ambitious class of Muslim city notables who were willing to drop old ideas and adopt new ones, and so set the example for others.

While the Ottoman empire lasted, Arab nationalism among the Muslims of Syria remained for the most part the preserve of these city notables, and the mainly Sunnite intellectual circles with which they were associated. It did not reach the masses, and it only gained little headway among the Shiites and the Druzes. Similarly, when Arab nationalism reached Iraq, it made more headway among the urban Sunnites than among the largely rural or tribal Shiites.

During the first world war, however, the movement was given a tremendous boost by the Arab Revolt in the Hijaz. In Beirut and Damascus, Arab nationalist activists who were in sympathy with the revolt, and who were in secret contact with the Allies who backed it, were tried and executed as traitors by the Ottoman military authorities, giving the movement its first martyrs. Meanwhile, the revolt itself provided Sharif Husayn as its focus, and his son Faysal as its first hero. By the time Faysal entered Damascus to establish his Arab government there, it was already understood by all that the Ottoman empire was gone, never to return, and it was pointless to remain loyal to something that no longer existed. Following the lead of the Muslim and Christian Arab nationalists, increasing numbers among the Muslims in Syria, along with many Christians including a number of Maronites from Mount Lebanon, declared themselves openly for Faysal and for Arabism. When Faysal left Syria and became King of Iraq, the hopes of the Arab nationalists turned to focus, for the duration of his reign, on Baghdad.

Arab nationalism, as it came to exist in the Arab world after the first world war, was more of a romantic ideal than a political movement with clear precepts and a set programme. Moreover, it meant different things to its Muslim and Christian adherents. Although Muslim Arab nationalists, usually with great sincerity, spoke of Arabism as being secular, they could not dissociate it from Islam: if for no other reason, because Arab history is difficult to dissociate from Islamic history. The Christian view of Arabism could only be secular; but the Christian Arab nationalists could not deny that the central fact of Arab history was the mission of Muhammad, who was not only the Prophet of Islam but also the first leader to give the Arabs political unity under its religious and political banner. In this respect, he was the pre-eminent hero of historical Arabism, and they had to accept him as such.

While the Muslim Arabs tended to regard Arab history as being essentially Islamic, the Christians stressed the pre-Islamic history of the Arabs which was no less important a part of the national history: they pointed out that many of the Arabs of pre-Islamic times – most notably, the Ghassan Arabs of Syria – were Christian. They also emphasized the importance of the role played by Christians in Arab society in Islamic times. To all this, thoughtful Muslim Arab nationalists were more than willing to concede; yet they continued to speak of Arabism and Islam in the same breath, while the Christians did not. Among ordinary Muslim Arabs, the more Islamic the interpretation of Arab nationalism, the more popular it became.

Moreover, as Christians or as Muslims, the Arab nationalists of the period were an assortment of different elements, to each of which Arab nationalism was significant in a different way. First, there were the ordinary Muslims and Christians of the patriotic and civically-minded urban middle class, to whom Arab nationalism was the valid and proper expression of their sense of patriotism and civility. Among those were the intellectuals, in most cases Christian academics or quasi-academics, who tried to provide the idea with a body of historical and philosophical thought. In the works of two intellectuals, Constantine Zurayk and Nabih Amin Faris, Arab nationalism found its purest articulation. Both were professors at the American University of Beirut: the first, a Greek Orthodox Christian from Damascus; the second, a Protestant Christian from Palestine, whose family originally came from Mount Lebanon. From the same urban middle class came the men of political ambition who found in Arab nationalism a useful political platform. There were Christians as well as Muslims among those, but the majority were naturally Muslim; in a society which was predominantly Islamic, more Muslims than Christians could aspire for political power.

Among the urban lower classes, which were predominantly Sunnite Muslim, what really counted was the sentiment of Islamic solidarity, particularly at a time when there was no longer an Islamic state to provide the body of the faithful with a paramount leadership, and when Islam stood threatened by Christian imperial powers from the West, by Jewish ambitions in Palestine, and by Christian Arabs such as the Maronites who seemed to be making common cause with the imperialists against their fellow Arabs. To the Muslims of these classes, Arabism was little more than another name for Islam: a fact which politicians of the Arab nationalist platform, in their competition for urban popular support, could not afford to neglect.

Finally, there was the Arab rural and tribal population which was in the large majority Islamic, but included a number of communities of varying sizes which were not Sunnite Muslim – most notably, the Twelver Shiites of Iraq and Greater Lebanon; the Nusayris of the Syrian Republic; and the Druzes who were divided between Lebanon, Syria and Palestine. Among these communities, more especially the Twelver Shiites and the Druzes, there were notables and many individuals who had received a modern higher education, and they could appreciate, with varying degrees of sincerity, what Arab nationalism really stood for in principle. A number of them had been active in the Arab nationalist movement from the very beginning; and of the Syrians among them, some formed part of the political entourage of Faysal in Damascus and later followed him to Baghdad, or joined his brother Abdullah in Amman. In general, however, the non-Sunnites among the Muslim Arabs maintained a considerable degree of reserve towards Arab nationalism which they regarded as predominantly a Sunnite movement. In some cases, this reserve, though normally concealed, virtually amounted to hostility.

The fact was that these communities had historical scores to settle: in the case of the Twelver Shiites and Nusayris, with Sunnite Islam; in the case of the Druzes, with the Maronites who had been their historical associates and political competitors in Mount Lebanon. The Druzes were certainly no closer to Sunnite Islam than the Twelver Shiites or Nusayris. While Sunnite Muslims had tradition-ally regarded Twelver Shiism as no more than a regrettable political schism within Islam, taking little note of the fact that these Shiites also had a different religious interpretation of the common faith, they had always regarded the Nusayris, and more so the Druzes, as highly aberrant communities who were practically infidels. There had been in fact Sunnite persecutions of the two communities; yet both had finally learnt to accept Sunnite dominance and live with it by the practice of dissimulation. The Twelver Shiites were too numerous, in both Iraq and Greater Lebanon, to feel the need to practise dissimulation. That Twelver Shiism had been the official Islam of Iran since the early sixteenth century was a valuable political reassurance to its Arab adherents throughout the Ottoman period. What had historically irked the Arab Shiites, however, was that they normally lived under the rule of Sunnite regimes whose Islamic legitimacy they did not accept. The Sunnite and Shiite views of early Islamic history, moreover, were radically different, and neither recognized the possible validity of the other.

The idea of Arab nationalism appealed to the non-Sunnite Islamic communities in the same manner that it appealed to the Christians: in theory, it involved a principle of national equity which put Arabs of different religions and sects on one footing and promised to end political and social discrimination on confessional grounds. In practice, however, it did not always work in that manner. In Iraq, for example, many Shiites came to see in Arabism an ostensibly good doctrine put to improper use to justify the established Sunnite dominance over the country, where the majority of the population was generally reckoned to be Shiite.

In Greater Lebanon, the Sunnites took the Shiites politically for granted in the name of Arabism, while tending in general to leave them out of their inner councils. The Shiite restiveness in South Lebanon which marked the earlier years of the French mandate, and which remained essentially of a parochial nature, was given an Arab nationalist interpretation by the Sunnites – an interpretation which was accepted by some Shiites, but not by others. The Druzes were also taken politically for granted by the Sunnites in the name of Arabism, both in Lebanon and in Syria. Among the Druzes of Lebanon, however, the adoption of Arabism served a useful purpose. While the Druzes acquiesced to the establishment of Greater Lebanon, to which they were not opposed in principle, long experience had taught them – rightly – to be suspicious of Maronite political ambition. In the name of Arab nationalism, they could now oppose the Maronites and keep them perpetually annoyed, with the Sunnites in the country as their allies, and with general Arab support from outside. Moreover, when the Druzes of Jebel Druze rose in revolt against the French in 1925, as the French mandatory authorities insisted on introducing modern administrative measures which trespassed on traditional interests and established practices, the Arab nationalists in Damascus immediately advertised their cause as an Arab nationalist one. What had started as a strictly local rising of Druze tribesmen was rapidly transformed into a general Syrian revolt which took the French two years to crush, mainly because of the valour of the Druze warriors. As a result, the Druzes not only in Syria, but also in Lebanon, gained a special Arab nationalist respectability which subsequently proved eminently useful to them as a cover for their generally parochial pursuits – most of all, for the war of nerves which they seemed determined to pursue against their old Maronite foes.

The problem, in short, was the following: while there was much that could be said for Arabism as a valid nationalist ideal, most of the Arabs who adopted it were tribal or quasi-tribal communities of different kinds, and also of different religions and sects, who had not undergone a uniform social and civic development, and who were therefore still far from having achieved the attributes of a real nation. Ill prepared to face this problem, uncertain of the exact aims of their movement, yet impatient to achieve them in circumstances which involved serious international difficulties to start with, the Arab nationalist political leaders, wherever they happened to be, found their position hopelessly compromised. In nearly all cases, they ended up serving as umpires in the ongoing game of Arab tribal and regional particularism, passing favourable judgement on whatever side played the game according to their rules, which mainly involved the payment of lip service to Arabism, and unfavourable judgement on whatever side did not.

Even as umpires, these Arab nationalist leaders could not be fair, because Arab nationalism derived its social force principally from the Islamic solidarity among the Arabs, which had to be preserved at all costs. Any unfavourable judgement passed on an Islamic community, no matter how slight, could put this highly valued solidarity in jeopardy. On the other hand, there was little danger involved in passing such judgement on communities that happened to be Christian, such as the Maronites in Lebanon, of whom most rejected the notion of Arabism altogether and spoke instead of Lebanism.

Had the concept of Lebanese nationality, as advanced by the Maronites, been a truly civic one, rationally and realistically interpreted within the broader context of Arabism, its chances of success as the basis of a Lebanese state acceptable to all its people would have been good. In Greater Lebanon, after all, it was not only the Maronites, along with other Christians, who could see through the true nature of Arabism as it existed in practice; Shiites and Druzes had no more wish to be dominated by a Sunnite ruling class in the name of Arabism than Christians did. At the same time, neither they nor most Christians could deny the important fact that they were Arabs with a rich heritage of history and culture in common with other Arabs, especially those of historical Syria. As Arabs among Arabs, however, and tribal ones at that in the broad sense of the term as defined above, the Maronites had originally conceived of what they called Lebanese nationality in terms of their own tribal particularism, and they persisted in doing so. In Mount Lebanon, their particularism, long before it came to be postulated in terms of nationality, had been historically pitted against another tribal particularism, that of the Druzes. In Greater Lebanon, where the same Maronite particularism was somewhat broadened to cater for feelings of insecurity among other Christians, it was further pitted, this time as Lebanism, against the particularism of the Sunnite Muslims. The particularism of the Sunnites was articulated in terms of Arab nationalism, and was accepted outside Lebanon as being that, mainly by fellow Sunnite Muslims of other Arab countries, and most of all by those of Syria and Palestine. At the same time, the Lebanism of the Maronites held little attraction for the Shiites, although these same Shiites, judging by the experience of their co-religionists in Iraq, were also very wary of the negative social and political implications of Arabism where they were concerned.

Apart from the Druzes and the Shiites, there were also the non-Maronite Christians of Greater Lebanon, among whom the Greek Orthodox formed the largest group. While also fearing the implications of Arabism as a new guise for political Islam, the Greek Orthodox by and large resented the Maronite political dominance in the country, and therefore treated the concept of Lebanism advanced by the Maronites with considerable reserve. The Greek Orthodox, moreover, were far from restricted only to Lebanon: there were more of them in Syria alone, not to count those in Palestine and Transjordan, than all the Christian communities of Lebanon put together. To the Greek Orthodox, therefore, the concept of pan-Syrianism was more meaningful than the concept of Arabism. When one member of the community, Antun Saadeh (d. 1949), gave a forceful political articulation to this concept for the first time in the 1930s, pitting it against both Lebanism and Arabism, the Syrian Nationalist Party (Parti Populaire Syrien, or PPS) he organized found a ready following among his co-religionists. His idea of secular pan-Syrianism also proved attractive to many Druzes and Shiites; to Christians other than the Greek Orthodox, including some Maronites who were disaffected by both Lebanism and Arabism; and also to many Sunnite Muslims who set a high value on secularism, and who felt that they had far more in common with their fellow Syrians of whatever religion or denomination than with fellow Sunnite or Muslim Arabs elsewhere. Here again, an idea of nationalism had emerged which had sufficient credit to make it valid. In the Lebanese context, however, it became a ready cover for something more archaic, which was essentially Greek Orthodox particularism.

And so began the great confidence game in Lebanon. The game involved a succession of devious transactions between players who invariably pretended to stand for nationalist ideals and principles aimed at the common good, while they strove to outwit and overturn one another, motivated by atavistic loyalties and insecurities for which the professed ideals and principles normally served as a mere cover. Before long, the game had recognized rules which amounted to a set script, with different lines assigned to different participants; moreover, no participant was permitted to repeat lines assigned to another. Whoever played and recited lines to which he was not entitled found himself automatically ostracized by his own community, and openly or secretly despised by the others. Although the parties to the game were religious communities, the game itself did not involve debates on points of religion, except among the marginal class of the clergy who played a game which was exclusively their own. Only in cases of dire necessity, when a given religious community showed signs of political slackness, were the clergy called upon to help restore its militant solidarity by assuming the functions of party whips. Otherwise, at the religious level, a high degree of tolerance normally prevailed.

The plain fact remained that the religious communities in Lebanon were essentially tribes, or in any case behaved as tribes, and the game that came to be played between them was a tribal game. At an overt level, the game was a contest between different concepts of nationality for the country. At the covert level, tribal rivalries and jealousies were mainly involved. As long as this devious game was played only among the Lebanese, it could pass for day-to-day Lebanese politics, and the Lebanese state headed by the Maronites could somehow control it. There always remained a lurking danger, however, that the game could run out of control. From the very start, players from outside Lebanon could easily intrude whenever they wished to spoil its normal course; and more often than not they came by actual invitation.

3   Talking geography

Countries are created by history, but their territories belong to the realm of geography, where history is merely a bird of passage. Since antiquity, in the regions between the Mediterranean Sea and the Indian Ocean which the Classical geographers were the first to call Syria, Mesopotamia and Arabia, different countries have existed at different times. Some of them used to be no more than city-states or tribal cantons. Others were regional principalities or kingdoms, or provinces of some empire whose centre was sometimes inside the area, and sometimes outside it. Here was a land – essentially, a subcontinent – where political frontiers were forever shifting as a result of internal developments, or under the impact of foreign political interventions or military conquests. Nevertheless, the unity of the land in terms of natural and human geography always remained. In ancient times, it comprised the heartlands of the Semitic world. Later on, it came to form the original Arab world, which was expanded after the Islamic conquests of the seventh century AD to include Egypt and North Africa as far west as the Atlantic.

Geographically, the territory of Syria, Iraq and Arabia is composed of a central desert and its peripheries. In the east, these peripheries include the alluvial lowlands of Mesopotamia, or Iraq, which continue southwards as the coastal lowlands of eastern Arabia, all the way to the mountains of Oman. In the west, they comprise the broken highlands of coastal Syria, bordering the eastern Mediterranean, which continue southwards, with hardly an interruption, to connect with the highlands of western Arabia, bordering the Red Sea all the way to the Yemen. In southern Arabia, the hilly coastlands of the Arabian Sea link the Yemen and Oman. In the extreme north, Iraq and Syria are connected by the foothills of the Taurus mountains, which hug the northern parts of the central desert in the form of an inverted crescent – the Fertile Crescent, as it has been called in modern times. There, it is difficult to tell exactly where Iraq ends and Syria begins; unless the boundary between them is taken arbitrarily to be the upper Euphrates or one of its two major tributaries, the Balikh or the Khabur. Similarly, in the west, it is impossible to determine the exact point which separates the highlands of Syria from those of western Arabia; unless one takes Syria to end geologically with the last ridges of sedimentary rock south-east of the Dead Sea, and western Arabia to begin a little further south, in the vicinity of the town of Aqaba, with the first Precambrian ridges of the so-called Arabian Shield.

Rather than being a barrier between the lands of the different peripheries, the area's central desert, with its intricate network of highways, has historically provided natural connections between them. Each highway follows depressions in the land, known as wadis: dry river beds which form the drainage system of the desert in the rainy seasons. Down the ages, for example, the depression of Wadi al-Rimmah has been the natural highway between lower Iraq (the classical Babylonia) and western Arabia. The depression of Wadi Sirhan, on the other hand, has served as one of the principal natural highways between northern Arabia and Syria. Moreover, between the central desert and the more fertile Syrian, Mesopotamian and Arabian peripheries, the lines of demarcation are nowhere clear. Nearly everywhere, the desert closely dovetails with the more arable land. Normally, we tend to think of the

Syro-Arabian desert as ending in the east with the Euphrates. Actually the desert, in central and southern Iraq, continues across the Euphrates all the way to the Tigris, making of lower Iraq what may be perceived as a north-eastern extension of Arabia. In eastern, southern and western Arabia, the desert everywhere reaches the sea, cutting up the more fertile settled peripheries into countless strips. In Syria, it continues at many points beyond the first line of cities and towns fringing the coastal highlands from the east to permeate these very highlands, in the notable case of southern Palestine as far west as the Mediterranean shore. Thus, throughout the area, the desert is nowhere far away. From the dawn of history, and until the present day, its pastoral folk, traditionally organized as tribes, have been close neighbours of the sedentary peoples living in the cities, towns and villages of the settled lands.

At all times, the tendency in the area has been for the pastoral desert tribes living closest to the sedentary regions to merge with their rural and urban neighbours and settle among them. Usually, such settlement was gradual, taking long periods to bring about noticeable change. There were times, however, when the settlers from the desert arrived in the peripheries in massive waves, destroying whatever civic order existed in their different parts and bringing about the emergence of a new order. This normally occurred when the desert became over-populated, at a time when political control in the peripheries, for one reason or another, happened to be weak.

In the desert, the pastoral tribes must have originally spoken dialects of a mother tongue which ultimately developed into different but related forms of speech – the so-called Semitic languages, which in their turn were spoken in different dialects. From the desert, these languages, one after another, found their way to the peripheries in the wake of the major waves of tribal settlement there. In historical times, three of them came to dominate the greater part of the area, or the whole of it, in succession, dividing its history into what may be regarded as three linguistic phases: the Canaanite, the Aramaic and the Arabic. Of these three phases, certainly the Aramaic and the Arabic started in the wake of massive migrations from the central desert to the surrounding lands. The same must have been true of the Canaanite phase which preceded the Aramaic, Canaanite having been the language of ancient communities in the western parts of the area such as the Phoenicians and the Israelites – the language of the the Hebrew Bible, whose living traces continue to exist in the form of place names all the way from the extreme south of Arabia to the northernmost reaches of Syria. Side by side with the common language at each phase went a common traditional culture, modified here and there to varying degrees by different external influences. In the case of Syria, these external influences normally came from the West. In the case of Iraq and east and south Arabia, they normally came from the East: from Iran and Central Asia, or from the lands of the Indian Ocean basin.

Today, the modern political frontiers which feature so prominently on the map of the Middle East are artificial, and for the most part imaginary lines drawn across empty desert, making it difficult for us to conceive of the contiguous territories of Syria, Iraq and Arabia as being one unit of historical geography. In Greek and Roman times, however, the classical geographers treated them as such; so did the Arab geographers in Islamic times. In the geography of Strabo, for example, the eastern parts of peninsular Arabia are treated as an extension of Babylonia, in southern Mesopotamia, while the western parts are treated as an extension of Judaea and the adjacent parts of southern Syria. In the Arab tradition, the three regions together were called *bilad al-'Arab*, or the land of the Arabs (in later Ottoman usage, Arabistan), the distinction being made between *bilad al-Sham*, or the land of the North, meaning Syria; *bilad al-Yaman*, or the land of the South, originally denoting the whole of peninsular Arabia; and *bilad al-'Iraq*, meaning the land of the River Banks, or Mesopotamia. Later, when the term *bilad al-Yaman* came to refer in a special way to the south-western parts of the peninsula, which are today North and South Yemen, the Arab geographers began to speak of the peninsula as a whole as *jazirat al-Arab*, or the peninsula of the Arabs, as distinct from the greater *bilad al-Arab*, or land of the Arabs in the sense of *magna Arabia*.

In its original classical usage, the geographic term *Arabia*, for which there is no exact Arabic equivalent, was used to denote peninsular Arabia as well as lands further to the north, which comprise today the so-called Syrian Desert and its immediate peripheries. The Greeks, and the Romans after them, distinguished between an *Arabia deserta*, or desert Arabia; an *Arabia eudaemon*, or *Arabia felix*, meaning fertile Arabia, which referred in a special way to the south-eastern parts of the peninsula, in the region of the Yemen; and an *Arabia petraea*, or rocky Arabia, which was taken to comprise the Syrian highlands east and south-east of the Dead Sea along with the west Arabian ridges of the Hijaz. In Roman times, the territory of what came to be called the province of Arabia was virtually restricted to the parts of the Syrian interior south of Damascus. To the Arabs, this same territory, which the Romans considered Arabian, formed part of what they called Bilad al-Sham, which was their own name for Syria. From the classical perspective however, Syria, including Palestine, formed no more than the western fringes of what was reckoned to be Arabia, between the first line of cities and the coast. Since there is no clear dividing line between what are called today the Syrian and Arabian deserts, which actually form one stretch of arid tableland, the classical concept of what actually constituted Syria had more to its credit, geographically, than the vaguer Arab concept of Syria as *bilad al-Sham*.

Under the Romans, there was actually a province of Syria, with its capital at Antioch, which carried the name of the territory. Otherwise, down the centuries, Syria, like Arabia and Mesopotamia, was no more than a geographic expression. In Islamic times, the Arab geographers used the name, arabicized as *Suriyah*, to denote one special region of Bilad al-Sham, which was the middle section of the valley of the Orontes river, in the vicinity of the towns of Homs and Hama. They also noted that it was an old name for the whole of Bilad al-Sham which had gone out of use. As a geographic expression, however, the name Syria survived in its original classical sense in Byzantine and Western European usage, and also in the Syriac literature of some of the Eastern Christian churches, from which it occasionally found its way into Christian Arabic usage. It was only in the nineteenth century that the use of the name was revived in its modern Arabic form, frequently as *Suriyya* rather than the older *Suriyah*, to denote the whole of Bilad al-Sham: first of all in the Christian Arabic literature of the period, and under the influence of Western Europe. By the end of that century, it had already replaced the name of Bilad al-Sham even in Muslim Arabic usage.

At this point, it would be useful to make a rapid review of the historical geography of Syria, or Bilad al-Sham, since the Islamic conquests of the seventh century.

Under early Islamic rule, the land was divided for purposes of administration into five different provinces called *ajnad* (singular *jund*), each of which comprised a stretch of territory running from the borders of the desert to the Mediterranean coast. South to north, they were the Jund of Palestine, the Jund of the Jordan, the Jund of Damascus, the Jund of Homs, and the Jund of Qinnisrin comprising the vicinity of Aleppo and originally forming part of the Jund of Homs. These early Islamic divisions of Syria continued to be recognized as officially valid until Crusader times. Starting with the tenth century, however, as the central Islamic control of the area weakened, and occasionally collapsed, the *ajnad* became no more than a nominal cover for a baffling kaleidoscope of shifting tribal territories, regional principalities and local baronies, many of the latter consisting of no more than the castle of a local adventurer – usually a robber baron – and its immediate surroundings. During the first half of that century, the great Arab poet al-Mutanabbi earned his living by travelling from one part of Syria to another, visiting the different princes, barons and tribal chiefs in their respective territories and singing their praises. The names of a number of them are only known from his poetry.

During the twelfth and thirteenth centuries, the coastal parts of Syria were ruled by the Crusaders as the kingdom of Jerusalem (1099–1291), the county of Tripoli (1109–1289) and the principality of Antioch (1098–1268), while the inland parts remained under the Islamic rule which continued in Aleppo and Damascus. Between Aleppo and the territory of Mosul, in northern Iraq, the Crusaders also held for a time the county of Edessa (1098–1146). Towards the end of the thirteenth century, however, the Mamluk sultans of Egypt expelled the Crusaders from their last coastal outposts and redivided the Syrian territory into six provinces or vice-regencies called mamlakas (Arabic *mamalik*, singular *mamlakah*). These, in order of importance, were the mamlakas of Damascus, Aleppo, Tripoli, Hama, Safad, and Karak. The Mamlaka of Damascus, which was unmanageably large, was subdivided into four administrative divisions called safaqas (Arabic *safaqat*, singular *safaqah*), meaning marches. Of these, the so-called mountain and coastal safaqa comprised the territory of Palestine; the southern safaqa (the inland parts south of Damascus, including Transjordan); the western safaqa (the area north of Damascus, including the town and vicinity of Homs); and the northern safaqa (the Bekaa valley and the mountain territory beyond it, all the way to the coastlands of Sidon and Beirut).

When the Ottomans conquered Syria from the Mamluks in 1516, they maintained the mamlakas of Aleppo and Tripoli as separate provinces which they called eyalets (and later vilayets), expanding the territory of Aleppo southwards to include the territory of the abolished Mamlaka of Hama. In the central and southern regions, the mamlakas of Safad and Karak were also abolished, and their territories incorporated in what became the Eyalet (and later Vilayet) of Damascus. Later, in 1660, a fourth eyalet, that of Sidon, was created out of the coastal parts of the Eyalet of Damascus which included the territory of the former Mamlaka of Safad along with the coastlands of

Sidon and Beirut and their mountain hinterland. These Ottoman divisions in Syria continued, with occasional readjustments, until the second half of the nineteenth century, when major modifications were introduced.

In 1864 the Vilayet of Damascus was reorganized as the Vilayet of Syria, which introduced the Arabic form of this classical name for Bilad al-Sham into official use for the first time, albeit in a restricted sense. In 1888, a new Vilayet of Beirut was created to include, for the most part, the territories of what used to be the vilayets of Tripoli and Sidon.

If Syria, for most of historical times, was no more than a geographical expression, so too was Lebanon: a name which features prominently in the Hebrew texts of the Bible. In Greek and Roman times, the Lebanon and the Anti-Lebanon, to the classical geographers, were the western and eastern mountain ranges separated by the Bekaa valley, which form the central part of the highland fringes of Syria. In the local usage, the name of the western range (in Arabic, *Jabal Lubnan*) was probably applied, originally, only to its higher, northern ridges which over-look the stretch of coast between the towns of Tripoli and Jubayl. This, apparently, was the Jabal Lubnan of the Arab geographers, who described it as a mountain in Bilad al-Sham, in the territory of Homs. It was certainly the Mount Lebanon of the Crusader historians of the twelfth and thirteenth centuries, who spoke of it as the homeland of the Maronites in the hinterland of Tripoli. To the older Maronite historians, it comprised no more than three districts: Jubbat Bsharri, Bilad al-Batrun and Bilad Jubayl. To the north and south of this Mount Lebanon, or Jabal Lubnan, the Lebanon range continued under different names. In the north, it ended with the ridge of Jabal Akkar. In the south, it stretched across Jabal Kisrawan to include the ridges of the Matn, the Gharb and the Shuf, known collectively as Jabal al-Shuf.

Of the parochial history of the Lebanon range in antiquity, little is known for certain. In Islamic times, however, its northern parts (Jabal Lubnan to Jabal

Akkar), and its central and southern parts (Jabal Kisrawan and Jabal al-Shuf), invariably formed parts of different provinces. Under early Islamic rule, Jabal Lubnan belonged to the Jund of Homs, while Jabal Kisrawan and Jabal al-Shuf, along with the Bekaa valley, belonged to the Jund of Damascus, and were administered from Baalbek. During the Crusader period, Jabal Lubnan formed part of the Frankish County of Tripoli; Jabal Kisrawan and the northern parts of Jabal al-Shuf (the Matn and the Gharb) were claimed as part of the territory of Islamic Damascus; while the southern parts of Jabal al-Shuf (the Shuf proper) formed part of the Seigneury of Sidon, which was one of the four major fiefs of the Frankish kingdom of Jerusalem. North of this seigneury, the territory of the kingdom of Jerusalem also comprised a narrow strip of coast forming the Seigneury of Beirut, which was one of its twelve minor fiefs. Under the Mamluks, Jabal Lubnan became part of the Mamlaka of Tripoli, while Jabal Kisrawan and Jabal al-Shuf were assigned to the northern Safaqa of the Mamlaka of Damascus and administered, along with the adjacent coastlands, in two districts of that safaqa: the Wilayah of Beirut (which included Kisrawan, the Matn and the Gharb), and the Wilayah of Sidon (which included the Shuf proper). This same division of the mountain territory continued under the Ottomans, when the territory of the Mamlaka of Tripoli simply became the Eyalet of Tripoli, while the wilayas of Beirut and Sidon became two sanjaks of the Eyalet of Damascus, and afterwards of the Eyalet of Sidon.

It was only by the early decades of the nineteenth century that the whole of the Lebanon range, except for its northernmost parts, came to be referred to as Jabal Lubnan, or Mount Lebanon, in local usage. To understand why this happened, there is some history to consider.

After their conquest of Syria in 1516, the Ottomans were faced with considerable difficulties in trying to control the Druzes who inhabited the different parts of Jabal al-Shuf. After repeated attempts to subdue these Druzes by force, the Ottomans turned to one of their more powerful chiefs, who was called Fakhr al-Din Maan, and appointed him in about 1590 to administer the two-sanjaks of Beirut and Sidon on their behalf, leaving it to him to establish himself the full master of the coastal and mountain territory involved. By 1605, this Druze chief, whose official title was Sanjak-beyi, or Amir-i-Liwa (hence the common reference to him as Emir Fakhr al-Din), had come to control the whole territory of the two Sanjaks, which included Jabal Kisrawan along with the different parts of Jabal al-Shuf. Meanwhile, the Ottomans had assigned him other parts of the Eyalet of Damascus to administer, notably the Sanjak of Safad, which included the whole territory of Galilee along with the coastal towns of Tyre and Acre. In later years, the emir also came to control the sanjaks of the Eyalet of Tripoli, including the territory of Mount Lebanon proper, or Jabal Lubnan. Subsequently, he fell afoul of the Ottomans. In 1633, the emir was tracked down and captured in one of his mountain hideouts and taken as a prisoner to Istanbul, where he was put to death two years later.

After the downfall of Fakhr al-Din, the Ottomans experimented with different ways to keep the Kisrawan and Shuf mountains under reasonable control, but without success. In 1660, the Eyalet of Sidon was specially created to maintain a closer administrative and military watch over these parts, and also over the turbulent Shiites of the Sanjak of Safad further to the south; but the creation of this new eyalet, alone, did not solve the Ottoman problem. What was needed in the mountain districts, in addition to direct Ottoman control from Sidon, was another, less ambitious and more manageable Fakhr al-Din whose authority would be restricted to these districts, to the exclusion of the coastal towns; such a man was found in the emir's grandnephew, Ahmad Maan. In 1667, only seven years after the Eyalet of Sidon was created, Ahmad Maan was allowed to take over the whole of the Shuf mountains and Kisrawan as a *multazim*, or tax-farmer, answerable to the *beylerbeyi* (Ottoman governor) of Sidon, his *iltizan*, or tax-farming concession, being subject to annual renewal.

Locally, the man, like his granduncle before him, was called an emir. When he died in 1697, leaving no male heirs to succeed him, the iltizam of the Shuf and Kisrawan passed on to a branch of the Shihab family who were descendants of the Maans in the female line. These Shihabs, unlike the Maans, were Sunnite Muslims, not Druzes, and they originally came not from the Shuf, but from the district of Wadi al-Taym, in the south-eastern Bekaa. To exercise power in the trouble-prone mountain districts of which they became the alien multazims, they needed every local assistance they could get.

Even the great Fakhr al-Din, in his time, had faced problems in trying to govern the Shuf districts, where he appears to have had more enemies than friends among his fellow Druzes. To boost his power there, he established strong relations with the Maronites, many of whom were already settled in Kisrawan, and opened the Druze country, for the first time, to large-scale Maronite settlement. Later, his grandnephew, as multazim of the Shuf districts and Kisrawan, did the same. The Shihab emirs, as Sunnites and newcomers to the Shuf, had hardly any real friends among the Druzes, whose only true loyalty was to their own tribal chiefs; so these Shihabs were forced to seek political support mainly among the Maronites and other Christians, whose numbers in the Druze country were constantly increasing. By the second half of the eighteenth century, many members of the Shihab family began to convert to Christianity and become Maronites, and after 1770, or 1788 at the latest, only Shihabs who were Maronites were appointed as multazims of the Shuf and Kisrawan. One of those, Emir Bashir Shihab II (1788–1840), succeeded in expanding the area of his iltizam, by 1821, to include the original Maronite homeland of Jabal Lubnan, or Mount Lebanon proper, where his predecessors had only exercised occasional control in some districts. Thus, for the first time, the whole of the Lebanon range from Jabal Lubnan southwards, to the exclusion of other adjacent coastal or inland districts, fell under one Shihab rule. Until that time, the Shihabs, like the Maans before them, had been spoken of as emirs of the Shuf, or as the emirs of the Druzes, which is actually what they were called by the French traveller Volney who visited Syria in 1785. Now, for the first time, they could be spoken of as emirs of Mount Lebanon, or of 'the Lebanon', in the broader sense of the term, not only locally but also by European travellers, and even in the chanceries of the Western world.

In the 1840s, as eminent a man as Clemens Metternich, the chancellor of the Austrian empire, considered Mount Lebanon as a *pays* or country on its own, separate and distinct from the rest of Syria. Officially, however, the emirate of the Shihabs had never carried that name, being composed of no more than different mountain districts normally but not always held by the same Shihab emir, whose iltizam of them was subject to annual renewal. Every year, the terms of this iltizam had to be negotiated afresh: for the northern districts, with the Vali or governor of Tripoli; for the southern districts, with the Vali of Sidon. In the local usage, the fiscal arrangement involved in either case was called a muaamala (Arabic, *mu'amalah*, or 'transaction'). Thus, rather than being considered one country, the emirate of the Shihabs by the nineteenth century was regarded as consisting of two muaamalas: the muaamala of Tripoli, and the muaamala of Sidon. The gorge which formed the dividing line between the two, at the northern end of Kisrawan, continues to this day to be called al-Muaamalatayn – literally, the two fiscal transactions.

By the end of 1841, the involvements of the Shihabs in the thorny international politics of the so-called Eastern Question had brought about their downfall, to the satisfaction of both the Ottomans who had long been losing patience with them, and the Druzes who had never fully accepted the legitimacy of their government and who had ultimately come to regard them as scheming enemies. This Shihab downfall was preceded by the first open clashes between the Maronites and the Druzes, which continued, off and on, for two decades, ending with a large-scale Druze massacre of the Christians of the southern Lebanon and Wadi al-

Taym in 1860. Meanwhile, after 1841, the former territory of the Shihab iltizam was reorganized in two self-governing divisions called kaymakamates – literally, lieutenancies. The territory of the former muaamala of Tripoli was extended southwards to include Kisrawan, the Matn and small strip of the Gharb, and placed under a Maronite lieutenant-governor, or kaymakam, to become the Kaymakamate of the Maronites, renamed after 1845 the Kaymakamate of the Christians. What remained of the former muaamala of Sidon was placed under a Druze lieutenant-governor and called the Kaymakamate of the Druzes. In the chanceries of Europe, however, as among the Maronites who outnumbered the Druzes in their own kaymakamate, the former territory of the Shihab emirs continued to be regarded as one country or *pays* called 'the Lebanon', or Mount Lebanon.

Following the massacres of the Christians in the Druze kaymakamate in 1860, the French intervened militarily to put an end to the conflict, and a conference of representatives of European powers convened in Beirut to initiate the reorganization of Mount Lebanon as a political entity of special standing within the Ottoman system. The outcome, in 1861, was the establishment of the privileged Ottoman Sanjak or Mutesarrifate of Mount Lebanon under the guaranty of the six major European powers: Britain, France, Austria, Russia, Prussia (later Germany), and Sardinia (later Italy). Thus, at long last, Lebanon ceased to be a mere geographic expression and became the official and internationally recognized name of a territory of special administrative character within historical Syria. This happened three years before Syria, as a geographical expression, was given formal political rehabilitation for the first time since the Roman period, when the Ottoman Vilayet of Damascus was officially renamed the Vilayet of Syria. Following the first world war, the State of Greater Lebanon was established by the French seven years before the territories of the State of Damascus and the State of Aleppo were brought together to form, for the first time in history, a State of Syria.

Since 1920 it has been repeatedly argued that Lebanon, until that time, had been part of Syria. Politically, the argument is meaningless, because there was no nation-state before 1920 called Syria from which the State of Greater Lebanon was artificially separated. All that had existed, and only since the 1860s, was a Mutesarrifate of Mount Lebanon and a Vilayet of Syria comprising only the territory of Damascus, which included the four kazas of the Bekaa valley; and it was only these four kazas which were taken away from the territory of the former vilayet rather than nation-state of Syria and made part of Greater Lebanon. The other territories annexed to the territory of the Lebanese Mutesarrifate to create Greater Lebanon were taken, not from the Vilayet of Syria, but from the Vilayet of Beirut, and had belonged at an earlier time to two other Ottoman vilayets: that of Tripoli, and that of Sidon. This, however, is no more than a pointless splitting of hairs. In terms of historical geography, there had always been a territory of special character, between the desert and the Mediterranean coast, which the ancient Greeks were the first to call Syria. In this Syrian territory, Lebanon was no more than the name of a small cluster of mountain ridges which geographers in classical and modern times, but not in the intervening centuries, applied by extension to a longer mountain range.

As an adjective derived from Lebanon, the term Lebanese is exclusively modern. After the creation of the Mutesarrifate of Mount Lebanon, the term came to have a limited administrative use. Most of the people of the mutesarrifate simply called themselves Syrians, and only the most ardent among the early Christian advocates of Lebanese national particularism spoke of themselves as Lebanese. When the State of Greater Lebanon finally came into existence, its people became officially Lebanese, but many among them, including Christians and even Maronites, continued to refer to themselves in a more general way as Syrians, without necessarily implying any rejection of their new Lebanese nationality. Under the French mandate, after all, Lebanon and Syria were two countries under the same higher mandatory administration. It was only after the end of the mandate in the 1940s, when the independent Lebanese and Syrian republics began to go their different ways, that the Lebanese ceased to consider themselves Syrian, unless they happened to be Syrian nationalists. The Arab nationalists among them, when they felt disinclined to identify themselves as being Lebanese, preferred to call themselves not Syrians, but Arabs.

Yet, today, there is a country called Lebanon whose people have generally come to identify themselves as Lebanese, regardless of whether or not they consider themselves a special historical nationality; and another country called Syria whose people now alone call themselves Syrian. Between the two countries, there is a long historical heritage in common; there is also a common ethnicity and a traditional and formal cultural heritage which both of them share with other countries of the modern Arab world. On the other hand, however, there is a fundamental difference. In Syria, no serious attempt has ever been made to justify the existence of the country as an independent and sovereign state within its standing frontiers in geographical, historical or other philosophical terms. To the Syrian people, Syria is simply a country which happens to be there, perhaps fortunately, to serve as 'the throbbing heart of Arabism', as the country is often poetically described. With Lebanon, it is a different matter. Even before the present Lebanese state came to exist on the political map of the modern Arab world, a number of theories had been developed, sometimes locally, sometimes by external parties, which depicted Lebanon as a national entity of special historical character. Are any of these theories historically or philosophically plausible?

4   Rose among the thorns

In 1510, Pope Leo X paid the Maronites a great compliment, recognizing them for the first time as an Eastern Christian community of special historical standing. In a bull addressed to their patriarch, Peter of Hadath, the pope thanked Divine Providence for having preserved them through the hardest of times, planted among infidels, schismatics and heretics as in a 'field of error', as a 'rose among the thorns'.* According to the Christian interpretation of the Song of Songs, from which the wording of the compliment was taken, the Rose among the Thorns (2:2) was none other than the True Church, the beloved of Christ who refers to it saying: 'Come with me from the mountains of Lebanon, my bride; come with me from Lebanon' (3:8). The pope must have congratulated himself many times on the happy choice of this particular Biblical expression for the occasion. After all, the Maronites did come from the mountains of Lebanon.

Less than a hundred years earlier, the predecessors of Leo X had not thought as highly of the Maronites. True, their patriarchs had formally recognized the supremacy of Rome since about 1180. Two of them, in the course of the

---

* For the original Latin text of the bull see Tobia Anaissi, *Bullarium Maronitarum* (Livorno, 1921).

72

thirteenth century, had actually visited the Holy City: one of them, Jeremiah of Amshit in 1215, in order to attend the opening sessions of the Lateran Council, whose proceedings he could not follow because he knew no Latin; the other, Jeremiah of Dimilsa in 1282, to solicit papal recognition of his appointment to office against the claims of a rival patriarch called Luke of Bnahran. Since then, however, the Maronites had been virtually forgotten in Rome. Under Mamluk rule, it was not easy for their patriarchs to travel to Italy, and it was also difficult to maintain regular correspondence with the popes by other means. Even had they tried, the Great Schism within the Roman Catholic church during the fourteenth century would have left them at a loss to decide whether to communicate with the popes of Rome or those of Avignon. Meanwhile, to the extent that the Maronites were still remembered by the divided Roman curia of the period, the prevailing tendency then was to view them as an outlandish communion of Eastern Christian heresiarchs who had entered into union with Rome while under Crusader rule, probably because they had found it politically expedient at the time, but who had long since lapsed into their former ways.

From the point of view of Rome, the Maronites had originally been Monothelites who believed that Christ had Two Natures but only One Energy and Will. This doctrine, established as Roman state orthodoxy for a time under the emperor Heraclius (610–41) and his immediate successors, had been condemned as a pernicious heresy in 680 by the Sixth Ecumenical Council, the Third Council of Constantinople; but the Maronites, it was maintained, had rejected the decisions of the council and had separated themselves from the body of the faithful by beginning to elect patriarchs of their own to the see of Antioch. Even after their return to orthodoxy through union with Rome, the popes could not recognize the validity of the apostolic succession of their patriarchs to the see of Antioch; the Maronites themselves, however, insisted that they had never had anything to do with the Monothelite heresy, and that theirs was actually the only valid claim to that particular apostolic see whose founder, Peter, was the same Apostle who had founded the see of Rome.

Until 1456, and except for the Crusader period when the see of Antioch was occupied by a succession of Latin patriarchs deriving their apostolic authority from the popes, the true patriarchs of Antioch, in the eyes of Rome, were the Melchite occupants of the post. True, the Syrian Melchites were among the Eastern Christians of the Greek rite who had not been in communion with Rome since the Byzantine schism of 1054; but the Melchites, as Christians of the Byzantine rite, had never been regarded by the Latin church as heretics, and the validity of all their sacraments, including the crucial one of ordination, was therefore officially accepted. A Melchite priest or bishop did not have to be reordained by the Latin church if he decided to return to communion with the papacy. In the case of the Maronites, it was a different matter. Before their formal union with Rome, all the sacraments of their church, and therefore also the ordination of their clergy, had not been performed under an apostolic authority which the popes would accept as legitimate. Even as patriarchs of the Maronites, and not as patriarchs of Antioch, the heads of their church, to gain the apostolic authority required for their office, had to seek it from Rome by formally applying for a papal confirmation of their election and appointment. Since the end of Crusader rule in Syria, no such confirmation had been applied for, although the Maronite patriarchs still considered their church to be in full union with Rome. From the point of view of Rome, however, this union had ceased to exist.

In 1414, the Council of Constance put an end to the internal problems of the Roman Catholic church for a time, and the papacy could again turn its attention to external matters; but the Maronites, now barely remembered, were low in the list of priorities. Having succeeded in putting an end to the schism within their own Western church, the popes now hoped to negotiate an end to the schism with Constantinople and the other Eastern churches following the Greek rite. The circumstances then seemed particularly favourable. From Constantinople, the Byzantine emperor was sending urgent appeals to the popes for Western Christian help against the Ottoman Turks, who were beginning to press against his capital from every direction; in return for such help, he promised to secure an end to the schism between the Byzantine and Roman churches on Roman terms. Encouraged by these appeals and promises, which were repeated time and again, Pope Eugene IV at last decided to act. Upon his initiative, a special ecumenical council was convened in Florence in 1439 to finalize matters.

Considering the urgency of the situation in Constantinople, Eugene IV must have hoped at first that the council, which was organized at lavish expense, would not take long to complete its business. He soon discovered, however, that the Patriarch of Constantinople, unlike his emperor, was unwilling to barter the ecclesiastical independence of the Byzantine church against promises of Western military support for the Byzantine state. After the opening sessions in Forence, an outbreak of plague in the city forced the council to adjourn to Ferrara, where its meetings continued until 1444; but the council finally disbanded without any achievement. To the pope, this was a bitter personal disappointment; to the Roman see, it was a lesson. Under no circumstances could the papacy make any headway with the Greeks.

In 1453, Constantinople fell to the Ottomans. The Byzantine church, as the other Eastern churches had before it, became a tributary of the State of Islam; but its prelates, along with those of the other Eastern churches, continued to pride themselves on their independence from Rome. Only one tiny Eastern Christian communion in the mountains of Lebanon held a different perspective; so Eugene IV learnt at the opening sessions of the Council of Florence from a Franciscan friar arriving from Beirut. The friar carried a special message to the pope from the Maronite Patriarch John of Jaj, who was then living in the village of Mayfuq, in the hill country south of Tripoli. The patriarch, said the message, had wanted to come to Italy in person to attend the council and receive the blessings of the pope for himself and his people, but circumstances had not permitted him to do so. He wished the pope to know, however, that the pope could always consider him as a 'Frank' – an ordinary, faithful member of his own Latin parish.

During the five years that followed, Eugene IV pursued the tiresome proceedings of the council, first in Florence, then in Ferrara, not knowing what the mounting costs of the useless exercise were ultimately going to be; and the simple, trustful words of the Maronite patriarch, relayed to him from the obscure village of Mayfuq, must have remained in his mind. In the East, Rome was courting the proud and forgetting the humble. In Byzantium, it was chasing rainbows. In Mount Lebanon, there was solid rock on which to build. By the time the council had ended, the pope had made up his mind: from now on, there was to be no more neglect of the Maronites. As far as the Roman Catholic church was concerned, this poor mountain folk of goatherds and peasants was henceforth to be considered of far more worth than all the other Christians of the East put together.

Almost immediately following the Council of Florence, the Franciscan friars of the Terra Santa mission in Jerusalem and Beirut received special papal instructions to look after the Maronite church and attend to its needs. Shortly after, in 1450, one of these friars, called Brother Gryphon of Flanders, became the first Roman Catholic resident adviser to the Maronite patriarch. Six years later, the head of the Maronite church was addressed for the first time in a papal bull as Patriarch of Antioch. After the failure of the Council of Florence, and the subsequent fall of Byzantium to the Turks, there was no longer any point in reserving the title for the heads of the Syrian Melchite church with whom the papacy, in any case, had not had any direct contact for centuries. Clearly, Rome was already beginning to see its relations with the Maronite church in a new light; and the operation, though highly rewarding, was not costly: every now and then, the travel fare and

pocket expenses for a papal Visitor to Mount Lebanon; a
mitre, a pallium and a signet ring to be sent to each
patriarch upon his election, in token of his confirmation;
occasionally a small present for the church, such as an
ornamental chalice, or some lengths of brocade from which
to make proper ceremonial vestments for the higher clergy.

In 1470, Brother Gryphon was still advising the Maronite
patriarch when he inducted three young Maronites into the
Franciscan order, then made arrangements for them to go
and study in Italy. One of the three, called Gabriel Ibn al-
Qilai, returned to Mount Lebanon in 1493 as a Roman
Catholic missionary to his own people. The Maronite
patriarch, to whom he first acted as resident adviser,
subsequently appointed him as bishop for the Maronite
diocese of Cyprus, in Nicosia, where he died in 1516. As a
student in Italy, Ibn al-Qilai had been taunted by his
teachers and fellow students about the heretical origins of
his community. In response to these taunts, he had argued
that the Maronites had been the original champions of
Christian orthodoxy in the see of Antioch, and that they
had always been ardent Eastern Christian followers of the
Latin church, unlike the Melchites who from the very
beginning denied the supremacy of the Roman see and
followed Byzantium instead. On the other hand, while in
Italy, Ibn al-Qilai must have been deeply impressed by the
way the Maronites had come to be commonly regarded
after the Council of Florence as the chief defenders of
Roman orthodoxy against the Christian schisms and
heresies of the East, and as the only Eastern Christians
who dared to maintain contact with their fellow Christians
in the West while under the rule of Islam. Out of these
impressions, after his return from Italy, Ibn al-Qilai wove a
fanciful account of the history of his community, which he
wrote in vernacular Arabic verse and called *Madihah 'ala
Jabal Lubnan*, (A hymn on Mount Lebanon).* This small
epic, composed of about 280 quatrains, and full of local

---

* First published by Bulus Qara'li under the title *Hurub al-Muqaddamin*
(Bayt Shabab, 1937).

colour, represents the first attempt by a Maronite to draw a historical portrait of his community against the background of its mountain homeland. What exactly did it say?

The Maronites, said Ibn al-Qilai, were *Sha'b Marun*, meaning the People of Marun – Marun being the Syrian saint of the early fifth century revered by the Maronite church as its special patron. Their history in Jabal Lubnan dated back 600 years, which would mean that they first came to be established in Mount Lebanon in about AD 900. In those days, there were kings and heroes among them who defended the mountains and the coastlands. From the heights of the mountains, their valiant chiefs would descend together with their men as a torrential fall of rain to rout Muslim invaders whenever they attacked. At one time the Maronites had controlled the Bekaa valley, but the wanton behaviour of one of their kings had caused them to lose it. In Mount Lebanon, their bishops were established all the way from the coastal foothills of Jabal Akkar to the borders of Jabal al-Shuf, where the Druzes lived. Among those were the dabblers in the occult whose specialty was the making of talismans. East of the Maronite country, in the direction of Damascus, lived the *Arfad*, or Dissenters, which was the name normally given by the Sunnite Muslims to the Shiites. Around the strategic mountain passes, there were settlements of Kurds. In their own territory, however, the Maronites lived in perfect security, because their rulers and their patriarchs co-operated as brothers, being united by their common devotion to the orthodox Christian faith, as defined by the see of Peter in Rome. At the time, no heretics and no sorcerers had access to Mount Lebanon, and no Muslims could live there. As for the Jews, their very graves would be spotted from the sky by the ravens who would descend and destroy them.

From this ideal state, however, the Maronites soon began to degenerate. Satan himself, in envy, undertook to divide their ranks by unleashing various heresies against them, such as the 'sins' of the Jacobites, and the 'poison' of the Melchites. Among those who succumbed to the lure of these heresies at different times were monks, priests, mountain chiefs, and on one notable occasion even a patriarch, who was called Luke of Bnahran (the rival of Jeremiah of Dimilsa in 1282). The Muslims, quick to take advantage of any weakness among the Maronites, attacked Mount Lebanon every time they heard that its people were divided by heresy. In the end, they succeeded in taking Tripoli (the reference here is to the Mamluk conquest of Tripoli from the Crusaders in 1289), and the Maronites were subjected to Muslim rule as a punishment from God for their sins.

The mercies of God, however, always remained. Even under Muslim rule (which Ibn al-Qilai referred to with poetic licence as the Rule of Hamdan), the plight of the Maronites was alleviated to some degree each time they recanted their heresies and returned to Roman orthodoxy. Once, when the district of Bsharri happened to have a *muqaddam*, or chief, who followed the correct faith and obeyed the patriarch, a deposed Muslim sultan who was travelling around the country stopped in the valley of Qadisha, where he was offered hospitality by a Maronite monk living in one of the many ruined monasteries in its cliffs. The sultan marvelled at the way of life of his host and his fellow Maronite hermits. When he regained his throne, he made rich endowments to reconstruct the monasteries of the Qadisha valley. The sultan in question must have been Barquq, the Mamluk sultan of Egypt (1382–99), who was actually deposed and imprisoned in Syria in 1389, but escaped from prison and returned to his throne in Cairo in 1390. The Bsharri district then began to prosper under its orthodox muqaddams, who came to enjoy an immunity from direct 'Egyptian' interference in their affairs, and held the title of *kashif* (in Mamluk usage, the title of a fiscal official). In addition to this title, the Maronite patriarch made the first of them a *shidyaq*, or hypodeacon, of the church, so that he governed the district in a spiritual as well as in a secular capacity. In a small way, this was a return of the lost golden age to Mount Lebanon.

New misfortunes, however, shortly followed. Attracted

by the prosperity of the Bsharri district under its orthodox muqaddams, the Jacobites began to flock to the area from every direction. The Jacobites were the followers of the Monophysite church in Syria, whose founder in the sixth century was Jacob Baradaeus; hence their name. According to Ibn al-Qilai, these Jacobites, having arrived in Mount Lebanon, began to preach their wicked heresy maintaining that Christ had only One Nature; and Maronites of weak will and weaker faith fell easy prey to their preaching. One among them was Abd al-Munim Ayyub, who was the Muqaddam of Bsharri in Ibn al-Qilai's own time. Ibn al-Qilai warned this muqaddam that if he did not return to orthodoxy, Emir Ahmad (whoever he was) stood by awaiting the first opportunity to attack Bsharri and bring it to ruins, and furthermore God would help him achieve his ends because of the muqaddam's erring ways. On the other hand, if the muqaddam rejected the Jacobite heresy and returned to the orthodox fold, Bsharri would be saved, and Mount Lebanon would return to what it had once been, and what God had always wished it to be: a standing fortress for the True Faith, guarded by vigilant Maronites against Islam and heresy alike.

Ibn al-Qilai was still alive and active as Maronite Bishop of Cyprus in 1510, when Pope Leo X wrote to his patriarch describing the Maronites, among the Christians of the East, as a rose among the thorns. Seven years later, this pope, in Europe, faced the beginnings of the Protestant Reformation, the response to which, in the middle decades of that same century, was the Catholic reformation, called by Protestants the Counter-Reformation. The Jesuit order, which was organized at the time, rallied to the support of the Roman Catholic church in its hour of need, both in Europe and abroad. Before the end of the century, the Jesuits had replaced the Franciscans in Mount Lebanon as the main link between Rome and the Maronites. Meanwhile, the interest of the popes in the Maronites, as the main bulwark of Roman Catholicism in the Christian East, had been noticeably increasing. A special Protector of the Maronites was now appointed from among the Roman cardinals; and in 1885, Pope Gregory XIII, best known for his reform of the Christian calendar, established the Maronite college in Rome, next to the church of San Pietro in Vincoli, for the training of young Maronites in the Roman ecclesiastical discipline. Next, in 1596, the Jesuit Father Girolimo Dandini was sent to Mount Lebanon where he convened the first Maronite synod at the patriarchal residence of Qannubin, in the Qadisha valley, to look into the reorganization of the Maronite church along modern lines.* The work started by Dandini was completed in 1736 by another such synod – that of Luwayza.

Twelve years after the Synod of Qannubin, in 1608, a graduate of the Maronite college in Rome, John Makhluf, was elected Maronite patriarch for the first time, and others followed. One of them was Istifan Duwayhi, who was elected patriarch in 1668 and remained in office until his death in 1704. In his time, the first regular Maronite monastic order was established. More importantly, however, Patriarch Duwayhi was a trained historian and polemicist knowledgeable in a number of languages, including Greek. Dividing his time between church administration and scholarship, Duwayhi wrote several important works, among them a general chronicle which he first called *Tarikh al-Muslimin* (History of the Muslims), then *Tarikh al-azminah* (History of the times), and a special study of Maronite origins which he called *Tarikh al-tai'ifah al-Maruniyyah* (History of the Maronite community).† In the general chronicle, as in the special study, Duwayhi had a great deal to say about Maronite history, upon which he developed a special theory.

Duwayhi fully endorsed the view of Ibn al-Qilai that the Maronites had never been Monothelites, and that they had always been faithful, orthodox followers of the Roman Catholic church. Actually, in his special study on the

---

* Girolamo Dandini, *Missione apostolica al patriarca, e Maronite de Monte Libano* ... (Cesena, 1656); trans. as *A Voyage to Mount Libanus* ... (London, 1698).
† *Tarikh al-azminah* was first published in Beirut, 1952; *Tarikh al-ta'ifah al-Maruniyyah* was first published in Beirut, 1890.

Maronites, a full section of the work is devoted to the refutation of the 'accusations' and 'false claims' that the community was of heretical origin, and that it only reverted to orthodoxy and joined Rome in about 1180 or later. Unlike Ibn al-Qilai, however, Duwayhi lived at a time when Maronites were already living in the Druze country under Druze protection, and the Druze Emir Ahmad Maan, in the Shuf, was his personal friend. Moreover, in his time, the Maronites were already gaining a recognized political importance in Ottoman Syria. Ibn al-Qilai, in Syria, had never been outside Mount Lebanon, and it does not appear that he had any important Muslim contacts. Duwayhi, on the other hand, had served as a Maronite bishop in Aleppo before being elected patriarch, and he had also travelled in other parts of the Syrian interior. Most important of all, he had read the Muslim historians, and was highly knowledgeable of Islamic affairs. He was not as certain as Ibn al-Qilai that the Maronites, in their early history, had been in a continuous state of war with Islam, and that it was the Muslims who had driven them into Mount Lebanon. In fact, he was careful to point out that the Maronites whose church was originally established in the valley of the Orontes, near Hama, had to move the seat of their patriarchate to Mount Lebanon as a result of Byzantine, not Muslim persecution. This, according to him, had happened in 685, and not in about 900, which was the date suggested by Ibn al-Qilai.

What was especially important about Duwayhi's theory regarding Maronite origins was his claim that they had originally arrived in Mount Lebanon as Mardaites from Anatolia. Duwayhi had learnt about these Mardaites mainly from the ninth-century Byzantine historian Theophanes Confessor. They were tribes from Anatolia – possibly Armenians – who were settled by the Byzantines in early Islamic times in the Amanus mountains of north-western Syria, between Antioch and Alexandretta, where they served as a first line of defence against the Umayyad caliphs of Damascus. To the early Arab historians, these Mardaites were known as *Jarajimah*, after their main settlement in the Amanus mountains – a village called Jurjuma. From there, according to both the Byzantine and the Arab historians, the Mardaites made several incursions into Syria in the middle decades of the seventh century, where many bandits, outcasts and runaway slaves joined their ranks. In 685, however, a treaty of peace was concluded between the Umayyads and the Byzantines, under the terms of which the Umayyads agreed to pay an annual tribute to the Byzantines, provided the Byzantines removed the Mardaites or Jarajima from the Amanus mountains and settled them elsewhere. In keeping with this treaty, the Mardaites were actually removed by the Byzantines from that region and dispersed in Anatolia, after which nothing about them is known.

Duwayhi, however, took a different view of the matter. According to him, the founder of the Maronite church in the late seventh century, known as John Marun of Sarum, was a Mardaite of princely descent. Sarum, Duwayhi guessed, must have been at one time a village of the Amanus mountains, near Antioch. The Mardaites, as he envisaged them, were a race of Christian heroes, and they had important contacts with Western Europe. In fact, John Marun's mother, Duwayhi asserted, was a Frankish princess of the Carolingian line – an anachronism which escaped the Maronite historian's notice, as the Carolingians did not appear in Western Europe until the following century. Being related to the 'King of France' on his mother's side, it was only natural, in Duwayhi's opinion, that John Marun should have had close contacts with the Roman papacy, of which he was a faithful follower. In 680, when the Sixth Council condemned the Monothelite doctrine as a heresy and deposed the Monothelite Patriarch Macarius from the see of Antioch, John Marun was elected to replace him as the candidate of Rome; and thus the Maronite church came into existence, from the very beginning, as the representative of Roman orthodoxy in the East, to the displeasure of Byzantium.

Before his election to the see of Antioch, John Marun had been the head of an important monastic foundation in the

Orontes valley, near Hama, with the name of Saint Marun. He himself was called John Marun after this saint, who had been in his time a champion of Christian orthodoxy (a certified fact). After his election as patriarch, John Marun continued to reside in the monastery of Saint Marun on the Orontes, and his Mardaite and other followers came to be called Maronites after it. In 685, however, there was the treaty between the Umayyads and the Byzantines, which stipulated that the Mardaites must be removed from Syria. Thereupon, the Byzantine emperor Justinian II (685–95, 705–11), who favoured the Monothelite heresy (in fact, he did not), sent his Greek forces into Syria to persecute the Maronites in the Orontes valley, after the Mardaite strongholds in the Amanus mountains had been dismantled. In the emergency, one of Patriarch John Marun's nephews, who was called Ibrahim, and who was a valiant Mardaite warrior, secured the withdrawal of his uncle and his faithful followers to the safety of Mount Lebanon. When the Byzantines pursued them there, Ibrahim routed their forces in a decisive battle. In Mount Lebanon, this Ibrahim became the founder of a dynasty of Mardaite muqaddams who continued to lead the Maronite community for centuries, in co-operation with the patriarchs.

On the surface, Duwayhi's theory that the Maronites were originally north Syrian Mardaites seemed plausible. The Maronites wanted to know what made them so different from the other Christians of the East, such as the Melchites and the Jacobites; and Duwayhi provided a ready explanation: they belonged to a different ethnic breed. Unlike the Melchites and the Jacobites, they were not the descendants of the effete Christian peasants and townsmen of Syria who had vied with one another in ready submission to Islamic rule in the seventh century, to live in humiliation thereafter. Rather, their own ancestors were the virile Mardaites who had undertaken the heroic defence of the cause of Eastern Christendom at the time, and with remarkable success, until they were betrayed by the perfidious Byzantines. It was obviously from their valiant Mardaite ancestry that the Maronites inherited their warlike instincts and skills which preserved them in Mount Lebanon as a free and defiant Christian people in their Islamic surroundings. Was it not the same valour inherited from their Mardaite forebears that made them also rise in the defence of the True Apostolic Faith of Rome against the wicked schisms and heresies of the East, to deserve in the end the supreme compliment paid to them by no less a person than the pope himself: that they were, truly, a rose among the thorns?

Today, no serious historian would accept Duwayhi's theory that the Maronites were originally Mardaites, but many Maronites continue to uphold it – if for no other reason, to disclaim for themselves an Arab origin. Remarkably, however, Duwayhi himself, who made such an issue of the Mardaites in his special study on Maronite origins, appears to have otherwise considered his people to be Arabs. In his general chronicle, while speaking of the Ottoman conquest of Cyprus from the Venetians in 1570, he pointed out that the Maronites there received special treatment after the completion of military operations because the commander of the Ottoman forces on the island happened to be an Arab and sympathized with them. From this same chronicle, we learn that the Maronites of one mountain district – that of Aqura – were divided into Qaysi (north Arab) and Yemenite (south Arab) factions, much as other tribal Arabs in Syria were. There is also the available Maronite literature. Unlike that of other Syrian Christians, it is entirely in Arabic, though written until the nineteenth century in the Syriac script. To the Maronites, unlike the Jacobites, Syriac appears never to have been anything more than a language of liturgy. Even the colophons one finds on their Syriac scriptural or liturgical texts are never written in Syriac, only in Arabic. From the Muslim historian Masudi, who lived in the tenth century, one learns that Arabic was certainly the language written by the Maronites in the century before. Even had they been of non-Arab origin, the Maronites must have been arabized by then. Yet, is there actually any evidence that they could have been of non-Arab origin? Also, what evidence is there that they were, in the early centuries of their history, in a continuous state of war with Islam?

To answer these questions, one must turn from considering what Maronite historians have said about the origins and early history of their community and examine the facts. The Maronites have long maintained that they have always been a historical community of special importance. This they certainly were, but perhaps not in the way that is commonly envisaged.

5 The Maronite record

The Maronites, as a Christian community in historical Syria, are roughly as old as Islam. According to Eastern as well as Western Christian sources, their church was founded as a Syrian Monothelite communion in 680, which was the year in which the Monothelite doctrine of the Two Natures but only One Will and Energy in Christ was condemned as heresy by the Sixth Ecumenical Council. Patriarch Duwayhi also maintained that the Maronite church was founded in that year, although he argued that it was established, from the very beginning, as a staunchly orthodox Eastern Christian communion recognizing the supremacy of Rome.

The earliest known references to the Maronites, however, are to be found in the works of two Muslim scholars of the tenth century, the historian al-Masudi and the theologian Abd al-Jabbar, both of whom described the Maronites as Monothelite Christians, explaining exactly what that meant.* In their time, the Maronites still had their main settlements in the valley of the Orontes, in the Syrian interior – a fact which al-Masudi notes in some detail.

---

* The reference is to Al-Masudi, *Kitab al-tanbih wa'l ishraf* (Cairo, 1938); and al-Qadi Abd al-Jabbar, *Al-Mughni* (Cairo, 1965).

Actually al-Masudi had a direct knowledge of the community, for which he appears to have had a special regard. He was also acquainted with the work of their earliest known Maronite historian, Qays al-Maruni, who must have died shortly after 902, and whose writings have since been lost.

Unlike the Christian historians of later times, al-Masudi indicates that the Maronite church was founded as a Monothelite communion in the valley of the Orontes not in 680, but about a century earlier, during the reign of the Byzantine emperor Maurice (582–602). This would mean that the Maronite church was already established in northern Syria when the Prophet Muhammad first began to preach Islam in Mecca in 610. It also implies that, contrary to the commonly held view, the Monothelite doctrine – which was declared the official interpretation of Christianity in 638, then condemned as a heresy by the Sixth Council in 680 – was not originally devised by the emperor Heraclius (610–41) and his theologians as an expedient to reconcile the belief in the Two Natures in Christ (which was Byzantine and Roman orthodoxy) with the Monophysite doctrine of the One Nature (as upheld by the Monophysite churches of Egypt, Syria and Armenia). Rather, it was adopted by Heraclius for that purpose from a heterodox interpretation of Christianity which was already in existence. Al-Masudi may well have been right on this matter. From the acts of the Sixth Council, we learn that the originator of the Monothelite doctrine was a certain Theodore of Pharan, from Arabia, who does not appear to have been a theologian of the immediate entourage of Heraclius, nor necessarily his contemporary. In the early centuries of the Christian era, Arabia, the home of this Theodore, was well known as a breeding-ground for heterodox interpretations of Christianity: so much so that it was sometimes referred to as *Arabia heretica.*

According to their own traditions, as collected and recorded in the seventeenth century by Duwayhi, the Maronites first arrived in Syria as immigrants from another land. In some Maronite districts of Mount Lebanon, folk memory recalls a South Arabian origin for the community. Interestingly, the Shiites of Jabal Amil, and also the Druzes, maintain that they were originally immigrant tribes from the Yemen. There was actually nothing unusual about the movement of Arab tribes from Arabia to Syria in Roman and Byzantine times. Since the second century AD, if not earlier, the ups and downs of tribal politics in the peninsula had frequently triggered off such migrations.

By the sixth century, the Arab tribes of Syria which were generally recognized as being of South Arabian or Yemenite origin were beyond count, and included such groups as the Lakhm, Judham and Qudhaa of Palestine and Transjordan; the Ghassan of the Damascus region; the Awzaa of the Anti-Lebanon, in the vicinity of Baalbek; the Amilah of upper Galilee, who gave their name to Jabal Amilah, now called Jabal Amil; the Thaaliba of the Bekaa valley, among them the Taym, who gave their name to Wadi al-Taym; the Saleeh and Bahra of northern Syria, the last of whom lent their name to Jabal Bahra, today called the Alouite mountains. A number of these tribes could have originally arrived in Syria as Christians. Certainly, by the sixth century, most if not all of them were Christian. Starting with the reign of the emperor Justinian I (527–65), the chiefs of the Christian Arab tribe of Ghassan, having entered the service of the Byzantine state, received official Roman titles and were recognized as client Arab kings over the Syrian territories they controlled around Damascus.

It is very possible that the Maronites, as a community of Arabian origin, were among the last Arabian Christian tribes to arrive in Syria before Islam. The area of their settlement, generally described as the valley of the Orontes, actually comprised the hill country on either side, including the northern reaches of Mount Lebanon to the west; those of the Anti-Lebanon to the east; and the line of hills extending from this point towards the north, all the way to Aleppo. They were still found in considerable numbers, in all these regions, in the tenth century, at the time of al-Masudi. Thus, contrary to the assertion of

Patriarch Duwayhi, their alleged flight from the Orontes valley to Mount Lebanon could not have occurred in 685. Ibn al-Qilai, whose views on the early history of the Maronites were considered in the preceding chapter, was more correct in estimating that Mount Lebanon became the principal homeland of the Maronites in about 900. Considering that al-Masudi found the community still inhabiting the Orontes valley in the middle decades of the tenth century, the date of their final eviction to Mount Lebanon must have been closer to the year 1000.

Even if they had never been Monothelites, which is what their own historians since the fifteenth century have asserted, the Maronites, as newcomers to Syria in the late sixth century, would have had reason to establish themselves as a separate Christian communion – if for nothing else, to distinguish themselves from the older Christian Arab communities existing there, who were either Jacobites or Melchites. At all times, and in all religions, tribe and sect have frequently gone hand in hand, the sectarianism of the tribe serving to underline its sense of particularism as a community. Certainly since the twelfth century, from which time their history is better known, the Maronites have behaved as a tribe or confederation of tribes, often more than as a sect. As certainly, since the ninth century, their language has been Arabic, which indicates that they must have originated as an Arab tribal community, even if they had not actually arrived in Syria from Arabia. The fact that Syriac remains the language of their liturgy, in this respect, is irrelevant. Syriac, which is the Christian literary form of Aramaic, was originally the liturgical language of all the Arab and Arameo-Arab Christian sects, in Arabia as well as in Syria and Iraq. In the days of the Prophet Muhammad, the Christians of the Hijaz, who appear to have been Ebionites, or Jewish Christians, read their Gospel in that language, and not in Arabic.

The Maronites still inhabited the valley of the Orontes and other parts of northern Syria, including the northern reaches of Mount Lebanon, towards the middle of the tenth century. By the end of the eleventh century, when they next appear on the historical scene, their homeland is already restricted to Mount Lebanon, except for a small community in the city of Aleppo, where members are still to be found. To explain what happened in the meantime, we again have only circumstantial evidence. In 969, the Byzantine emperor Nicephorus Phocas invaded northern Syria and occupied Antioch. His immediate successor, John Tzimisces (969–76), swept through Syria as far south as Damascus in the interior, and Sidon along the coast, but the only lasting conquest he made was that of the Orontes valley. Under the next emperor, Basil II (976–1025), this valley continued to be controlled by the Byzantines from Antioch. In northern Syria, only Aleppo, under the Arab tribal dynasties of the Hamdanids and the Mirdasids, held out against the Byzantine onslaught. In the Orontes valley, Byzantine control began to recede after the death of Basil II, until it came to an end in about 1070. In Antioch, the Byzantines held out until 1085. Duwayhi, it appears, was right. It was not the Muslims, but the Byzantines who drove the Maronites out of the Orontes valley, but this did not happen in 685, as Duwayhi had supposed. The whole of Syria, at the time, was under Umayyad rule. Between 969 and 1071, however, the situation was different. The Byzantines were in actual control of the Orontes valley; but they had no foothold in Mount Lebanon, and Aleppo remained under Muslim rule. In the Orontes valley, they must have subjected the Maronites to enough persecution to force them to abandon the place and join their co-religionists in Mount Lebanon, either in one massive exodus or by stages. In Muslim Aleppo, however, the community survived, as it does to this day.

For the history of the Maronites in Mount Lebanon before the twelfth century, our only source is the fanciful account of Ibn al-Qilai, whose contents were sketched in chapter 4. Judging by this account, the Maronites, in Mount Lebanon, were initially organized more as a tribal confederation of clans than as a sect. The community had forty bishops, none of whom appears to have had a fixed parish or defined ecclesiastical functions. One is left with the impression, rather, that they merely served as the ecclesiastical representatives of their respective clans in an establishment which functioned more as a supreme tribal council than as a regular curia. The patriarch, chosen by the bishops to be the first among equals, behaved more as a tribal chief than as the head of the church. Until about the middle of the fifteenth century, there was no fixed residence for the patriarchal office. Each patriarch resided in a monastery of his own choice; in times of trouble, he could move his residence to a place where he could count on his own clan for support and protection.

Apart from the patriarchs and the bishops, who officially headed the Maronite community as a church, different districts and villages of the Maronite territory of Jabal Lubnan – or Mount Lebanon proper – were headed by local chiefs called muqaddams, or centurions. In one case, Ibn al-Qilai actually refers to one of them as *Qentrona*, which is the Syriac transliteration of the Latin military title. As seen by Ibn al-Qilai, these muqaddams were officially subservient to the church, and ultimately to the patriarch, their main function being to lead their followers in war. Some of them he extolled as great heroes; others he dismissed as despicable villains. By and large, one is left with the impression that the Maronite muqaddams were not true tribal chiefs who owed their position to a spontaneous loyalty they commanded among their followers, but petty mountain barons who assumed power in their villages or districts either by force or through political connections.

In the spring of 1099, the arrival of the armies of the first Crusade outside Tripoli, on their way from Antioch to Jerusalem, proved a turning point in the history of the Maronites. The Crusaders had stopped outside the village of Arqa to celebrate Easter. Since their departure from Antioch, they had passed through hostile territory. Now, however, a large party of Maronites descended from their lofty mountains to greet them with 'brotherly affection' and offer their services. On that occasion, the Maronites advised the Crusaders to take the easiest and safest road to

Jerusalem, namely the one that ran along the coast. When Jerusalem was captured in July of that year, it is said that the Maronite patriarch of the day, Joseph of Jirjis, insisted that his personal congratulations on the event be communicated to the pope by the Frankish delegation which was sent to report the news to him; in return, the pope sent the patriarch a present which included a mitre and a pallium. If the story is true, this would have represented the first historical contact between the Maronite church and the Roman papacy.

From the very beginning, however, the Maronites were more divided than united over the question of relations with the Crusaders and the church of Rome. Why this was so cannot be known for certain, but the facts are there. Sometimes, the Frankish historians would be extravagant in their praise of the Maronites: they were 'a stalwart race of valiant fighters' who rendered the Franks invaluable services. At other times, they deplored the treacherous behaviour of the 'men of the blood' among them* – possibly a reference to the brigand Maronite clans inhabiting the higher reaches of the mountains, who were given to selling their criminal services to the highest political bidder.

In about the year 1134, the Maronite Patriarch Gregory of Halat reportedly made the first overtures to a visiting papal legate about the prospect of a union between his church and the Latin communion. Barely three years later, in 1137, the Frankish count of Tripoli led an expedition into the mountains to punish Maronite tribesmen whose treachery had brought about the murder of his father in a Muslim ambush. A large number of these tribesmen were reportedly killed. In his account of the times, Ibn al-Qilai cites the case of one Maronite mountain chief, Muqaddam Kamel of Lihfid, who distinguished himself in repelling an attack by Muslim forces from Baalbek on the Seignery of Jubayl, this being the southernmost fief of the County of Tripoli held by the

---

* For example see William of Tyre, *History of Deeds Done Beyond the Sea*, trans. E. A. Babcock (New York, 1943).

Genoese family of the Embriaci. His heroic defence of the seigneury was rewarded by his induction into the order of knighthood headed by the 'king' (in fact, the seigneur) of Jubayl. Ibn al-Qilai further alleges that this same 'king' of Jubayl, in a further show of honour to Muqaddam Kamel, took his daughter as a bride for his son and heir, so that the 'queen' of Jubayl became in due course a Maronite from the village of Lihfid. Yet, Ibn al-Qilai himself speaks of other Maronite muqaddams, and also Maronite priests and commoners, who were far from faithful to the Crusader cause; and some of those he condemns as outright heretics and traitors.

Remarkably, the Muslim historians writing about the Crusades and about Frankish rule in Syria made no mention of the assistance rendered to the Crusaders by the Maronites. In a state of war between Muslims and Christians, such behaviour on the part of a Christian community, albeit a local one, could hardly have been considered by the Muslims as treason. Moreover, the Maronites were not the only natives of Syria who helped the Crusaders. When the first Crusade arrived in Syria, there existed two states in the country which claimed Sunnite Islamic legitimacy: one in Aleppo, the other in Damascus. The rulers of these two rival states were brothers belonging to the Turkish imperial dynasty of the Seljuks; their first cousin was the Seljuk sultan reigning in the Persian city of Isfahan, as the associate of the powerless Abbasid caliph of Baghdad who remained in theory the head of the State of Islam. Outside the territories of Aleppo and Damascus, there were countless principalities and baronies, some headed by urban notables or Turkish officers, others by Arab or Turkoman chiefs, the Turkomans being the pastoral Turkish tribes already settled in different parts of Iraq, Anatolia and Syria. In addition, there were large tracts of Arab tribal territory, some in the mountains, others on the peripheries of the desert, where no formal government existed.

To complicate matters further, two Islamic caliphates ruled at the time: that of the Sunnite Abbasids in Baghdad, and that of the Ismaili Shiite Fatimids in Cairo. In Syria, some of the local princes and barons professed allegiance to one caliph, some to the other, and a number of them sat on the fence between the two. Moreover, in 1094, a split had occurred among the Ismaili Shiites producing the runaway Ismaili sect of the so-called Assassins. Although their principal base was in the Iranian mountains bordering the Caspian Sea from the south, these Assassins also had a strong presence in Syria. Here they were accorded privileges by the Seljuk ruler of Aleppo, who hoped to make use of them against his political enemies. Before long, they acquired other bases for themselves in the territory of Damascus, whose rulers hoped to use them against the Fatimids. As an esoteric sect, however, the Assassins could not be counted on for loyalty by any Sunnite Muslim ruler in the long term. Moreover, there were large communities of Twelver Shiites in different regions whose loyalty went neither to the Sunnite State of Islam and its representatives in Syria, nor to the Fatimid caliphate in Cairo.

Of all the Muslim rulers and princes of Syria, it was only those of Damascus who persisted in taking the war against the invading Franks seriously in the name of Sunnite Islam. All the others, from the very beginning, showed a tendency to compromise, and among them were Sunnites as well as Shiites. In the resulting confusion, a number of princelings and tribes got away, now and then, with giving help to the Crusaders, while posturing to the contrary; and the rulers of the Frankish states in Syria, most of all the counts of Tripoli, found no difficulty in recruiting Muslim mercenaries to serve them — the so-called Turcoples. Against this background of Islamic perfidy, the Christian perfidy of the Maronites, understandable in the circumstances, must have appeared so negligible as to be hardly worth mentioning, let alone dwelling upon. Moreover, there were actually many Maronites who were opposed to the Franks, and who were occasionally willing to help the Muslims against them.

The Maronite support for the Crusaders appears to have been mainly the policy of the Maronite patriarchs and their

leading bishops, who were eager to gain a stronger
ecclesiastical command over their tribal followers with the
help of the Latin church, now firmly established in both
Antioch and Jerusalem. The higher Maronite clergy had
reportedly flirted with the idea of entering into some kind
of union with Rome ever since the the first arrival of the
Crusaders in Syria. In about 1180, while Amaury, the
Latin Patriarch of Antioch, was paying a visit to Jerusalem,
a number of Maronite bishops and priests met him; they
declared themselves openly in support of Roman orthodoxy,
and agreed to join the Roman Catholic communion. The
historian William of Tyre, who was the Latin bishop of that
city, was apparently present on the occasion, and declared
this formal Maronite conversion to the Roman church to be
a 'wonderful change of heart'. Among the Maronites,
however, there were many who remained strongly opposed
to the conversion. In fact, no sooner had this first formal
union with Rome been concluded than the community was
thrown into a state of civil war. Maronites who had no
liking for the Franks, and who refused to turn Uniate,
forthwith began to wage armed attacks on those who
supported the Franks and approved of the union. Monasteries and churches were not spared; and in some cases
bishops, priests and monks were killed or maimed.

With the Crusaders still present in Syria in force,
particularly in the County of Tripoli where the Maronites
actually lived, the party among the Maronites opposing the
established union with Rome could cause considerable
trouble, but had little chance of ultimate success. Various
measures were taken to strengthen the hand of the pro-
union party, among them the formal invitation extended
by Pope Innocent III to Patriarch Jeremiah of Amshit to go
to Rome in person to attend the Lateran Council held there
in 1215 – an event alluded to in the preceding chapter.
Certainly, Innocent III did not expect Patriarch Jeremiah
to make any important contribution to the proceedings of
the council, but the very fact that he was invited to attend
enhanced his position among his own people, which was
probably the main intent. Before leaving Rome to return to

Mount Lebanon in 1216, the pope issued the patriarch a special bull absolving all repentant Maronite dissidents of their sins of disobedience to the mother Church, except for those who had killed or maimed clergymen. The original texts of both the papal invitation (issued in 1213) and the bull, addressed to 'Jeremiah, Patriarch of the Maronites', survive in the Vatican archives as the earliest known documents relating to the history of the Maronite church.

After his return from Rome, Jeremiah of Amshit was apparently able to run the affairs of his church in peace until his death in 1230. The patriarch was hardly dead, however, when troubles broke out again. According to Ibn al-Qilai, his immediate successor, Daniel of Shamat, unable to face these troubles, was forced to abandon his original residence and spend the remaining years of his life in a remote mountain village, surrounded by his clansmen. By the late thirteenth century, as it became increasingly clear that the days of Frankish rule in Syria were nearing their end, the anti-union party among the Maronites gathered strength. In 1282, when the patriarchal office fell vacant, they secured the election of their own candidate, Luke of Bnahran, as the new patriarch. Opposed to his election, the Franks of the County of Tripoli prevailed on another Maronite cleric of the pro-union party – an obscure monk called Jeremiah of Dimilsa – to accept the same office; and the man was immediately dispatched to Rome to secure papal confirmation for his appointment. For a brief while, the Maronite church had two patriarchs: one living under the protection of the Franks of Tripoli; the other, who had been duly elected, defying Frankish intervention in Maronite affairs from a fortress he established for himself on a promontory of the mountains overlooking the city. To the good fortune of the pro-union party, Patriarch Luke's career – and possibly his life – came to a sudden and violent end when Turkoman bands acting under the orders of Qalawun, the Mamluk sultan of Egypt (1279–90), attacked and captured his fortress. From one important Mamluk source one learns that this patriarch was as much an enemy of the Mamluks as he was an enemy of the

Franks. Six years later, in 1289, the County of Tripoli was finally destroyed when Qalawun captured the city. Shortly after, in 1291, the last Franks were expelled from Syria when Qalawun's son and successor, al-Ashraf Khalil (1290–3), captured Acre and put an end to what remained of the Latin kingdom of Jerusalem.

Paradoxically, the cause of the Maronite union with Rome, on the Maronite side, was stregthened rather than weakened by the end of Crusader rule in Syria. Under the Islamic rule of the Mamluks, the Maronites came to feel more keenly the advantages of having a Western Christian sponsor. To their good fortune, the Mamluks were on excellent terms with one important Western Christian power – the Venetian republic in Italy, who was their partner in the now thriving spice trade between the countries of the Indian Ocean basin and the Mediterranean world. It was probably in a friendly gesture to Venice that they permitted the Franciscan Lesser Brothers to establish their Terra Santa mission in Jerusalem as early as 1291, as well as a branch in Beirut – a town which regained its importance during the Mamluk period as a major Syrian seaport for the spice trade. It was through the intermediary of the Franciscan missionaries in Beirut that Maronite Patriarch John of Jaj was finally able to re-establish proper contact with the Roman papacy in 1439 – a contact which was to lead, by stages, to the thorough reorganization of the Maronite church along Roman Catholic lines.

The story of the developing relations between the Maronite church and Rome after 1439 has been told in chapter 4. Reference was also made to the dynasty of muqaddams who governed the Bsharri district under the later Mamluks as kashifs, or fiscal officers, enjoying an immunity from direct Mamluk interference in the internal affairs of their district. From Duwayhi, we learn that the founder of this dynasty of privileged Maronite muqaddams was Yaaqub Ibn Ayyub, who first assumed power in the town of Bsharri in 1382. Duwayhi further indicates that these muqaddams claimed to derive their authority as local kashifs directly from Cairo, and not from their immediate overlords, who were the Mamluk viceroys of Tripoli. In fact, they boasted of the possession of the original deed of appointment issued to their ancestor Yaaqub Ibn Ayyub by Sultan Barquq in person, which was reportedly inscribed on a sheet of brass. Duwayhi also spoke of a sheet of brass which was issued by the same Barquq to the monk in charge of the monastery of Qannubin, in the cliffs of the Qadisha valley, as a guaranty for the immunities of the monastery – among other things, apparently, from taxation. From the Mamluk sources of the period we learn that the district of Bsharri and other parts of the northern Lebanon which were strictly considered as *wilayat*, or administrative districts, of the Mamlaka of Tripoli, were administered in an irregular fashion; no reports on their affairs were sent from Tripoli to the Mamluk chancery in Cairo. Moreover, the title of kashif, which the muqaddams of Bsharri held, was one which was commonly given in the Mamluk period for district fiscal officers in Egypt, but its use as an actual title is not attested for this same period in Syria, except in the case of the muqaddams of Bsharri. All this upholds the reported claims of these muqaddams that they had a special, privileged relationship with the Mamluk state. One might attempt a guess as to why it was so.

Until 1382, which was the year in which Yaaqub Ibn Ayyub became the Muqaddam and Kashif of Bsharri, the Mamluk sultans in Egypt were the descendants of Turkish slave officers (Arabic *mamalik*, singular *mamluk*) who had once been in command of the crack forces of the Ayyubids – a dynasty of sultans founded by Saladin (1174–93), the renowned hero of the Islamic holy war against the Crusaders. When the last of these Ayyubid sultans died in 1250, his Turkish Mamluk officers refused to accept his profligate son or any other member of the degenerating Ayyubid dynasty as his successor, and assumed power in Cairo themselves, claiming legitimacy for their rule in the dead sultan's name. The last of these Turkish Mamluk officers to become sultan was Qalawun (1279–90); and he became the founder of a dynasty of sultans whose legitimacy, as accepted successors to the Ayyubids, was

generally recognized. After 1341, however, the descendants
of Qalawun began to quarrel over power, which threatened
the security and continuing prosperity of the Mamluk
empire. Meanwhile, since the time of Qalawun, Circassians
rather than Turks had been recruited in Egypt as slave
troops, and powerful officers emerged among them. In
1382, one of these Circassian officers, Barquq, overthrew
the last sultan of the Turkish line of Qalawun and replaced
him on the throne. Under the last Ayyubid sultan, the
Turkish Mamluk troops used to have their barracks on the
island of Roda in the Nile, so their officers who subsequently
became sultans, and their descendants after them, were
commonly called the *Bahri*, or River Mamluks. Starting
with the reign of Qalawun, the Circassian Mamluks had
their barracks in the citadel (Arabic, *burj*) of Cairo, so they
came to be known as the *Burji* Mamluks. Thus, Barquq
was the first Mamluk sultan in Egypt of the Burji rather
than the Bahri line.

To the supporters of the old Bahri dynasty, Barquq was
no more than a Burji usurper, with no legitimate claim to
power. To secure himself on the throne, he needed all the
help he could get, and sought it wherever he might find it.
In 1389, his opponents managed to overthrow him and
retore the Bahri regime. Probably not to alienate his fellow
Burji Mamluks who dominated the army, the deposed
sultan was not killed but sent to prison in the fortress of
Karak, in southern Syria, in the hill country east of the
Dead Sea. From there, however, Barquq soon managed to
escape. With the help of the supporters he had in Syria,
including some powerful Arab tribes, he defeated his
enemies outside Damascus, then proceeded triumphantly
to Egypt to regain his throne in 1390.

In Syria, Venice had a strong presence at the time, as
well as contacts with the local tribes. Venetian merchants
stationed in Damascus, Tripoli and elsewhere were alert to
all the details of the local political developments, as is clear
from the intelligence reports they sent home which survive
in the Venetian archives. Venice, one would assume, had
an interest in having a stable Mamluk government in

Egypt and Syria with which it could deal; and there was no stability in the Mamluk government under the Bahri Mamluk regime after 1341. It is extremely likely, therefore, that Barquq should have actually enjoyed the political support of Venice – a support which could well have helped him take over the Mamluk throne in 1382, then regain it in 1389. From their trading stations in Tripoli, the Venetians had ready access to the Maronites of the mountain hinterland, to whom their intelligence reports make at least one reference. From Duwayhi, one learns that there were Maronite 'notables' living in Tripoli itself at the time, and with these city Maronites the Venetians were most probably in regular contact.

Could it have been through the intermediary of Venice that Barquq was first put into direct contact with the Maronites of the Bsharri district? Whatever the case, one thing appears certain. Barquq had hardly come to the throne in 1382 when he appointed the Maronite Muqaddam Yaaqub Ibn Ayyub as Kashif of Bsharri in an extraordinary capacity, as already indicated. According to Maronite legend, the sultan, after his escape from prison in Karak, stopped in the Bsharri district and stayed in the monastery of Qannubin, to which he later made generous endowments. It was thanks to these endowments that this monastery, which had reportedly been in ruins for centuries, was rebuilt to become the permanent residence of the Maronite patriarchs after 1440, enjoying a guaranteed immunity until the end of the Mamluk period.

In the history of the Maronites, the secular leadership of the muqaddams of Bsharri stands out as the first serious rival to the traditional leadership of the church. Actually, after 1440, the Maronite patriarchs resided in Qannubin under their protection. Outside the Bsharri district, the patriarchs until then had not enjoyed complete security. In 1367, one of them, Gabriel of Hajula, had been burnt at the stake outside Tripoli. According to Ibn al-Qilai, forty Maronites had brought charges of adultery and fornication against him before the Muslim judiciary in Tripoli, and he was tried and condemned to death on that account. Ibn al-Qilai maintained that the patriarch was innocent of these charges, and that he died at the stake, condemned by a Muslim court, as a martyr for his Christian faith. Later, when Patriarch John of Jaj sent a Franciscan friar to represent him at the Council of Florence in 1439, Muslim feeling in Tripoli was incensed against him. The council, it was known, had been convened to concert military efforts of Western Christendom and Byzantium against an important Muslim power, namely the Ottoman state. Undoubtedly, the Mamluks were not happy with the emergence of the Ottomans as rival claimants to the sultanate of Islam; but the Ottomans were making great conquests for Islam in Eastern Europe, and Sunnite Muslim opinion, in Syria as elsewhere, was with them. In 1440, a Muslim mob from Tripoli attacked the residence of the Maronite patriarch south of Mayfuq, setting it on fire. The agitation continued until the Maronite 'notables' living in Tripoli intervened with the local Mamluk authorities to stop it. Thereupon, John of Jaj decided to move his residence to Qannubin, in the Qadisha valley, where the security of his person and office could be guaranteed by the muqaddams of Bsharri, and by the immunity which their district enjoyed. The successors of this patriarch continued to reside in Qannubin until the nineteenth century.

After the Ottoman conquest of Syria in 1516, the Bsharri district did not continue to enjoy its immunity for long. In 1547, Husam al-Din of Ayn Halya, who was a Maronite from a village of the Anti-Lebanon and a descendant of Yaaqub Ibn Ayyub in the female line, arrived with a mixed force of Melchites and Shiites from the Baalbek region to kill the last Muqaddam of Bsharri in the male line, massacre his family, and replace him in the government of the district. The Ottomans, who had no wish to see old partisans of the Mamluks remain in power in Syria, must have been happy with the change, and may even have encouraged it.

Certainly, as muqaddams of Bsharri, Husam al-Din and his successors of the Ayn Halya line were far more subservient to the government of Tripoli, under the

Ottomans, than their predecessors in the same office had been under the Mamluks. The Bsharri district, under their rule, ceased to enjoy its former immunities; and, before long, the *kishlak*, or forced quartering of Ottoman troops, was imposed there, as in other rural parts of Syria. Moreover, the Shiites of the Baalbek region, having helped bring Husam al-Din of Ayn Halya to power in Bsharri in 1547, gained access to the district for the first time; by the following century, a number of them had arrived to settle in some of its villages, and their sheikhs of the house of Himada consequently began to wield a disturbing influence on local Maronite affairs. At Qannubin, the Maronite patriarchs occasionally had problems with the Himada sheikhs. The Ottomans, however, left these patriarchs at liberty to run their church as they pleased in co-operation with Rome, except that the monastery of Qannubin and its estate were now subjected to regular Ottoman taxation. On the whole, one gets the impression that the Bsharri district and the other parts of the northern Lebanon underwent a steady deterioration and impoverishment during this period.

It is against this background that the Maronite migrations of the Ottoman period, from the northern Lebanon south-wards, must be considered. These migrations began in the sixteenth century, when large numbers of Maronites, starting in about 1545, left Jabal Lubnan, or Mount Lebanon proper, to settle in Kisrawan. This region, since 1306, had been under the control of Turkoman clans who were settled there by the Turkish Mamluks; however, they had later fallen afoul of the Circassian Mamluks, because their sympathies lay with the Ottomans who were Turks like themselves. In 1516, the chief of one of these Turkoman clans, called Emir Assaf, was put in charge of the region, now established as a *nahie* (administrative district) of the Sanjak of Beirut, and his descendants succeeded him in that office until 1593. To manage the affairs of Kisrawan, whose inhabitants until then were predominantly Shiites, the Assaf emirs recruited a certain Sheikh Hubaysh and his sons, who were Maronites from the Jubayl district with some education and competence, and appointed them as their chief stewards, with extensive administrative privileges. These Hubayshes, consequently, became the most prominent Maronite family of the period, and they put the Assaf emirs in contact with the Maronite patriarchs at Qannubin. They also encouraged Maronites from the Jubayl district and other parts of the northern Lebanon to settle in the Kisrawan, where the Assaf emirs, who were Sunnite Muslims, welcomed their presence as a loyal element which could be counted on to counterbalance the turbulent Shiite element in the region.

On the political background of the Maronite migration into the Druze country of the Shuf in the seventeenth and eighteenth centuries, enough has already been said in an earlier chapter. What must be pointed out here, however, is that this migration also had an important connection with the development of silk production in the Shuf mountains under the Maan and Shihab emirs. In some parts of the Shuf, silk had been produced certainly since Mamluk times, but mainly for a limited local market. Under the Mamluks, Syria was only open commercially to Venice, and the Venetians were more interested in the spice trade coming to the Syrian seaports from the lands of Indian Ocean basin than in the local commodities. The situation changed after the Ottoman conquest, more particularly by the latter decades of the sixteenth century, when English, Dutch, French and other European merchant companies gained free access to the area and became highly active in its markets. From being a marginal product, the silk of the Shuf now became a commodity for which the European merchants competed.

Starting in the days of Fakhr al-Din Maan (1590–1633), the production of silk in the Shuf mountains and in Kisrawan was encouraged first by the Maan then by the Shihab emirs, who exported it to Europe from Sidon and later also from Beirut. To increase the production of silk in the Shuf, more labour was required than could be furnished by the local Druze peasantry, and the Maronite immigrants arriving in large numbers from the north provided the additional labour force that was needed. To attract the Maronites to come to work on their estates, the Druze chiefs did everything possible to facilitate their settlement in Druze villages; some of the villages appear to have been virtually deserted at the time, apparently in consequence of the repeated Ottoman invasions of the Druze country earlier on. More than that, Druze chiefs made donations of land to the Maronite church: the first donation was made by Fakhr al-Din Maan as early as 1609. Starting in the late seventeenth century, Druze land was also donated to the Maronite monastic foundations, which became particularly active in the management of local silk production. Meanwhile, other Christians from different parts of Syria came to settle among the Maronites in the Druze country, and some of those, notably the Greek Catholics, were also accorded favoured treatment. Before long, a whole micro-economy emerged there, centring around the silk trade, and dominated by the Christians – and most of all the Maronites – as the peasants who produced the silk; the money-lenders who advanced money on the crop; the intermediaries who facilitated the production; the brokers who bought the crop from the local markets to carry it to Sidon or Beirut; and the town merchants who arranged for its export to Europe.

In all these lucrative activities that developed in connection with silk, the Druzes had hardly a role, except that the Maronite and other Christian villagers who produced the commodity in the Shuf mountains worked in most cases as sharecroppers on lands owned by Druze tribal chiefs. In Kisrawan, the Maronites who cultivated the silk worked on lands which were owned by a new class of Maronites: the feudal sheikhs. The first among those were the Hubayshes, who had risen to prominence in the region under the Assaf emirs. In 1605, however, when Fakhr al-Din Maan took over Kisrawan, he entrusted its management to another local Maronite family, called the Khazins, who rapidly came to overshadow the Hubayshes in importance. Until the nineteenth century, the Khazins, first under the Maans, then under the Shihabs, remained the most prominent Maronite family in Lebanon.

Meanwhile in Europe, France had emerged as the leading Roman Catholic power under Louis XIV (1643–1715); and the Khazins, from the beginning of his reign, began to be appointed French vice-consuls, then French consuls, in Beirut, considerably enhancing their prestige. From that time, the Maronites began to consider France as their special European friend and protector, with the Khazins in a special way serving as the intermediary. In Kisrawan, the Khazins, with the encouragement of the Maans and the Shihabs, began to purchase the lands of the Shiites, including whole villages, and they invited more Maronites from the north to come to settle in these villages. Before long, clashes between the new Maronite settlers and the original Shiite inhabitants of these villages began to occur, and the gradual eviction of the Shiites from Kisrawan followed, sometimes by force, sometimes by monetary settlement. By the end of the eighteenth century, the Khazins had already come to own nearly the whole of Kisrawan, and only a few Shiite villages survived. As the Shiites were evicted from Kisrawan, their position in the Maronite districts further north naturally weakened, and they were gradually forced to withdraw from that area too.

And so, by the last decades of the eighteenth century, we come to the point when the Maronites, from their small beginnings in the northern Lebanon nine centuries earlier, had grown to become a community to reckon with in every part of the Lebanon range, including the Druze country of the Shuf. Theirs, throughout this period, was a success story unique in the annals of the Christians of the Muslim world. In all this time, they had never known persecution, unless the trial and execution of Patriarch Gabriel of Hajula in 1367, or the one attack on the patriarchal residence at Mayfuq in the exceptional circumstances of 1440, are considered persecutions. Somehow, the Maronites in Mount Lebanon, at every stage in their history, managed to accommodate to the prevailing political conditions in a manner which secured for them a privileged position, which they exploited until the early nineteenth century with discretion. Most important of all, beginning in the fifteenth century, they succeeded in developing and maintaining special relations with Western Europe through their union with Rome, without giving undue offence to the Islamic states under whose rule they lived.

Inspired by their history of success, by the nineteenth century the Maronites had developed a high degree of self-confidence as a community, and they felt they could now dream of greater achievements. There were certainly many obstacles in the way, but the Maronites had friends in the world – most important of all, France – who had an interest in helping them overcome these obstacles. The Maronites understood this, and subsequent developments were to prove that their calculations were correct.

6 The imagined principality

When Emir Bashir Shihab II by 1830 was at the height of his power, he controlled the whole territory of the Lebanon range except for the northernmost ridges of Jabal al-Dinniyya and Jabal Akkar. To the Ottomans, he was still, officially, no more than a multazim of the local taxation, answerable to the Pasha of Tripoli for the northern parts of his territory, and to the Pasha of Sidon (now actually resident in Acre) for the southern parts. In the chanceries of Europe, however, Bashir was already spoken of as 'Emir of the Lebanon'. From Cairo, the great viceroy of Egypt Muhammad Ali Pasha (1805–47) made a point of courting his friendship.

In the Lebanon, the emir's predecessors had resided in the Shuf in a modest palace previously the seat of the Maan emirs in the town of Dayr al-Qamar. By 1811, however, Bashir was already established in truly princely splendour in a magnificent palace recently completed outside Dayr al-Qamar, on the picturesque promontory of Beit el-Din. To supply the new palace and its terraced gardens with water, he undertook the construction of a canal from the headwaters of the river of Nahr al-Safa, several kilometres away. The waters carried by this canal, now used to irrigate the fruit orchards along the way, still fall in cascades outside the Beit el-Din palace as a living testimony to the emir's enterprise. In all parts of his territory, the emir initiated the construction of roads and bridges, some of which still stand. Under his stern and watchful eye, law and order prevailed everywhere.

Bashir was born a Maronite, and died a Maronite, as the surviving text of his will testifies; but he made no show of the Christian faith he formally professed. His palace had no chapel. Above the seat reserved for him in the hall where he held court, one can still read the verse inscribed on the ornate wooden panelling which he appears to have taken as the motto of his government: 'An hour of justice is better than a thousand months of prayer.'

To the Maronites and other Christians living under his rule, Bahir II was a reigning prince, and the scion of a dynasty of reigning princes. The Druzes, however, looked upon him differently. They knew precisely what he officially was: a mere fiscal functionary of the Ottoman state, whose iltizam, or tax-farming concession, was subject to annual renewal. Originally, the emir had secured this iltizam in 1788 against competitors from his own family with the help of the Jumblats of the Shuf, who were the strongest and most revered of the Druze tribal sheikhs. He had subsequently suppressed his rivals among his Shihab kinsmen by having the more prominent and ambitious among them killed, blinded, imprisoned or banished. Next, he had turned against the more powerful Druze sheikhly families, playing them off against one another until all were brought to their knees. The Jumblats alone continued to oppose him until 1825. In that year, however, Bashir Shihab had prevailed on the Pasha of Acre to have the head of that family, Bashir Jumblat, seized and hanged. With the power of their tribal chiefs thus reduced, and in some cases destroyed, the Druzes were left in no position to oppose the emir, as they had opposed his predecessors. For the duration of his rule, they openly accepted his overlordship as they secretly nursed their deep hatred of him and awaited the opportunity for revenge.

In 1830 it seemed inconceivable that the great emir would be overthrown and within ten years sent into exile to die in 1851 in a modest house in Istanbul on the shores of the Bosphorus, with only a few of his more faithful servants around him. His Christian subjects, at least, thought that his reign, and that of his descendants after him, would endure. Living with him in the palace of Beit el-Din at the time was his young Greek Catholic secretary Nasif al-Yaziji, who was later to gain great renown as an Arabic scholar and man of letters. From Yaziji's pen, we have an essay written in 1833 describing the Shihab regime in the Lebanon as the Christians of the country had come to view it, and as they continue to remember it to this day. A critical assessment of this essay, long accepted by scholars at face value, was recently made by Abdul-Rahim Abu Husayn, of the American University of Beirut, which puts the whole question of the Lebanese emirate in a new light.*

Mount Lebanon, said Yaziji, was a country of tribes (Arabic, *bilad 'asha'ir*). In fact, it ranked first among the tribal parts of Syria. At the head of its tribes stood the Shihab emirs who were its governors (Arabic, *wulat*, singular *wali*). The tribes of Mount Lebanon had grown so accustomed to having the Shihabs as their governors that they would submit to no other. They preferred to have a mere child of the Shihab family as their governor rather than a seasoned adult of any other family. Under the Shihab government, Mount Lebanon was divided into a number of feudal cantons called *muqata'at* (singular *muqata'ah*); and the management of these cantons was entrusted to different families of emirs or sheikhs, mostly Druze, but some among them Maronite. The heads of these families maintained law and order in their respective feudal cantons and collected local taxes according to arrangements worked out between them and the ruling Shihab emir. In each canton, the family wielding feudal

* As edited by Constantine Basha, Yaziji's essay is entitled *Risalan fi ahwal Lubnan fi 'ahdih al-iqta'i* (Harisa, 1936). Its first publication was in 1885. Abu Husayn's study of this essay was presented at the Third International Conference on the Social and Economic History of Turkey, Princeton University, 1983.

power could impose punishments for crimes and felonies except the death sentence, which was reserved for the Shihab emir alone. The feudal families of Mount Lebanon, however, were of different ranks and stations, and correspondence between them and the ruling emir was governed by a strict protocol. They also sat in his presence according to rank, and the emir accorded them formal greeting in different ways, again according to rank. In short, the Mount Lebanon of the Shihabs, as depicted by Yaziji in his essay, was a dynastic principality of established feudal structure, where everyone knew his place in the hierarchy. At the head stood the Shihab emir, who governed the country as a feudal suzerain in consultation with the heads of the different cantons.

Here was a highly idealized picture of the Shihab emirate which was not accurately descriptive of the reality at any time. Certainly by 1830, contrary to Yazjiji's claim, Bashir Shihab was running the affairs of the Lebanon as a despot rather than as a feudal suzerain. To the Christians, he was a benevolent despot; the Druzes, however, generally regarded him as a malevolent one. Actually, it was only the Christians who accepted Shihab rule in Mount Lebanon as legitimate and accorded it their loyalty. The Druzes never did: a fact which Yaziji perhaps deliberately ignored.

Moreover, there were essentials about the nature of the different feudal families which escaped the notice of Yaziji, or which he preferred not to dwell upon. In speaking of the Druzes, he did mention that they were divided into three parties: the Jumblatis at one extreme headed by the house of Jumblat; the Yazbakis at the other extreme headed by the house of Imad; with the house of Abu Nakad and their Nakadi partisans sitting on the fence between the two. Actually, these three parties were traditional Druze tribal factions, each of which had its recognized dynastic head; and certainly the two major factions – those of the Jumblatis and the Yazbakis – already existed in the early seventeenth century, at the time of Fakhr al-Din Maan. The sheikhly families who headed these factions wielded a power over their followers which, at a fundamental level, was completely independent of their association with Shihab rule.

To break the Druze tribal resistance to their rule in its early days, the Shihabs after 1711 had taken measures to involve the three leading Druze sheikhly families – the Jumblats, Imads and Abu Nakads – in the fiscal management of the Shuf mountains by assigning special cantons to each; this transformed them from a tribal aristocracy of unbridled powers to a feudal one dependent on a suzerain. The Shihabs had further given sheikhly rank at that time to two other families of Druze chiefs originally of secondary rank, the Talhuqs and the Abd al-Maliks, to each of whom a special fiscal canton was also assigned. The Imads, who headed the Yazbaki Druze faction, were much weaker than their Jumblat rivals. For this reason, if for no other, they tended to co-operate more closely with the Shihab regime in the Druze mountain. To strengthen their position against the Jumblats, the Imads made common cause with the two new Druze sheikhly families, the Talhuqs and the Abd al-Maliks, associating them in the leadership of the Yazbaki faction. Much as they tried, however, the Shihabs never managed to reduce the command of the Jumblats over the tribal followers. Similarly, they made little headway with the Abu Nakads, who carefully avoided playing the Shihab game.

Thus, in the Druze mountain, the traditional tribalism of the Druzes continued to lurk under the cover of the Shihab feudal system. It was only the Maronite and other Christian peasants of the different cantons of the Shuf mountains who regarded the Jumblats, Imads, Abu Nakads, Talhuqs and Abd al-Maliks as feudal overlords operating under the suzerainty of the ruling Shihab emir. To their own Druze followers, the heads of these families – and most of all the Jumblats – remained tribal chiefs whose traditional authority, at the Druze level, by far transcended the powers they enjoyed as heads of cantons under the Shihab system.

In the cantons of Kisrawan, the Maronite sheikhs of the Khazin and Hubaysh families had an altogether different standing. Those, and also the Maronite sheikhs of other cantons which were established by the nineteenth century in the northern Lebanon, were not chiefs who had tribal followings, but simply Maronite notables to whom the Shihabs assigned the local tax farming. Among these families, the Khazins were the actual owners of all but the northernmost strip of Kisrawan, which was the canton of the Hubayshes. In their own canton, the Khazins, apart from holding the local tax farm, were also manorial lords whose peasants were virtually their serfs. While the Druze sheikhs in the Shuf mountains were tribal chiefs to their Druze followers, and feudal overlords only to the Christians who lived in their respective cantons, the Khazin sheikhs in Kisrawan were feudal overlords to the local Maronite 'commoners' (Arabic, al-'ammiyyah) and nothing else.

Before arriving in Kisrawan and the Shuf mountains to become peasants working on the lands of Maronite or Druze feudal sheikhs, the Maronites, in their original home districts in the northern Lebanon, had been no less tribal than the Druzes. Those among them who did not leave the northern Lebanon actually remained so. In those parts, the loyalty of the Maronites to their different tribal affiliations had always transcended their loyalty to the village or district muqaddams, and even to their church. This situation did not change after the Shihabs gained control over the northern Lebanon, dividing it into fiscal cantons such as those already existing in Kisrawan and the Druze mountain. In the canton of al-Zawiya, for example, the Shihabs handed over control to the Dahir family, whom they appointed as the local tax-farming sheikhs. The Maronites of al-Zawiya, however, continued to be loyal to their old tribal sheikhs, among whom the most prominent at the time were the Karams of Ihdin.

Having lost their original tribal organization as they turned into peasants and share-croppers working for Maronite or Druze manorial lords, the Maronites of Kisrawan and the Shuf mountains could only keep their social solidarity as a community by turning to their clergy for leadership. Thus, paradoxically, the Maronite church in these regions, with its secular priesthood and monastic foundations, became stronger than it had ever been on its original home grounds in the north. This may explain, at least partly, why the Maronite patriarchs at the time of Bashir II moved their main winter residence from Qannubin, in the Bsharri district, to the village of Bkerke, in Kisrawan, keeping only a shorter summer residence first at Qannubin, then in nearby Diman. In Kisrawan, the Khazin and Hubaysh sheikhs used their influence to secure the election of members of one or the other of the two families as patriarchs for a time. In 1854, however, a Kisrawan 'commoner', Bulus Masaad, managed to succeed to the patriarchal office in Bkerke, and the two sheikhly families of the region consequently lost the control they had attempted to keep over the Maronite church organization.

Meanwhile, as observed in the preceding chapter, a class of well-to-do Maronites had been emerging among the 'commoners' in the villages and market towns of Kisrawan and the Druze mountains, as well as in Beirut. As a result, social stirrings began to occur among the Maronites in both regions; and these stirrings came to be encouraged, after 1854, by the church. In the Druze districts, Christian political ambitions were already growing and impinging on the traditional prerogatives of the local Druze sheikhs, most of whom owed large debts to Christian money-lenders who held much of their property as collateral. In 1858, matters came to a head in Kisrawan, where the 'commoners' rose in revolt against the Khazin sheikhs and evicted them from Kisrawan. For about two years, the region fell under the control of a jacquerie of armed villagers led by a farrier called Taniyus Shahin. Encouraged by the success of the Maronite 'commoners' in Kisrawan, the Maronites of the Shuf districts, egged on by their clergy, began to prepare for similar revolts against their Druze overlords, taking heart from the fact that they already formed a considerable majority of the population in all these districts. The Druzes, however, rallying in a body around their threatened tribal sheikhs, were swift to act. The planned Maronite revolts in the Druze territory were aborted within a few weeks in 1860 by a series of ghastly bloodbaths.

In short, the realities regarding the Lebanese emirate of Ottoman times differed greatly from the picture of the well-ordered dynastic principality of set feudal structure and elaborate protocol, as depicted by the young Yaziji in 1833. By the end of 1841, the Mount Lebanon of the Shihabs, whatever its true nature, had ceased to exist. Within a year, new Ottoman administrative arrangements had divided the mountain into two kaymakamates, one for the Christians, the other for the Druzes. In the Christian kaymakamate, the new system did not work. The authority of the appointed Maronite kaymakams clashed with the entrenched feudal interests of the Khazins in Kisrawan, and with the growing power ambitions of the Karams of Ihdin who were now the paramount tribal chiefs in the northern Lebanon. The same applied to the Druze kaymakamate, where the appointed kaymakam remained a figurehead, while the different Druze sheikhly families, backed by their tribal supporters, were left free to keep the cantons formerly assigned to them by the Shihabs and manage them as they pleased. Yet, among the Maronites, the idealized image of the old Lebanon of the Shihabs remained. In 1859 it received historical elaboration for the first time in a book published in Beirut by Tannus al-Shidyaq – a Maronite who had once served different members of the Shihab family as a clerk, and who was subsequently employed by the American Protestant missionaries in Beirut as a teacher of Arabic, and possibly also as a proof-reader at their American Press. His book was actually among the earlier publications of this press, and it was entitled *Akhbar al-a'yan fi Jabal Lubnan* (Annals of the notables of Mount Lebanon).

As conceived of by Shidyaq, the history of the Wilaya (Arabic *wilayah*, here in the sense of 'political mandate') of Mount Lebanon began in early Islamic times, when the Mardaites established their dynastic rule among the Maronites of the northern Lebanon, whilst the Tanukh Arabs lay the foundations of what subsequently became the Druze emirate in the Shuf mountains. These Tanukh Arabs, Shidyaq explained, were the descendants of the pre-Islamic Arab kings of Hira, in southern Iraq; they had first arrived in the distirct of the Gharb, in the hinterland of Beirut, as Muslim Arab military settlers under the early Abbasid caliphs of Baghdad. One of them, called Arslan (a Turkish name which no Arab could have carried at the time), became the founder of the Arslan dynasty, which continued to control the Gharb and adjacent districts, including Beirut, until 1110, when the Crusaders captured the city during the reign of King Baldwin of Jerusalem and put its people to the sword. Survivors of the house of Arslan remained in the town of Shwayfat, in the lower Gharb, a short distance away from Beirut, where the emirs of this family maintained a canton of their own during the centuries that followed. In 1843, they reappeared on the political scene when members of the family were appointed as kaymakams of the Druzes. This, to Shidyaq, was a revival of their earlier wilaya, after an interruption of more than seven centuries.

After 1110, as Shidyaq saw it, the Wilaya of the Gharb passed from the Arslans to another family of the Tanukh tribe founded by a certain Emir Buhtur. Shidyaq called this new dynasty the Tanukhs. To avoid confusion, we might call them the Buhturs. These Buhturs remained emirs of the Gharb throughout the Crusader and Mamluk periods, and came to be closely associated with the Mamluks, in whose time they were firmly established in Beirut. When the Ottomans arrived to conquer Syria, the Buhtur emirs fought on the Mamluk side, and hence lost their wilaya in 1516 when the Ottomans defeated the Mamluks and took over Syria.

Meanwhile – according to Shidyaq – in the course of their wars against the Crusaders, the Muslim rulers of Damascus sent new Arab military settlers to the Shuf proper, in the hinterland of Sidon, which at the time was virtually uninhabited, with instructions to guard the area against Crusader encroachments. Among these settlers were the ancestors of different Druze sheikhly families. At the head of the settlers, however, were the emirs of the house of Maan. A similar settlement of Arab tribes at the time was established by the rulers of Damascus in Wadi al-Taym, at the western foot of Mount Hermon; leading these other Arab settlers were the emirs of the house of Shihab. The Maans and the Shihabs co-operated closely when fighting the Crusaders; they also began to intermarry from an early time, which resulted in the establishment of a firm bond of kinship between them. In 1516, when the Buhturs of the Gharb opted to side with the Mamluks against the Ottoman invaders, the Maans volunteered to fight with the Ottomans. To compensate them for their support, the Ottomans, once they had taken over Syria, assigned to them the Wilaya of the Druze mountain which, until then, had been held by the Buhturs. Within a century, the Maans, during the reign of Emir Fakhr al-Din, had succeeded in bringing the whole of Mount Lebanon under their rule by taking over Kisrawan and the northern Lebanon. When the Maanid line became extinct with the death of Emir Ahmad in 1697, the notables of Lebanon – Druzes and Maronites – agreed that their Shihab kinsmen should succeed them in the wilaya of the country. Thus the wilaya of the Shihabs in Mount Lebanon began, continuing without interruption until the end of 1841.

Shidyaq's vision of the historical development of Mount Lebanon as a hereditary emirate under a succession of ruling dynasties was neat, and on the surface convincing. Historians of Lebanon continued to accept it until recently, when a new generation of scholars, trained in modern historical methods, began to subject it to close scrutiny by a more careful examination of the sources. The most important of all was the available Ottoman historical material concerning Mount Lebanon, including the rich archives of Istanbul: the *Tapu Defteri*, or Ottoman land register, studied for different parts of Mount Lebanon by Adnan Bakhit of the Jordanian University; and the *Muhimme Defteri*, or Ottoman chancery register, more recently exploited in a study of the provincial leaderships in Ottoman Syria by Abdur-Rahim Abu Husayn of the

American University of Beirut. From these and other studies, it has become increasingly clear that Shidyaq's vision of the history of Mount Lebanon, accepted at face value for more than a hundred years, is not only riddled with internal contradictions and loopholes but is also fundamentally untrue. What was the historical reality?

Since pre-Islamic times, Mount Lebanon appears to have been densely populated by Arab tribes, as other rural parts of Syria certainly were. With the coming of Islam, the tribes of Kisrawan and the Shuf mountains accepted the new faith and became Muslims; their Islam, however, as in the case of other rural and tribal Arabs in Syria and elsewhere, must have tended from the very beginning to be sectarian rather than orthodox, and in time it became in some cases highly sectarian. Thus, Twelver Shiism came to dominate in Kisrawan, and also gained ascendancy among the Muslim Arab tribes of the Baalbek region in the Bekaa valley, and those of Jabal Amil in upper Galilee. Ismaili Shiism, on the other hand, apparently in its more extremist forms, spread in the Shuf and Wadi al-Taym. Starting in the ninth century, the antinomian heresy of the Qaramita, which first appeared among the tribes of southern Iraq and eastern Arabia, reached Syria and penetrated the Bekaa valley, and perhaps also the Shuf mountains. Commonly believed to have been a sect of the Ismaili Shiites, the Qaramita, judging by what available sources have to say about their blatant antinomianism, could equally have been a Shiite sect which developed independently of Ismailism.

It was actually the Ismaili Fatimids of Egypt who undertook the suppression of the heresy of the Qaramita in Syria. This had already been accomplished when the caliph al-Hakim (996–1021) came to the throne in Cairo. According to the Ismaili Shiite doctrine, each of the Fatimid caliphs, in succession, was in a sense divine, personifying in his time the metaphysical soul of the universe by virtue of being the descendant and rightful successor of Ali, the first cousin of the Prophet Muhammad and the husband of Fatima, the Prophet's daughter. All the Shiite sects regarded Ali, who was the fourth caliph to succeed the Prophet, as having been in his time the rightful and infallible Imam or divinely-guided leader of the community of Islam. The Ismailis, however, were among the Shiite sects who regarded his person, and the persons of his rightful descendants, as having qualities which transcended humanity and shared in divinity. During the reign of al-Hakim, some Ismailis in Cairo developed a special doctrine about the person of this particular caliph. While all his Fatimid predecessors, admittedly, had reigned as living manifestations of some aspect of divinity, he himself was more than that. His living person manifested the unity of God.

The small group of Ismailis who first articulated this doctrine in Cairo called themselves *Muwahhidun*, or Unitarians. Historically, however, the followers of the doctrine have been known as the Druzes. Because the Druze religious doctrine represented such a radical departure from all accepted forms of Islam, Sunnite and Shiite alike, it was kept in strict secrecy. Unsuccessful in attracting any substantial following in Egypt, its originators, starting in about 1017, undertook its preaching in Syria among Arab tribes who already subscribed to esoteric interpretations of Islam, such as those of the Ismailis or the Qaramita. Among the Syrian regions where this Druze preaching was successful were the Shuf mountains, in the southern Lebanon, and Wadi al-Taym, in the Anti-Lebanon. Within a few decades, the preaching stopped, and the doors of conversion to Druzism were closed.

Among the Syrian tribal chiefs to whom the founders of Druzism addressed one of their epistles in 1026 was the head of a clan of the Tanukhs who was then established in the village of al-Bira, in the Gharb — today a ruin outside the town of Souk el-Gharb, which overlooks Beirut. Historically, the Tanukhs were a south Arab tribal confederation who came to be established in southern Iraq by the third century AD, where they founded the Arab tribal kingdom of Hira. One tribe of this confederation, the Lakhm, are known to have been established in Hira as well as in Palestine. It is entirely possible, therefore, that other Tanukhs, since pre-Islamic times, should have been established in different parts of Syria as well as in Iraq. On the other hand, it is highly unlikely that the Tanukhs of al-Bira in the hills of the Gharb were actually the descendants of the pre-Islamic Arab kings of Hira, which it appears is what they claimed.

Apart from the fact that the epistle addressed to the Tanukh Emir of al-Bira in 1026 survives in the Druze scriptures, nothing is known about him or his family at the time. In 1147, however, a descendant of his, called Buhtur, was recruited into the service of the Sunnite state of Damascus. This was the year in which the armies of the second Crusade advanced from Palestine against Damascus, but failed to capture the city and were decimated in retreat. The Crusaders, at the time, were established in Beirut and Sidon. From Sidon, they controlled the whole of the Shuf proper, as the surviving assizes of the Latin kingdom of Jerusalem indicate. From Beirut, however, they were unable to penetrate the hill country of the Gharb, where Buhtur led stiff local resistance. In a decree addressed to him by the ruler of Damascus in 1147, Buhtur was urged to keep up this resistance, and prevent the Franks from making any inroads into the Gharb. In return, he was recognized as Emir of the Gharb, and its territory was granted to him as an iqtaa (Arab *iqta'*, or 'land grant'). In the usage of the time, an iqtaa involved the right granted to army officers, known as emirs (Arabic *umara'*, singular *amir*), to collect and keep the taxes of assigned villages or districts as the main part of the compensation for their services.

The history of Buhtur and his descendants, beginning in that year, is well known from the works of two Druze historians. The first was a descendant of Buhtur called Salih Ibn Yahya, who died in about 1435. Eager to record the deeds of his ancestors, Salih Ibn Yahya gathered all the information concerning them which he could find. He also had at his disposal a large collection of family documents, most of which he reproduced verbatim in his work. The second Druze historian of the house of Buhtur, called Ibn Sibat, was a trusted clerk who served the family in the late fifteenth and early sixteenth century. Ibn Sibat wrote a history which summarized the work of Salih Ibn Yahya and provided it with a continuation until 1523, shortly before his death. Until it was discovered among the manuscripts of the Louvres, in Paris, towards the end of the nineteenth century, the single autograph manuscript of the history of Salih Ibn Yahya was unknown, because it had been originally kept as a family secret. Since then, two editions of it have been produced.* The history of Ibn Sibat, on the other hand, was written for general use. Among the Maronite historians, Patriarch Duwayhi was the first to depend on it in relating the history of the Druze mountain. Shidyaq also quoted from it profusely. The work, however, though existing in several manuscripts, remains unpublished.

From the writings of these two Druze historians, it is clear that the Buhturs were never reigning princes in the Gharb. In their time, they were simply the most prominent family of Druze notables in the region. Starting in 1147, the family maintained a policy of close relations with whatever Islamic regime was established in Damascus, and gave its prime loyalty to the cause of Sunnite Islam. Now and then, their loyalty wavered when Sunnite Islam did not appear to be doing too well, or when its ranks stood divided. This happened, for example, after 1250, when the Mamluks of Egypt were bidding for the Sunnite Islamic hegemony against the Ayyubids of Syria, and the Buhturids found themselves at a loss as to which side to take. When they finally opted for the Mamluk side, the Ayyubids of Damascus sent a punitive expedition against them which ravaged some of their villages in 1256. Later – when the Mongols, having established themselves in Persia and sacked Baghdad in 1258, invaded Syria and occupied

---

* The first edition, by Louis Cheikho, entitled *Tarikh Bayrut* (Beirut, 1927); the second, by Francis Hours and Kamal Salibi, under the same title (Beirut, 1969).

Damascus in the following year – the Buhturids decided to divide their ranks between the Mongols and the Mamluks. At the battle of Ayn Jalut in 1260, where the Mamluks arrived to defeat the Mongols near Lake Tiberias and drive them out of Syria, there were Buhturids fighting as expert archers in the Mongol as well as in the Mamluk army. After 1260, however, the family finally committed itself to the service of the Mamluks. While the Crusaders remained in Syria, the Mamluk state continued to be highly suspicious of them. Between about 1270 and 1277, three of their leading members were actually kept in prison, and in 1283 the iqtaas of the family were revoked. It was only after the Mamluks had completed the reconquest of coastal Syria from the Crusaders in 1291 that they took the Buhturids into their service again. This time, they were assigned commissions in the so-called Halqa corps (the locally recruited cavalry), as emirs, or officers, of different ranks, each with his own small iqtaa. Their military duties were carefully specified: they were required to assist in the defence of Beirut against attacks from the sea, and keep watch over its important harbour, in co-operation with the Mamluk military command in Baalbek. This made it necessary for them to take up residence, while on duty, in Beirut. When off duty, they returned to their homes in the Gharb hills, in the villages of Abey, Ainab and Aramun.

Once established in Beirut, some of the stronger Buhturid emirs grew rich, apparently by taking shares from the proceeds of the spice trade in the Beirut harbour. In the hills of the Gharb, they owned extensive olive groves from whose oil they made soap for the local market and for export. In the first half of the fourteenth century the leading emir among them, known as Nasir al-Din al-Husayn (d. 1341), built a palace for himself in Beirut, and another in the mountains, in the village of Abey. In both palaces, he held court as if he were a reigning prince, and a number of second-rate poets, attracted by his munificence, paid him visits and sang his praises. Two biographical dictionaries of the period have entries concerning him which emphasize the social prominence he enjoyed in his time. Strictly, however, Nasir al-Din al-Husayn, though he behaved as a prince, was no more than a Halqa officer of middle rank; and so were his descendants, until the Halqa corps was disbanded later in the century.

In 1389 when Sultan Barquq, the founder of the Burji Mamluk regime, was momentarily overthrown and imprisoned, the Buhturids remained faithful to him. The Turkomans of Kisrawan, who opposed Barquq and supported his Bahri Mamluk opponents, attacked the Gharb and ravaged some of the Buhturid villages during the troubled months that followed. When Barquq regained his throne in 1390, however, he sent a force against Kisrawan to subdue the Turkomans and kill their leading chiefs, and the Buhturids participated in the expedition. Until that time, the Turkoman chiefs of Kisrawan had been the chief rivals of the Buhturid emirs in Beirut, but now they went into eclipse, while Barquq and his successors showered favours on the Buhturids. In the course of the following century, and until the Ottoman conquest, at least two members of the family were appointed governors of the Wilaya or adminsitrative district of Beirut; and certainly one of them, called Sadaqa, who was the cousin and contemporary of the historian Salih Ibn Yahya, held the wilayas of Beirut and Sidon together for some time.

Of the history of the Maans in the Shuf district before the late fifteenth century, nothing is known. Apparently, they were a family of local muqaddams, or regional chiefs, who held the more important villages in the district, among them Dayr al-Qamar and Baruk. In 1494, one of them, called Fakhr al-Din Uthman, built a mosque in Dayr al-Qamar, possibly to endear himself to the Mamluk authorities, as the Druzes did not use mosques. This same Fakhr al-Din Uthman, at one time, was involved in a rising against the Mamluks in the Bekaa valley, which brought about his temporary imprisonment in Damascus. When the Ottomans conquered Syria, the Maans were among the Syrian provincial chiefs who were regarded with suspicion, no less than the Buhturids who were known to have been the supporters of the Mamluks. Certainly, the Maans did not fight with the Ottomans against the Mamluks in 1516, nor did the Ottomans award them with an emirate over the Druze mountain which was taken away from the Buhturids. Firstly, there was no Druze emirate, in the sense of a dynastic principality, to be taken from one dynasty and given to another. Moreover, to the Ottomans at the time, no Druze could be trusted. Shidyaq's story of the Maanid succession to the Buhturids as emirs of the Druze country in 1516 is pure invention, though the invention was not actually his. The first historian who actually mentioned this alleged succession was Haydar Shihab (d. 1835),* who was a cousin of Bashir Shihab II, and a former employer of Shidyaq. It appears that the Shihabs, or their Maronite partisans, had invented the story earlier to provide the Shihab regime in the Lebanon, as the successor of the Maanid regime, with an Ottoman legitimacy dating back to the time of the conquest.

For the greater part of the sixteenth century, the Maans remained muqaddams in the Shuf, different members of the family holding different villages, more as local strongmen than as tribal chiefs. The actual tribal leaders in this region, as elsewhere in the Druze country, were the sheikhs who headed different groupings of Druze clans, and those could be friends or enemies of the muqaddams depending on the circumstances. In the sixteenth century, the prevailing conditions caused the Druze clans to rally around the Maans for leadership. Between 1516 and 1521, the newly established Ottoman rule in Syria was faced with considerable resistance from local political elements which had formerly been loyal to the Mamluks; and there was even an abortive attempt at the time to revive the Mamluk regime in Damascus. From the Venetian documents of the period, it is clear that Venice, as the old friend and business associate of the Mamluks, was unhappy about the

---

* The work in question by Haydar Shihab is *Al-Ghurar al-hisan fi tarikh hawadith al-zaman*, published by Na'um Mughabghab (Cairo, 1900).

Ottoman conquest of the Mamluk empire. In Syria, the agents of Venice were in strong sympathy with the local resistance against the Ottomans, and they apparently began to supply the elements involved in this resistance with firearms – at the time, muskets. Even today, the Arabic word for a musket or a rifle is *bunduqiyya*, which is the standard Arabic form of the name of Venice.

From the work of Abu Husayn on the Ottoman materials of the period, one learns that the tribes of the Lebanon continued to receive consignments of firearms from Cyprus until the island was conquered by the Ottomans from the Venetians in 1570; also, that these firearms excelled those of the Ottoman army in quality, which caused the Ottoman state grave concern. When the Ottoman conquest of Cyprus was completed, the whole of the Venetian arsenal in the island was apparently dumped in the Lebanon. Among the chief recipients of this considerable ordnance were the Druzes; and the Ottomans, if they were to consolidate their rule in the strategic coastal parts of Syria, had first to disarm these Druzes. Between 1523 and 1586, Ottoman expeditions were repeatedly sent to the Shuf mountains for this purpose, and a succession of muqaddams of the house of Maan led the Druze resistance against them. One of these muqaddams, in about 1544, was reportedly captured and beheaded by the Ottomans. Another, called Korkmaz, somehow met his death in 1586 as he fled the last and most formidable of the Ottoman attacks.

In that year, it appears, the Druze country was finally subdued. In Syria, however, the Ottomans soon began to face a problem of another kind. The Safavids, since the early years of the century, had established Twelver Shiism as the religion of the new kingdom they had founded for themselves in Persia, and imposed it on their subjects. At that time, the leading men of learning among the Twelver Shiites were active in the villages of Jabal Amil, in the hinterland of Tyre, south of the Shuf, and a number of these scholars were invited to Persia to provide the newly established state religion there with doctrinal guidance. From the very beginning, the Safavids, who were originally in control of Iraq, were at war with the Ottomans. In 1524, when the Ottomans conquered Baghdad and took over Iraq, the Safavid kingdom in Persia went into a period of recession. In 1587, however, with the accession of Shah Abbas I (Abbas the Great, d. 1629) to the Persian throne, Safavid power began to revive, and the wars between the Safavids and the Ottomans were soon resumed.

In Syria, the Safavids could use local Shiite political leverage against the Ottomans, not only in Jabal Amil, which formed part of the Sanjak of Safad, but also in the Baalbek region. There, it seems, they had long been in secret contact with the local Shiite emirs of the house of Harfush, to whom the Ottomans normally entrusted the management of the Nahie (administrative district) of Baalbek. With the resurgence of Safavid power in Persia, the Harfush emirs began to seek an extension of their power to the strategic town of Mashghara, in the southern-most reaches of the Bekaa valley, no doubt with a view of securing direct contact with their fellow Shiites in nearby Jabal Amil. The Ottomans were determined to stop such contact being established, and kept a watchful eye on the Shiites, in Baalbek as in Jabal Amil. This, again, is clear from the work carried out on the Ottoman documents of the period by Abu Husayn.

To reduce the lurking Shiite danger in these parts, the Ottomans turned to the Druze Maans of the Shuf, who stood chastened and subservient after the successful Ottoman expedition sent against them in 1586. Their choice fell on Fakhr al-Din Maan, the son of Muqaddam Korkmaz who had died in the course of that expedition. In about 1590, this Fakhr al-Din was appointed *amir-i-liwa*, or governor, of the Sanjak of Sidon, to which the Sanjak of Beirut was subsequently attached. In 1598, as the wars between the Safavids and the Ottomans broke out again, he was also appointed *amir-i-liwa* of the Sanjak of Safad, which gave him direct control over the pro-Safavid Shiites of Jabal Amil.

Since the 1920s, Lebanese schoolchildren have been taught to speak of Fakhr al-Din Maan as an emir of

Lebanon, and to regard him as the historical founder of the Lebanese state. Certainly, Fakhr al-Din, in the later years of his career, came to control the whole territory of what is today Lebanon. It was he, in 1621, who put an end to the Maronite muqaddamate of Bsharri by having the last local muqaddam, who was little better than an ordinary criminal, seized and drowned in the Qadisha river. Fakhr al-Din's political ambitions in Syria, however, went far beyond the Lebanon mountains. Throughout his career, the Shuf remained his power base. To him, however, the control of the Sanjak of Safad, and also of the Sanjak of Ajlun and other parts of Transjordan, were at least as important, politically, as the control of the sanjaks of Beirut and Sidon, or the different mountain nahies of the Sanjak of Tripoli, in the Eyalet of Tripoli.

In the annals of Ottoman Syria, this Maanid emir stands out as a brilliant figure by any standard. His political ambitions apart, he was a man of enlightenment in an age when such were hard to come by in the Ottoman world. Beirut, Sidon and Acre prospered under his rule, as did their mountain hinterland. He invited experts from Italy to help modernize the local agriculture; and it was he who first attended to the promotion of local silk as a cash crop for which there was a ready world market. An English traveller visiting Beirut in 1697, and surveying the decaying remnants of Fakhr al-Din's public buildings and gardens, could not help observing that this remarkable emir, who had died several decades earlier, was obviously a man 'above the level of ordinary Turkish genius'.

Fakhr al-Din, however, was never emir of Lebanon, and he did not found a Lebanese state. From the work of Adnan Bakhit, he emerges as a Syrian strongman who was given leeway by the Ottomans to subdue and destroy other provincial leaderships in Syria on their behalf, and who was himself destroyed in the end, to make way for a firmer control by the Ottoman state over the Syrian eyalets. Politically, his only enduring achievement was the subtle symbiosis that developed under his patronage between the Maronites of Kisrawan and the Druzes of the Shuf mountains. After his downfall, the Ottomans experimented with different ways and means to break up this symbiosis, but all efforts in this direction failed. In the end, after taking the sanjaks of Beirut, Sidon and Safad away from the Eyalet of Sidon, and reconstituting them in 1660 as a separate Eyalet of Sidon, they returned to the Maans in the person of Emir Ahmad, the grandnephew of Fakhr al-Din, and entrusted him in 1667 with the iltizan of the five mountain nahies of the sanjaks of Sidon and Beirut: the Shuf, the Jurd, the Gharb, the Matn, and Kisrawan. Thus began the history of what historians came to recognize in retrospect as the 'Lebanese emirate' – a term which neither Ahmad Maan, nor any of his Shihab successors except the last, ever used to describe the regime.

Of the true nature of the Maan and Shihab government of different parts of Mount Lebanon, between 1667 and 1841, as an Ottoman iltizam, or tax farm, enough has been said in earlier chapters. This iltizam amounted to a dynastic principality only in the minds of the Christian partisans of the Maan and Shihab multazims. The Druzes, even when they did not oppose these multazims, always recognized them for what they really were, and never entertained any illusions of their being reigning princes. Nevertheless, the fact remains that the Shihabs, starting in 1711, introduced a unique system of fiscal cantons in the Shuf mountains and Kisrawan, and later in the northern Lebanon, which gave their regime a special character within the broader Ottoman system. The Shihab emirs were certainly appointed as multazims of their territories on an annual basis, and their position in this respect was always precarious. Yet, whatever the extent of the territory over which they had charge at any given time, they remained at the top of what amounted to a feudal hierarchy – a hierarchy which, until 1841, held the different parts of this territory together, more or less in the manner described by Yaziji in his essay of 1833. Under their government, the Druze and Maronite sheikhs of the different cantons did work in co-operation. Even the Druze sheikhs who were most vehemently opposed to the Shihab regime could not conceive of a workable alternative to the Shihab system, much as they would have liked to, for as long as this system remained operative.

To this extent, the so-called emirate of the Shihabs after 1711, while it was not exactly a dynastic principality of traditional legitimacy, bore a close resemblance to one. It was certainly not the continuation of an emirate of the Druze mountain whose history dates back to the earliest centuries of Islam; to the period of the Crusaders and the Mamluks; or to the Ottoman conquest. On the other hand, it was definitely the historical precursor of the Mutesarrifate of Mount Lebanon which was established in 1861, and which became, in its turn, the precursor of the Lebanese Republic of today. Historians of Lebanon who limit themselves to this view of the significance of the period of the emirate in the history of the country stand on firm ground.

7 The mountain refuge

Henri Lammens (d. 1937) was a Jesuit priest of Flemish origin, and a professor of oriental studies at the Saint-Joseph University which his order had founded in Beirut in 1875. He was a prolific and highly imaginative scholar, and ranked among the leading orientalists of his time, although he was gerenerally criticized for giving free rein to prejudice and conjecture in his work. His students were strongly influenced by his ideas, and among them was the generation of Christians, mainly Maronites, to whom the French, in many cases upon his personal recommendation, entrusted the government and administration of Lebanon after 1920. In that year, the Jesuit father was hard at work completing a general survey of the history of Syria, which was published by the Catholic Press in Beirut in 1921. The book appeared in two volumes under the title *La Syrie: précis historique.*

Lammens undertook the writing of this history of Syria shortly after the end of the first world war, clearly with a political purpose, and possibly upon the suggestion of the French authorities in Beirut who had a high regard for his scholarship. His earlier witings had been mainly on Islam and early Islamic history; and of Islam the Jesuit father held an extremely negative view. To him, as to the Christians in Beirut who were pressing at the time for the political separation of a Greater Lebanon from its Syrian surroundings, the Arab nationalism which had recently been spreading in Syria, largely among the Muslims, was little more than political Islam under a new name and guise. During the war years, Britain had espoused the Arab nationalist cause among the Syrians, backing the Arab Revolt of Sharif Husayn in the Hijaz, and permitting the Sharif's son Faysal to enter Damascus in 1918 and establish his Arab government there.

In the following year, the Paris Peace Conference stipulated that the former Arab territories of the Ottoman empire would be distributed between the leading Allied powers as mandates under the newly established League of Nations. The American King–Crane commission was sent to Syria to assess local opinion on the matter, in keeping with the principle pressed by President Woodrow Wilson at the peace conference that all the peoples of the world had the right to national self-determination. The report of the commission emphasized the Arab nationalist opposition among the Syrians to having a French mandate imposed upon them. Short of complete independence, the people of Syria, according to the report, preferred to have their country placed under American mandate; and if that was not possible, under a British mandate. The French regarded the King–Crane report, which was highly publicized at the time, as an Anglo-Saxon ploy deliberately devised to obstruct their own regional interests.

In 1920, France finally secured its mandate over its share of the 'Levant' territory, ousted King Faysal from Damascus, and proclaimed the creation of the State of Greater Lebanon as a first step towards the political reorganization of the mandated territory. But Arab nationalism remained a serious force to reckon with, secretly backed against the French by the British, and more openly supported by the Americans who had a firmly established intellectual base in the area: the Syrian Protestant College, founded in 1866 and soon to be renamed the American University of Beirut. Meanwhile, Charles Crane, one of the two heads of the King–Crane commission, and a businessman who had close connections with American oil interests, maintained the contacts he had established with the Arab nationalists in Syria in 1919 and continued to give them moral encouragement. His Syrian Arab friends nicknamed him Harun al-Rashid, after the most famous of the Abbasid caliphs; and as late as 1938 the first history of the Arab nationalist movement, entitled *The Arab Awakening* and written by the Christian Arab George Antonius, was dedicated to him. Greatly embarrassed first by the British then by the American sponsorship of Arab nationalism, the French were anxious to find some other idea forceful enough to be pitted against it, and the book of Henri Lammens on Syria appeared in time to provide such an idea. The Syrians, Henri Lammens argued in his book, had been historically in existence as a people long before the coming of the Arabs, and they had all the potential to develop into a nation on their own.

The idea of Syria as a natural and historical nation was not entirely new. It had been in the air since the nineteenth century, particularly after the Vilayet of Damascus was renamed the Vilayet of Syria in 1864, borrowing the name from European and Christian Arabic usage (as indicated in an earlier chapter). To the Christians of the country, more particularly the Melchites, the name had a special emotional appeal, because it denoted their historical diocese of Antioch. In 1920, one year before Lammens completed his history of Syria, the concept of Syria as a historical nation was articulated by George Samne, a Greek Catholic from Damascus, in a book which he entitled *La Syrie*. In the work of Lammens, however, this concept received further elaboration.

Syria, as Father Lammens saw it, was a natural country, with natural frontiers the like of which are rarely found: the Taurus mountains which separated the country from Anatolia in the north; the desert which separated it from Iraq in the east and Arabia in the south; and the sea which served to connect it with the world of the Mediterranean basin in the west. To this extent, one could say that Syria had been originally willed by Divine Providence to be the cradle of a nation. On the other hand, an extremely rugged topography cut up the country internally into self-enclosed compartments, where different communities had always lived without direct contact with one another. It was as if the same Divine Providence that had originally willed Syria to be a nation had also willed that the Syrians should never be able to interact to achieve this end.

Nevertheless, to Lammens, the potential for the achievement always remained. The Syrians, as a people, had traits in common which transcended the superficial regional and confessional differences between them. At all times, they had demonstrated a high degree of intellectual and practical resourcefulness and initiative; a love of freedom; a hatred for oppression. At all times, moreover, they had been open to constructive cultural influences more from the West than from the East, and they had also influenced the West in return. In their history, their Hellenistic heritage, Greek and Roman, was of paramount importance. Did not Christianity carry the distinct marks of its Syrian Hellenistic origin? Did not five emperors from Syria sit on the imperial throne in Rome? Was Beirut not the leading centre for the study of law in late Roman times?

In the seventh century AD, however, Islam appeared in Arabia, and Syria was conquered by Arabs arriving from the hostile aridity of the desert under the banner of the new religion. Of all the country, only the Lebanon mountains remained unsubdued, so that the true history of Syria, so to speak, came ultimately to be concentrated there. In the Syrian interior, as in the towns of the coast, Islamic rule, Lammens maintained, was highly oppressive, except for a brief century at the start when the exceptionally enlightened Umayyads ruled as caliphs in Damascus (661–750). Their rule was more like a Syrian than an Arab dynasty, he thought, in which the rigour of Islam was tempered by a remarkably open-minded liberalism. After the overthrow of the Umayyads by the fanatical and ruthless Abbasids, Syrians who could not abide tyranny fled to Mount Lebanon, which thus became the refuge of all the persecuted of the country who valued their freedom –

l'Asile du Liban, as the Jesuit father called it. The persecuted in Syria, of course, were not only the Christians; there were also the dissident Muslims, among them the Twelver Shiites and the Druzes. Then followed one tyranny after another, relieved only by the interlude of the Crusades. After that came the worst: the squabbling and brawling rule of the Mamluks, followed by the intolerable oppression of the Ottomans and their venal and humourless pashas. Yet, even in these darkest of times, 'to all those who were put off by the tyranny of the pashas, the mountain stood open.' It was then that the great Emir Fakhr al-Din Maan brought the Maronites and the Druzes together under his leadership in resistance to the Ottomans, and established the first Lebanese mountain state which continued under his Maan and Shihab successors. His remarkable achievement was to secure for the *Asile du Liban*, at long last, a special political status as an autonomous principality within Syria, in the interest of all the fugitive communities which formed its population.

By depicting Syria as a natural country awaiting the opportunity to actualize its nationhood, while reserving a special historical place for Lebanon within Syria as the traditional mountain refuge for the oppressed, Father Lammens struck two birds with one stone.

On the one hand, he drew a fine line of distinction between what he maintained to be legitimately Syrian national history, and the accidental though prolonged and in his opinion fundamentally unwelcome intrusion of Arabism and Islam into this history. This provided historical justification for the emergence of a secular, interconfessional nationalist movement in geographical Syria which was independent of Arabism; and such a movement did not take long to come of its own accord, as a natural development of the Syrian national sentiment which had already been gaining ground in some Christian circles since the previous century. In the mid-1930s, as already noted, a Greek Orthodox Christian from Mount Lebanon, Antun Saadeh, became the founder of a Syrian Nationalist Party – the Parti Populaire Syrien (PPS).

Through the medium of this party, Syrian nationalism came to be accepted by many Christians in different parts of Lebanon, Syria, Palestine and Transjordan; also by many Shiites, Druzes and Nusayris, and even by some liberal and secular-minded Sunnite Muslims who found Arabism too Islamic in character for their taste.

On the other hand, Lammens was careful to draw an even finer line of distinction between his *Asile du Liban* and the rest of Syria, thus providing a specific historical justification for the State of Greater Lebanon, which the French had created only a few months before his book was published. To the Syrian nationalists wherever they happened to be, and also to the Christian Lebanists in Lebanon, the *La Syrie* of Father Lammens became a standard work of reference. As it was, naturally, to the French High Commission in Beirut, for whose policies the book provided intellectual cover.

The argument of Lammens for the historicity of a nationality peculiar to the Syrian people had much to commend it, but more that was against it. After all, hardly anyone could seriously contend that the Syrians of medieval and modern times were not fully Arab in language and culture, regardless of any differences that could have existed between them and other Arabs. Moreover, to maintain that the Syrians came to be arabized after the conquest of their country by the Muslim Arabs was simply not correct, because Syria was already largely inhabited by Arabs – in fact, Christian Arabs – long before Islam. On the other hand, the concept of Lebanon as a historical refuge for the persecuted of Syria, as advanced by Lammens, appeared to have far more to its credit. All Christians in Lebanon accepted it as valid, and so did their Shiite and Druze compatriots who could find no other historical explanation for why they were as concentrated in Lebanon as they were. Sunnite Muslims, in Lebanon and elsewhere, balked at the idea that historically they had been the persecutors from whom the different Christian and dissident Muslim communities had fled for refuge to the Lebanon mountains. They had to admit, however, that while they formed the majority in the coastal towns and the cities and villages of the Syrian interior, Mount Lebanon and its immediate vicinity was mainly populated by religious minorities. Thus, even to Sunnites, the idea of Lebanon as a Syrian mountain refuge from their own oppression appeared to be historically plausible, though hardly complimentary, and they ultimately came to give the idea a grudging acceptance.

As an explanation of the social and political origins of Lebanon, the idea of the *Asile du Liban* remains highly seductive. To determine its historical accuracy, however, two questions must be asked. First, to what extent is it true that Mount Lebanon, historically, has provided refuge for different communities fleeing political tyranny and religious persecution in other parts of Syria, presumably at the hands of the Sunnite Muslim majority? Second, was Mount Lebanon in Islamic times, given the ruggedness of its terrain, ever so immune to Islamic rule that it could actually provide safe refuge for communities preferring not to live under this rule?

Since the time of Ibn al-Qilai in the late fifteenth century, the Maronites have generally maintained that they had first arrived in Mount Lebanon as fugitives from intolerable Muslim persecution in northern Syria. In the seventeenth century, however, their leading historian, Patriarch Duwayhi, asserted that the persecution which forced them to abandon the valley of the Orontes, in the Syrian interior, and flock to Mount Lebanon took place at the hands of the Byzantines, not the Muslims, and all available evidence points in this direction. It was demonstrated in an earlier chapter that this persecution of the Maronites by the Byzantines must have occurred about the year 1000, when the Byzantines were actually in control of the area, and not in 685, as Duwayhi thought. This means that the Maronites were content to live under Islamic rule in the Syrian interior for more than three centuries, until the Byzantine reconquests in northern Syria made it impossible for them to remain in the area. When they fled the Orontes valley, some went to settle in Aleppo, while most others arrived in Mount Lebanon. In both cases, they sought refuge in territory which was actually under Islamic control.

In the course of the eleventh century, the Druzes of the Shuf mountains and Wadi al-Taym did not arrive as fugitives from elsewhere, but were converted to the Druze faith on home territory. The Druze scriptures still preserve the text of an epistle, dated AD 1026, which was sent to one of the local Druze chiefs who had accepted the new faith as preached by its originators in Cairo during that period. There was, in fact, a persecution of a Druze community in northern Syria in that century, but no Druzes are known to have fled the area in consequence to seek refuge in Mount Lebanon. It was only in 1811, when the countryside of the Syrian interior was repeatedly raided by Wahhabi Muslim tribes arriving from central Arabia, that the Druzes of the Aleppo region, falling under pressure, were invited to settle among their co-religionists in the Shuf mountains by Bashir Shihab II, upon the suggestion of Bashir Jumblat, who was the paramount chief of the Shuf Druzes at the time.

There is no evidence whatsoever that there was ever a massive exodus of Twelver Shiites, Ismailis or Nusayris into the territory of present-day Lebanon from any area. On the contrary, there is evidence that the Ismailis and the Nusayris used to be found at one time in considerable numbers in some parts of the present Lebanese territory where they no longer exist. This may mean that they were once persecuted in these very areas, from which they fled to other parts of Syria. Indeed, under the Ottomans, some Shiite scholars did flee Damascus to settle among their co-religionists in Jabal Amil, but their flight could not be described as massive.

After accepting union with Rome in 1683, Uniate Melchites, or Greek Catholics, left the Aleppo region and other parts of the Syrian interior to seek refuge among the Maronites and the Druzes of Mount Lebanon. The persecution that caused their migration was not perpetrated by the local Muslims, but by their fellow Melchites, the Greek Orthodox. The same applied to the Armenian

Catholics, who were persecuted in Cilicia by the Armenian Orthodox, and began to seek refuge among the Maronites in Kisrawan after they had entered into union with Rome in 1721.

In the early nineteenth century, there was a considerable migration of Greek Orthodox Christians from the Syrian interior, not only into the territory of present-day Lebanon, but also into Palestine. Most of the migrants were from Transjordan and the Hawran region south of Damascus and were perhaps in flight from the Wahhabi raids that caused the Druzes to abandon the Aleppo region at the same time. Certainly, there were further Christian migrations from different parts of Syria into Mount Lebanon after 1860, when there were persecutions of Christians throughout Syria, and a terrible one-day massacre of about 12,000 of them in Damascus. It must be noted, however, that the Ottomans promptly punished the perpetrators of the massacre with the utmost severity, so that it would never be repeated. In one night, more than one hundred of the men held responsible, among them the Ottoman Pasha of Damascus and his leading officers, were given a summary trial and hanged. Large numbers of Muslim Damascene notables were also tried and imprisoned, or sent into exile, for not having used the social influence they wielded to stop the massacre. After 1894, and more so after 1915, Armenians from eastern Asia Minor and Cilicia began to flock into Lebanon in large numbers to escape massacre by the Turks; but many Armenians settled in parts of Syria other than Lebanon, where they appear to have felt equally safe among the local Arab population.

Certainly, the territory of present-day Lebanon did provide a refuge at times for communities fleeing persecution, though this persecution in a number of cases was not Islamic; and when it was so, it was not always perpetrated by the Muslim Arabs of Syria. Of the present Lebanese communities, the Shiites and the the main body of the Druzes did not arrive in Lebanon at any given time as fugitives from Sunnite persecution in Syria; and large numbers of Maronites were already living in the northern

Lebanon long before the Maronites of the Syrian interior, persecuted by the Byzantines, fled the Orontes valley to join them there. This creates the first big dent in the *Asile du Liban* theory, which also founders on other grounds.

The whole concept of Lebanon as a historical mountain refuge for the persecuted of Syria rests on the assumption that the Islamic state never succeeded in establishing full dominance over the rugged mountains. When the facts are examined, however, an entirely different picture emerges. Beginning from the time of the Arab conquest, Islamic control was never absent from the Lebanon mountains except at the time of the Crusades, when this control came to be restricted to the Gharb hinterland of Beirut, as already observed. Across the rugged heights of the Lebanon range, from the exteme north to the extreme south, ran vital lines of communication between the interior and the coast whose strategic importance no Islamic rule in Syria could afford to ignore. In early Umayyad times, the caliph Muawiya (661–80) brought newly Islamized Persian clans from Iran to settle in the hill country of Baalbek and Tripoli, and also in Kisrawan, in order to help guard the mountain passes and the coast for the Islamic state. The very name of Kisrawan must have originally been that of a Persian clan called the Kisra folk, who were among the local Persian settlers. The name is in the Persian plural form, the singular being *Kisra* (Arabicized form of *Khosro*), which has always been a common Persian name. Lammens knew about these important Persian settlements of the Umayyad period in Lebanon. In fact, he wrote a special article concerning these *Perses au Liban*.

Under the early Abbasids, the governors of Baalbek collected the taxes of northern Mount Lebanon. During the reign of the caliph al-Mansur (754–75) the Christians of the Munaytira district, in the Lebanon mountain heights just north of Kisrawan, refused to pay their taxes and, under the leadership of a man called Bandar who proclaimed himself to be their king, rose in rebellion. The governor of Baalbek attacked the district, subdued the rebellion and dispersed the local Christian population without much difficulty. This we learn from the Arabic historian Baladhuri who left an account of the event. The evicted Munaytira Christians had to appeal to a leading Muslim jurist from Baalbek, al-Awzai, who happened to be living at the time in Beirut, to help them return to their villages. When the revolt of the Christians of Munaytira occurred, a Byzantine war vessel was reportedly anchored outside Tripoli; and the leader of the revolt, following his defeat, managed to escape to Byzantium on this same vessel. This could indicate that the rebel Christians in question were Melchites rather than Maronites, and it is possible that their revolt against Abbasid rule was actually instigated by the Byzantines.

The whole incident, however, provides conclusive evidence that Islamic rule under the early Abbasids had access to the highest reaches of Mount Lebanon as well as regular fiscal control of those parts. The Syrian coastal towns came to be fortified and heavily garrisoned against Byzantine naval attacks during that same period; and to provide the town and garrison of Beirut with water, a Roman aqueduct in the valley of the Beirut river, which runs between the Shuf and Kisrawan mountains, was restored during the reign of Harun al-Rashid (786–809). Only a high degree of Abbasid control over the mountain districts on either side of the valley could have made the work of restoring this aqueduct possible.

The Abbasids, on the whole, appear to have had more trouble maintaining law and order in the towns and countryside of the Syrian interior than they had problems with Mount Lebanon. The chronicles report serious revolts against their rule in Palestine, Damascus, Homs and elsewhere, some of which reoccurred. On the other hand, the impression one gets from Arabic sources is that the Lebanon mountains, starting with the time of the Abbasids, were a relatively quiet and pleasant part of Syria where pious Muslims – and later on Sufi mystics – would go for religious retreats; and there are several references to the hospitality with which these Muslim men of religion were received in the Christian villages of northern Mount

Lebanon, which was Jabal Lubnan or Mount Lebanon proper. Among the Sufis, it was generally believed that this Jabal Lubnan was the dwelling place for many of the *abdal* whose existence provided the world with perennial blessing. Those were supposed to be seventy holy people, forty of them in Syria, whose individual identities no one knew, and who never decreased in number because Divine Providence saw to it that anyone among them who died was promptly replaced. It was probably the peace and serenity experienced by generations of Sufi ascetics in the Maronite villages of the northern Lebanon, so readily accessible to Muslim visitors from other parts, which convinced them that most of the Syrian *abdal* were to be found there rather than anywhere else.

Under the Fatimids, only the southern parts of Mount Lebanon were ruled from Cairo; the northern parts fell under the control of the Mirdasid Arab rulers of Aleppo who introduced Kurdish military settlers into some areas. In Ayyubid times, one Ayyubid prince maintained a castle at Musayliha, in a valley of the northern Lebanon uphill from the coastal town of Batrun, where the picturesque walls of this castle still stand as a local tourist attraction. Later, under the Mamluks, a major Shiite rebellion was subdued in Kisrawan by 1305, and Turkoman military settlers were introduced into the area to keep it under firm control. (These Turkomans of Kisrawan were discussed in chapter 6.) Other Turkoman settlements were established in Jabal Akkar, at the extreme north of the Lebanon range, either by the early Mamluks, or by the early Ottomans.

The chronicles do not report any Maronite or Druze rebellions against Mamluk rule in northern Mount Lebanon and the Shuf mountains. The Mamluks in their time had such easy access to the Shuf that they regularly exploited the forests of *quq* trees (apparently a kind of fir) in the heights of Mount Baruk, from which they made arrows for their troops in Damascus. Unable to stop the exploitation, which was no doubt accompanied by the forced quartering of Mamluk troops in the Druze villages at the foot of Mount

Baruk, the local Druzes finally decided to destroy their *quq* forests: this was the only means they had to keep the Mamluks away.

In the last years of the Mamluk period, when the Maanid Muqaddam Fakhr al-Din Uthman of the Shuf felt free to join a rebellion against the Mamluks in the Bekaa valley, he was immediately seized and imprisoned in Damascus for the duration of the rebellion. This was during the period when Mamluk power in Syria was at its weakest. It was only in the sixteenth century, when the Druzes of the Shuf mountains happened to be armed to the teeth with the best Venetian firearms then available, that the Ottomans faced serious problems in bringing the area under their control. Once this had been achieved, the local Druzes were left to run their local politics as they pleased under the Maan and Shihab multazims, provided that their tribal chiefs co-operated with these multazims in collecting the taxes of the region.

What all this indicates is that no part of the Lebanon range ever enjoyed any demonstrable immunity from Islamic rule. Certainly, the Islamic state never had a continued, direct presence in every village or district in the Lebanon mountains; but this was universally true of all formal government at the time, in the world of Islam as in Byzantium and elsewhere. Today, modern military technology makes it possible for a state to maintain fixed frontiers which can be no more than imaginary lines drawn on a map; also to keep up strict police control over every bit of its territory. Before the age of modern technology – more so before the age of gunpowder – this was not possible. States then had to content themselves with the control of cities and towns which they could defend. In the open countryside, control had to be exercised from fortified castles, and there were limits as to how many a state could maintain. Consequently, the control of the countryside was normally inefficient. In Syria, this applied in Islamic times to the mountain regions of the Lebanon as well as to other parts. In the pastoral desert of the interior, where fortresses could not easily be maintained, the Islamic state had hardly any regular control, except by the occasional means of punitive expeditions against the desert tribes, or by the purchase of the co-operation of the chiefs of these tribes with money and honours.

In short, there was nothing especially unique about the Lebanon mountains in Islamic times. Geographically, they do not constitute the only rugged hill country in Syria, although they do stand at much higher altitudes than the Alouite hill country to the north and the Galilean and Palestinian hill country to the south. Because the winds that bring rain to the area in winter come from the west, the Lebanon mountains, with their high altitudes, act as the main rain trap in Syria, which makes them exceptionally well watered. Gradations of climate, from sea level at the coast to the mountain heights which in the northern Lebanon exceed 3000 metres, lend an unusually rich variety to the local vegetation. While plains are hard to come by in the Lebanon valleys, most of which are steep gorges, the mountain slopes, with their rich soil, have traditionally been terraced for intensive agriculture; and where such terracing is difficult, there are excellent mountain pastures for sheep and goats to graze. Clearly, there was something other than their mountain fastness that made the Lebanon mountains highly attractive to human settlement not only in Islamic but also since the most ancient times. Travelling around the country in the 1960s, the American geographer Joseph Van Riper, of the State University of New York at Binghampton, remarked that people must have always arrived to settle in the Lebanon not only in search of social or political security, but because it was 'such a nice place in which to live'; it was also healthy and had an envigorating mountain climate. The essentially ecological advantages that the Lebanon held over other parts of Syria, most particularly with respect to the abundance of water, made it far more attractive to settle in than the relative rather than absolute security of its rugged mountain terrain.

All things considered, the Muslim rulers of Syria, except

for the Ottomans after 1841, did not recognize a special autonomous status for the Lebanon mountains. They simply accorded the local Maronites, Druzes and Shiites the treatment which the Islamic states normally reserved for tribes. As long as they gave no trouble, they were permitted to run their affairs according to their own norms, subject to the bare minimum of government intervention. In this respect, Yaziji was correct when he began his essay on Mount Lebanon with the statement that it was a *bilad 'asha'ir*, or a country of tribes.

Of the three major religious communities in the mountain and its immediate neighbourhood, the Maronites and the Druzes were politically more successful than the Shiites because their tribal organization was fortified by religious institutions: the church in the case of the Maronites; the councils of religious *'uqqal*, or Initiates, among the Druzes. For the Maronites, the church existed to lead the community from the very beginning and serve as a repository for its historical experience. Among the Druzes, the tight religious organization of the community came somewhat later, in the course of the fifteenth century, under the leadership of a member of the Abey branch of the Buhturid family called Abdallah al-Tanukhi (d. 1487), who is still revered by the Druzes as *al-Sayyid*, or the Master. It was apparently this Sayyid Abdallah who first instituted and headed a council of the Initiates which united the Druzes of the Shuf mountains under its leadership and exercised moral power over them. According to Ibn Sibat, Sayyid Aballah in his days enjoyed such prestige that it was sufficient for him to ban the recalcitrant from admission to his council in order to bring them to their knees. He never resorted to force, and frowned on its use.

Such organization did not exist among the Shiites of Mount Lebanon and the neighbourhood. There was a long tradition of religious scholarship among the Shiites of Jabal Amil which was widely respected throughout the Shiite world, but the local Shiite scholars, who came from the peasant class, apparently kept aloof of the local tribal politics, which was left in the hands of the leading tribal chiefs. The same appears to have been true among the Shiites of Kisrawan who kept chronicles of their affairs which no longer exist, but to which some reference is made in Maronite writings of the seventeenth and eighteenth centuries. From the Mamluk sources, one learns that they also had men of religious learning with whom Sunnite scholars from Damascus had long arguments before recommending that they could only be deterred from their obstinate heterodoxy by military means. Acting upon this recommendation, the Mamluks finally attacked and subdued Kisrawan in 1305. In northern Mount Lebanon and the Baalbek region, no tradition of religious learning is known to have ever existed among the local Shiite clans, who were not particularly religious; they were mainly goatherds, often living outside the pale of the law. All in all, the Shiites of Lebanon, wherever they happened to be found, never developed the social and political coherence of the Maronites or the Druzes.

On the other hand, the Maronites and the Shiites, unlike the Druzes, had important connections with external powers: the Maronites with Western Europe, because of their union with Rome, which became increasingly effective after the fifteenth century; the Shiites with Persia, which emerged as a Shiite Muslim power under the Safavids beginning with the sixteenth century. In the case of the Maronites, their connections with Western Europe, particularly with France from the seventeenth century, proved eminently useful. Their Western Christian friends were able and willing to come to their assistance in times of trouble. In 1860, for example, the West intervened on their behalf not only politically but militarily as well. In the case of the Shiites, their connections with Persia, from the very start, proved counter-productive. The Ottomans, highly suspicious of their strong political sympathies with the Persians, kept the community under close watch, and occasionally condoned the use of force against the Shiites of Jabal Amil by the Druzes of the Shuf mountains, first under the Maans, then under the Shihabs. In the late eighteenth century, Jabal Amil was thoroughly ravaged by the redoubtable Ahmad Jazzar, who was then the Pasha of Acre (1775–1804), and even the libraries of the local Shiite men of learning were not spared. It is believed that among the Shiite books lost at the time were some histories of the Shiite community in the region.

When the Maan and Shihab emirs, from their base in the Shuf, made a point of developing their relations with the Maronites, it was partly with a view to securing for themselves the Western European support which the Maronites enjoyed. Of these emirs, only Fakhr al-Din Maan had relations with Western Europe which were independent of the Maronites. His special European friends were the Medici of Tuscany, who dreamt at the time of leading a Christian reconquest of the Holy Land from the Ottomans, and hoped to use the Druze emir for that purpose as a local ally. When his secret relations with the Medici became known to the Ottomans, the emir, fearing Ottoman vengeance, fled by sea to Italy in 1613, where he stayed for five years in exile. There the notables of Tuscany put the question directly to him: what could he do to help should Christian armies arrive in Syria, with a view to recapturing Jerusalem? The answer of Fakhr al-Din is worth quoting: 'You know the power of Islam,' he said; 'if you want to take up arms against it, you should have no need of such a small ally as myself.' Fakhr al-Din had no illusions about an *Asile du Liban* where the power of Islam could be challenged with impunity.

It was actually on the initiative of Rome, which then fell under strong Medici influence, that the Maronite Patriarch John Makhluf first sought the protection of Fakhr al-Din Maan for himself and his community. Shortly after his election in 1608, this patriarch had received a special papal bull from Rome instructing him to develop relations with the Druze emir and regard him as a friend. In the following year, faced with troubles instigated against him by the muqaddams of Bsharri, John Makhluf actually sought refuge for a while in the Shuf. It was on that occasion that Fakhr al-Din made the first Druze donation of land in the Shuf to the Maronite church – the village of Majd al-Maush

– to serve the Maronite patriarchs as a local residence whenever they needed it.

After Fakhr al-Din, however, the Maan and Shihab emirs needed the Maronites more than the Maronites needed them, because the Maronites – particularly the Khazin sheikhs of Kisrawan, who served as French consuls in Beirut – could secure for them French backing. After the Khazins, the French consulate in Beirut was held by another succession of Maronite sheikhs, the Saads of the village of Ayn Traz, in the Jurd district of the Shuf mountains. Those, after the Khazins, provided the Shihab emirs from the mid-eighteenth century with the Western European connections they needed. It was no doubt with a view to further endear themselves not only with the Maronites, but also with France, that the Shihabs themselves ultimately chose to convert to Christianity and become Maronites.

Under the Shihabs, the parts of the Lebanon which they controlled did become to some extent a refuge: not for freedom-loving Syrians who could not abide the 'tyranny of the pashas', as was the opinion of Father Lammens, but for Greek Catholics persecuted by the Greek Orthodox; Armenian Catholics persecuted by the Armenian Orthodox; or Druzes and Greek Orthodox Christians fleeing for safety from the Wahhabi raids of the early nineteenth century against the towns and villages of the Syrian interior. In any case, it was certainly not the ruggedness of the Lebanon mountains that made such fugitives flock to the territory of the Shihab emirs for safety. Rather, it was the external connections secured by the Maronites for the Shihabs, most of all with France, which made of these Shihabs something more than the Ottoman multazims they actually were, enabling them to provide security in the territory entrusted to their management by the Ottoman pashas for whoever sought such security. Even then, the Ottoman pashas remained sufficiently strong to reassert the Ottoman state control over Mount Lebanon whenever the need arose.

European travellers visiting Mount Lebanon in the

eighteenth century, during the time when the country under the Shihabs was actually serving as a refuge for the persecuted of Syria, were struck by the high degree of social disorganization they discovered locally. In one instance, it was remarked that this social disorganization stopped just short of total anarchy. The French traveller Volney, who visited Mount Lebanon in 1785, did not disagree; yet he observed that he found 'a ray of freedom shining there', which he did not find elsewhere in Syria, and which he seems to have attributed to the Shihab government. Was this a responsible civic freedom peculiar to Mount Lebanon as a historical 'mountain refuge', as Lammens would have thought; or was it the chaotic freedom common to all tribal societies living outside the limits of orderly government? Since Volney found this freedom in Mount Lebanon coexisting with a baffling social disorganization, even with the Shihabs in control, it must have been a freedom of the latter kind. Had he gone to live among the lawless Arab tribes of the desert, he would have found a ray of the same type of unbridled freedom shining there as well amidst the prevailing anarchy.

Today, the Lammens thesis, that the history of Lebanon in Islamic times was that of a mountain refuge for the persecuted of Syria, is accepted almost by everyone as an article of faith. While there is much that is true about the thesis, however, there is also much that is untrue. The ancestors of the main body of the population of Mount Lebanon and its immediate neighbourhood did not arrive in Lebanon as fugitives from persecution in Syria in Islamic times. They had already been established locally, as different Arab tribes and clans, before Islam, some among them possibly from as early as the third century AD. Wherever these tribes settled, they must have merged with older elements of the local population who had been there since antiquity. The Lebanon tribes that ultimately accepted Islam did so in the manner of other tribal Arabs: they adopted the new religion in one of its several heterodox forms, rather than in the orthodox or Sunnite form which was finally given it by the Abbasid state in the second half of the ninth century. The Maronites, who did not accept Islam, maintained their tribal distinction from other Christian Arabs in Syria – Melchites or Jacobites – by keeping themselves organized as a separate sect with their own church.

In whatever parts of Mount Lebanon they happened to be living, the different mountain communities – Maronites, Shiites or Druzes – were not engaged in a continuous defence of the inviolate security of their mountain home-lands against the imperial sway of Sunnite Islam, from its Syrian base in Damascus. As all other tribal peoples, they had a strong antipathy for any form of law and order imposed by a central government; they disliked paying taxes to such governments; and they were prone to rebellion. Now and then, punitive expeditions had to be sent against them, as against tribes in other parts, whether deserts or mountains, in order to keep them under minimum control. The Maronites alone appear to have been left in their own mountain homeland in peace. They were better organized than the Shiites or the Druzes, because they had a church, and they could thus accommod-ate to changing political circumstances as a social body better than the others. Moreover, starting with the Mamluk period, they always enjoyed some kind of Western Christian protection, because of the union of their church with Rome.

There was no time when the Maronites and the Druzes took the historical decision, in the manner legend attributes to the Swiss, to join ranks under one generally accepted leadership for the defence of their common mountain homeland against Ottoman tyranny. The Maan emirs, and after them the Shihabs, were essentially Ottoman officials always answerable to higher Ottoman authorities. They were popular with the Maronites for reasons that have already been dwelt upon, but they were generally unpopular with the Druzes, among whom the Shihab hegemony in particular was never accepted. Even the leadership of the Maans, in their time, was never accepted by all the Druzes, although the Maans were themselves Druzes, unlike the

Shihab emirs who were Sunnites and later Maronites. To control the Druze country, the Shihabs needed the co-operation of the more powerful Druze tribal chiefs. For this reason, beginning in 1697, the Ottomans saw to it that these chiefs, in consultation with the heads of the Maronite community, approved the choice of each Shihab emir to the office of multazim before he was actually appointed, and special caucuses were held for that purpose. Those were not popular elections, as they have come to be generally depicted. The practice did not really involve rule by popular consent in an island of Lebanese democracy set in an ocean of Ottoman tyranny. Rather, it was introduced into the mountain, at a given time, by the Ottomans themselves for political convenience, and somehow managed to work amidst the social anarchy that prevailed.

All this puts the validity of the Lammens theory of *l'Asile du Liban* into serious question. The theory assumes that there was something unique about Lebanon in Islamic times, and more particularly during the Ottoman period. Was this actually the case? Moreover, if there was something unique about Lebanon in the Syrian and broader Arab world at that particular time, what precisely was it?

8   Ottoman Lebanon: how unique?

From the sixteenth century, two Islamic empires cast their shadows on Syria, Iraq and Arabia: the Sunnite Ottoman empire from the west, and the Shiite Persian empire from the east. The Ottoman empire was strong in the sixteenth century; began to show signs of weakness in the seventeenth; and rapidly declined in the course of the eighteenth. After this the Ottoman empire managed to survive by securing the support of one European power or another, taking advantage of the disagreement among these powers on the conditions for its destruction: this was the central issue of what was called at the time the Eastern Question. The Persian empire was strong in the early sixteenth century; had revived after a period of confusion by the early seventeeth; then declined for a long while. It revived for another brief period in the middle decades of the eighteenth century during the reign of the military adventurer Nadir Shah (1736–49), before plunging again into chronic decline.

For as long as it lasted, the Ottoman empire maintained a continuous control over Syria and the west Arabian Hijaz which varied from time to time in effectiveness. When the Ottomans happened to be strong, or enjoyed strong European support, their sway in west Arabia was extended southwards to include the Yemen. Except for some periods when the Persian empire happened to be strong, the Ottomans also controlled Iraq, and sometimes maintained footholds in eastern Arabia. On the other hand, when the Persian empire happened to be strong, it could dominate Iraq and gain sporadic control in eastern Arabia, or at least influence developments there. Off the eastern Arabian coast, the Persians held the islands of Bahrain continuously from 1602 until 1783 – their longest uninterrupted stay in any Arab land.

Fundamental to the decline of both the Ottoman and Persian empires, the signs of which were already visible in the course of the sixteenth century, was a change in the world economy set in motion by the initiative of Western Europe. In 1492, the Spaniards landed for the first time on the American continent. Only five years later, in 1497, the Portuguese rounded the Cape of Good Hope, and demonstrated that the lands of the Indian Ocean basin could be reached from Western Europe directly by sea. What followed was a rapid expansion of Western European world commerce which began, increasingly, to bypass the lands of what we now call the Middle East. This alone condemned these lands to relative economic stagnation; the final blow came by the eighteenth century with the decline of the coffee trade of the Yemen. Moreover, with the growth of Western European world commerce came an inflation. This was given a tremendous boost when American silver hit the European markets, then the world markets, beginning with the Spanish exploitation of the rich silver reserves of Potosi, in Peru, in 1555. In Western Europe, the increased liquidity produced by this great inflation, the natural outcome of Western European enterprise, was invested in further enterprise which led to further economic development and expansion. When the same inflation, by the seventeenth century, reached the Ottoman and Persian empires, it played havoc with the traditional economy of the Ottoman and Persian lands, which led to their rapid impoverishment. Whatever local commercial activity remained beyond the level of the parochial markets fell into the hands of European merchant companies.

Once the great trading nations of Western Europe – the Portuguese, followed by the English, the Dutch and the French – started making regular use of the direct sea route to the Indian Ocean, which rounded the African continent, they began to impinge directly on southern Arabia, eastern Arabia and Iraq from the east. Meanwhile, some were already beginning to press and probe in Syria from the west. By the latter decades of the sixteenth century, Dutch, English, French and other European merchants had already gained easy access to the Syrian seaports, as did travellers, missionaries and political agents – at least, so the literature and records of the period indicate. In the Syrian interior (as pointed out in an earlier chapter), the European merchant companies established offices for themselves in Aleppo, where the Venetians had already been active from an earlier time.

Whether they arrived in the area from the west or from the east, the Western European traders preferred to deal with weak local Arab potentates rather than with the stronger Ottoman or Persian states. Thus, wherever they happened to have a special commercial interest, they encouraged local autonomies to develop at the expense of the Ottoman or Persian imperial authority. In a number of cases, the weakening of Ottoman power from one direction, and that of Persian power from the other, had already paved the way for the emergence of such autonomies. Also, the continuing conflict and sporadic wars between the Ottomans and the Persians had created a balance of Islamic imperial power in the area which Arab and other regional chiefs who were politically ambitious could exploit. By the seventeenth century, for example, Ottoman Anatolia was already falling under the rule of local *derebeys*, or valley lords, among whom festered the so-called Jelali revolts.

In 1612, an adventurer of Persian or Kurdish origin called Afrasiyab established himself as the virtually independent master of Basra, in southern Iraq, sitting on the fence between the Persians and the Ottomans; his descendants, for a time with Portuguese support, continued to maintain a sort of principality there until 1668. The last Afrasiyabs enouraged a revolt against Ottoman rule in the Hasa region of eastern Arabia, where the Ottoman pasha was expelled and a tribal emirate – that of the local Banu Khalid – was established for about a century. Earlier, in northern Syria, a dynasty of Kurdish chiefs called the Janbulads had made themselves the masters of Aleppo between 1591 and 1607, and after 1603 in defiance of the Ottomans and in alliance with the Medici of Tuscany. In 1636, probably with secret encouragement from the Dutch or the English who were then competing for the coffee trade of the Yemen, the local Zaydi Imams staged a successful revolt against the Ottomans and took over independent control of the country. Shortly after, in 1649, the Ibadi Imams of the Yaarubid dynasty, again probably with Dutch or English help, expelled the Portuguese from Muscat and established themselves as independent rulers in Oman.

In the circumstances of the times, there was nothing unusual about the career of Fakhr al-Din Maan in the southern Lebanon. Here was a Druze chief or notable who was appointed by the Ottomans to govern the sanjaks of Beirut and Sidon on their behalf, and then the sanjaks of Safad and other parts of Syria. The man, being highly intelligent, alert and enterprising, opened the seaports under his control to European commerce, and developed the silk production in the Druze country and its environs as a cash crop for export to Europe. The Tuscans approached him and fanned his ambitions, as they did with the Janbulads who were his contemporaries in Aleppo; so began his problems with the Ottoman overlords. More cautious and circumspect than the Janbulads, Fakhr al-Din managed to mend his fences with the Ottomans every time they were broken. In the end, however, his ambitions led him too far, and the Ottomans finally realized that they had no choice but to deal with him as a rebel.

According to Adnan Bakhit, it was as a rebel of the Anatolian Jelali sort that Fakhr al-Din was finally subdued, captured and put to death. The only aspect that distinguished him from his Jelali contemporaries and other rebels of their type was that he happened to be a man of unusual enlightenment who left behind him some heritage in his home base in the southern Lebanon – particularly the silk economy which remained the local economic mainstay for a long time to follow.

During the seventeenth century, the Ottomans were still strong enough to reassert their control periodically in Syria. They continued to be able to do so in the eighteenth century, but only to a steadily decreasing degree. In the course of this century, a local dynasty of pashas of the Azm family controlled the Eyalet of Damascus on behalf of the Ottomans, and occasionally held other Syrian eyalets as well. Between 1750 and 1775, an Arab chief of the Tiberias region, Dahir al-Umar, controlled the southern parts of the Eyalet of Sidon and the adjacent parts of Palestine, and established himself as a virtually autonomous potentate in Acre. Meanwhile, by 1763, the Circassian Mamluks who formed the military elite of Cairo under the Ottoman governors established their own control over Egypt under the leadership of one of their officers, called Ali Bey *al-Kabir*, or Ali Bey the Great. In Iraq, a succession of Georgian Mamluk officers came to wield actual power, nominally as Ottoman pashas in Baghdad.

Between 1668 and 1774, while the Ottomans were preoccupied with a serious war against Russia, then under the rule of Catherine the Great, a Russian fleet – more correctly Greek, or 'Ionian' privateers under Russian command – cruised the waters of the eastern Mediterranean, and Russian contact was established with Ali Bey in Egypt, and with Dahir al-Umar in Acre. With Russian encouragement, and with local support from Dahir al-Umar, Ali Bey sent Mamluk forces into Syria which occupied Damascus. The end of the Russo-Turkish war in 1774 came in time to put a stop to this adventure. In Egypt, Ali Bey was killed and replaced by the commander of the army he had sent to occupy Damascus; and the Ottomans were able to reassert their control over Syria for the remainder of the century. To do so, however, they had to give a free hand to the most trusted and ruthless of their local agents, Ahmad Jazzar, the Pasha of Acre (1775–1804) who was also appointed Pasha of Damascus whenever the need arose. Although he remained faithful to the Ottomans to the very end, Ahmad Jazzar, in his Syrian domain, behaved virtually as an independent ruler. In 1799, the ageing pasha astounded the world when, with some naval help from the British, he stopped the advance of General Bonaparte from Egypt into Syria outside Acre – the first military defeat that Bonaparte experienced. Bonaparte was to remember Jazzar all his life.

For as long as the European powers were prohibited from access to the Red Sea, the Ottomans, in Arabia, continued to control the Hijaz. Elsewhere in the peninsula, the balance of European power which prevailed in the world of the Indian Ocean basin until the nineteenth century, coupled with the brief resurgence of Persian power under Nadir Shah between 1736 and 1749, led to the development of further Arabian autonomies, on varying scales. Beginning in 1745, the Wahhabi movement in the villages of Najd, in central Arabia, led to the emergence of the first Wahhabi state there under the house of Saud. In Oman, where the rule of the Yaarubid Imams had been disintegrating for some time, a new ruling dynasty, the Bu-Saids, succeeded in taking over power in 1743 first as Ibadi Imams, then as secular Sayyids. In the deserts of the Omani interior, and also in eastern Arabia, local tribes began to group together to form confederations. One among them was that of the Banu Yas, a branch of which established a tiny sheikhdom on the island of Abu Dhabi in 1734. From eastern Arabia, a branch of the tribal confederation of the Utub Arabs, led by the house of Al-Khalifa, occupied the Bahrain islands in 1783 and replaced the decaying Persian rule there with a sheikhdom of their own. Meanwhile, in the southern parts of the Yemen, the weakening grip of the Zaydi Imams of Sanaa, partly as a result of the decline of the Yemeni coffee trade, led to the emergence of a large number of local autonomies whose rulers called themselves by different titles, some settling for no less than the title of sultan.

Viewed against this broad regional background, the relative autonomy of the Shihabs in central and southern Lebanon during the eighteenth century falls into perspective. Here were multazims appointed by the Ottoman pashas of Sidon to keep order in the more unruly mountain districts of their eyalet and to collect local taxes on their behalf at a certain profit. Taking advantage of the weakness of Ottoman rule at the time, and of the support they could receive from France through the intermediary of their Maronite friends, the Shihabs got away with running the affairs of their mountain iltizam, now and then, with a free hand. Under Ahmad Jazzar, between 1775 and 1804, they were reduced to subservience. After his death, they were able to reassert their autonomy in the days of Bashir II largely with the support of Muhammad Ali Pasha of Egypt. Between 1832 and 1840 Muhammad Ali Pasha, having rebelled against his Ottoman overlords, had his son Ibrahim Pasha occupy Syria. For the duration of this Egyptian occupation of Syria, Bashir II remained in power in Mount Lebanon as a vassal to the Egyptians. When the British helped the Ottomans drive Ibrahim Pasha from Syria in 1840, Bashir II had to abandon his mountain emirate and go into exile. The Shihab regime in the mountain only outlasted him by about one year. The story of the Shihabs had parallels, or near parallels, all over Syria, Iraq and Arabia, and also in Egypt, at approximately the same time.

To this extent, there was nothing especially unique about the Lebanon of the Ottoman period before the middle decades of the nineteenth century. Yet, this only tells the political side to the story. Closely intertwined with it were other strains of narrative relating developments of a different order. One must bear in mind, to begin with, that the main political developments in the Lebanon story, from the very beginning, unfolded on the western side of the mountain range, whose terraced slopes nearly everywhere reach the Mediterranean Sea, their central parts enclosing the harbour town of Beirut and its small adjoining coastal plain, between the promontories of Nahr al-Kalb (the Dog

River) and Nahr al-Damur. From across the Mediterranean, by one means or another, came subtle influences to which the Maronites of Mount Lebanon, at the start, were more receptive than others, but which gradually came to have an impact on other communities as well.

In the fifteenth century, three young Maronites from the northern Lebanon were sent to study in Italy for the first time. After the establishment of the Maronite College in Rome in 1585, what started out as a trickle of Maronites going to Western Europe to study became a regular though relatively small stream. Among the more gifted of the Maronite graduates of Rome, a number remained in Western Europe, some of them adopting Latinized names and gaining distinction as scholars who helped lay the foundations of European orientalism: Abraham Ecchellensis (Ibrahim al-Haqilani); Joseph Assemanus (Yusuf al-Simaani); Sergius Risius (Sarkis al-Ruzzi). Others, however, returned home to become clerics or teachers of their native village folk. Some Maronite graduates of Rome joined Western monastic orders and became Lazarists or Jesuits. One of those, in 1734, founded the college of Ayn Tura in Kisrawan, which is still a flourishing educational institution. Another, also in Kisrawan, founded the college of Ayn Waraqa in 1774. Both colleges were essentially religious seminaries at the start, but each of them also offered a secular curriculum which became in time the more important, and which blended the traditional Arabic learning with an educational discipline of European type. Among the graduates of Ayn Waraqa, in particular, were the leading figures of the Arabic literary revival of the nineteenth century which flourished in Beirut.

The Maronite College was already active in Rome when Emir Fakhr al-Din Maan went to Italy in 1613 to spend five years in exile. From the pen of one of his secretaries, whose name remains unknown, we have a record of the observations of the Druze emir during his Italian stay, apparently as he personally recounted them to his entourage after his return home. The emir was struck by the organized economy he found in Italy; by the regular

maintenance of the highways; by the technological development in various fields; by the banking system; by the thrift
exercised in the preservation and employment of resources,
to the extent that the dung of captives and prisoners was
systematically collected from the dungeons and put to
agricultural use as fertilizer. He dwelt at length on the
magnificence of the public buildings and the orderly layout
of the cities, particularly Florence. He was surprised by the
ease with which women mixed with men in society, to the
extent of dancing with them in public; also by the fact that
Europeans, unlike Orientals, preferred beef to mutton and
lamb, so that beef fetched higher prices than mutton and
lamb in their markets. Most of all, he was struck by the
constitutional structure of government in the parts of Italy
he visited. There, he remarked, government was not
exercised according to the whims of the rulers, but
according to rules set down in 'books'. Whenever a problem
or dispute over any governmental practice arose, recourse
was had to these 'books'. Officials who committed offences,
or lost the confidence of rulers or of the public for any
reason, were tried according to the rules set in these same
'books' before they were dismissed. Following dismissal,
and after receiving the stipulated punishment, they retired
into obscurity, and were never restored to office simply
because the ruler altered his opinion of them. Everybody,
including the ruler, was accountable before the law.

The Druze emir greatly admired what he saw in Italy,
including the liberty enjoyed by women; but he was
disturbed by two aspects upon which he could not help
making negative comments. First, he discovered that
European hospitality was as limited by hard and fast rules
as European government. After the grandiose reception
with which he was first met, which included a great ball in
the Palazzo Vecchio in Florence, he was left to live on a
fixed stipend which barely met his needs. Second, he was
baffled by the religious intolerance he found in Europe. In
the Ottoman empire, as in earlier Islamic empires,
Christians and Jews were expected to observe certain
social restrictions specified by Islamic law. Otherwise, they

were not normally molested in the public practice of their religions. In the Syrian territories under his own control, Fakhr al-Din himself treated Christians and Muslims on an equal footing, and even showed special favour to the Christians. The emir was not only highly tolerant in his general behaviour, but actually unreligious. The English traveller George Sandys, who visited him in Sidon in 1607, reports that the emir was never known to pray, nor ever seen in a mosque. Fakhr al-Din, of course, was a Druze, and Druzes do not pray in mosques. In Italy, however, the emir probably feared that there were secret agents of the Ottoman state observing and reporting on everything he did or failed to do, so he made a point of dissimulating Sunnite Islam. When he and his Muslim companions in exile tried to hold public prayers in the courtyard of the mansion where they were staying, the local authorities intervened to stop them, and their prayers thereafter could only be held in strict privacy. Fakhr al-Din and his companions also had difficulty fasting during the month of Ramadan, for no facilities were extended to them by their hosts to help them.

Upon his return home, Fakhr al-Din tried to modernize his central domains in accordance with what he had admired in Italy, employing Italian advisers for the purpose. After his death, most of what he managed to achieve in this direction was undone; yet, the example was set. Meanwhile, the influence of Western Europe continued to trickle into Mount Lebanon through the intermediary of the Maronite church and its relations with Rome; also to Beirut through the intermediary of European commerce. Between 1749 and 1774, the Shihab emirs managed to gain and keep control over the town and harbour of Beirut, initially with the help of the Talhuqs – the Druze sheikhs of the Gharb who were then also manorial lords over the terraced maritime slopes of Ras Beirut, west of the town. During these years, members of the Shihab family settled in Beirut and its suburbs, as did a number of Christian families from different mountain districts – among them enterprising Maronites such as the Tyans, and rich Greek

Catholics such as the Pharaons, who became highly active in local export commerce.

These Christian merchant families of Beirut, and also some Sunnite Muslim merchant families such as the Barbirs, maintained regular trading contacts not only with Alexandria, in Egypt, but also with European commercial establishments in Italy, France and elsewhere. Members and relatives of the Barbir family still own pieces of ornamental glassware laced with gold which they received as presents from their European commercial associates during this period. The commercial contact between Beirut and Western Europe was interrupted when Ahmad Jazzar occupied the town in 1774, and remained broken until the death of Jazzar in Acre in 1804, when it began to revive again, first slowly, then in rapid strides. With the opening of Damascus to European trade in the 1840s, the commerce of Beirut burst into flowering as the town became the main seaport for Damascus and the Syrian interior. New merchant families emerged, Christian as well as Muslim, taking over control of the prospering business. Merchant firms from different European countries began to maintain regular offices in Beirut, which also became a centre for European consular representation. Here, as nowhere else in Syria and other parts of the Ottoman empire, the European residents were made to feel welcome, and could live free from all restrictions. Their local associates – mainly Christians, but also Muslims – came to form a Levantine class, cosmopolitan in attitude and socially refined, whose liberal and intelligent style of life, by the 1860s, was already shedding a special lustre on the city.

Shortly after Beirut began to revive as a centre for Syrian commerce with Europe in the early decades of the nineteenth century, Protestant missionaries from the United States and Britain began to arrive; and from Beirut, these missionaries subsequently extended their activities into the mountains. There, they were met by stiff resistance from the Maronites and the older established Roman Catholic missionaries who worked among them – groups such as the Jesuits and the Lazarists who, in reaction, began to reinforce their presence in Beirut. In the Maronite-controlled parts of Mount Lebanon, the Protestant missionaries could not gain any foothold, and Maronites and Greek Catholics everywhere were warned against sending their children to Protestant schools. In the Druze-controlled areas, however, the same Protestant missionaries were made welcome. In fact, Druze sheikhs such as the Talhuqs in the Gharb, the Abu Nakads in Abey, and the Jumblats in the Shuf vied with one another to invite the newcomers to establish schools in their villages. These missionaries were also able to establish mission houses and schools in the Matn, which had a mixed population of Maronites, Greek Orthodox and Druzes, and where the chiefs in control, namely the emirs of the house of Abul-Lama, used to be Druzes before they converted to Christianity and became Maronites. Thus, while Western influence had long been reaching the Maronite parts of the mountain through the intermediary of the Maronite church and its Roman connections, the same influence now began to touch the Druze areas through the intermediary of the Protestant missions.

Naturally, the Protestants made no religious headway with the Druzes; but their influence at a more subtle level nevertheless existed. At a time when the Maronites boasted of their relationship with Roman Catholic France, the Druzes turned to Protestant Britain for friendship. Later, in 1866, when the American missionaries founded the Syrian Protestant College in Ras Beirut (now the American University of Beirut), the land for its premises was purchased mainly from the Druze sheikhs of the Talhuq family. There, as elsewhere in Beirut, the educational activities of the American and British missionaries, and also the business activities of the European merchant firms, operated in Islamic rather than Christian surroundings.

Here we have another image of Ottoman Lebanon: not the mountain alone whose political history, in its basic pattern, had close parallels in many different corners of the Arab world between the sixteenth century and the nineteenth; but the marriage of the mountain with Beirut, both partners interacting, stage by stage, with influences from the West arriving through a variety of channels. In this marriage, the tribal mountain, with its feudal organization under the Maans and the Shihabs, could sometimes wield political control over Beirut. On the other hand, more discreet influences radiating from Beirut came with time to permeate the mountains – an aspect of the history of Lebanon which was first brought to notice and emphasized in the work of Albert Hourani. From the mountains came the tribal and manorial dynasties, with their clients and associates, who continued to dominate the politics of Mount Lebanon through the age of the mutesarrifate, and who ultimately came to form the core of the ruling establishment in Greater Lebanon. To the politics of Greater Lebanon, these dynasties brought a heritage of political experience, along with another heritage of bitter mountain feuds, which could now be played out on a larger arena. From Beirut, on the other hand, came the urbane and liberal Levantine tradition which gradually fused with the wilder heritage of the mountain and succeeded, now and then, in rounding off its harsher edges.

Viewed in this perspective, the attributes which truly make Lebanon, historically, a unique phenomenon in the Arab world of Ottoman times begin to stand out. Here was an Arab country – and let us permit ourselves, for the sake of the argument, to call it a country – where special social rather than political conditions prevailed:

1 A Christian mountain society maintaining strong traditional links with Western Europe.
2 A Druze mountain society so confident of the impregnability of its tribal solidarity that it had no reservations about having Christians living in its midst in steadily increasing numbers, and in the full enjoyment of religious and social liberties.
3 A harbour town, Beirut, surrounded on all sides by the Maronite and Druze mountains, traditionally open to commerce with Europe, with a Sunnite Muslim population

continually reinforced by enterprising elements from the mountains, and unusually receptive to influences from the West.

4   A long tradition of free Roman Catholic missionary presence in Beirut, supplemented in time by a vigorous American and British Protestant missionary presence, which was also made amply welcome in the Druze mountains.

5   A silk economy concentrated in these same mountains, and dominated by Christians, which naturally fed into Beirut and forged a strong economic and social link, starting in the seventeenth century, between the mountains and the city.

Add to these the developments of the nineteenth century, when Beirut grew to become not only the point on which European commerce with Syria converged, but also the leading centre for modern Western education in the Ottoman empire, and the chief repository of Western liberal ideas in the Arab world.

On the development of Mount Lebanon in Beirut in the nineteenth century, important contributions have been made by Dominique Chevallier and his students in Paris; by Leila Fawaz at Harvard; and by the late Marwan Buheiry of the American University of Beirut, whose untimely death left his major study on the economic history of Lebanon in that important period incomplete. Much work on the subject remains to be done. One thing, however, is certain: by the nineteenth century, something we might call Lebanon already existed with inherent attributes making of it a unique social rather than political phenomenon in Syria and the broader Arab world.

Strictly, it was not yet a country; yet it stood in the one corner of the Arab world where the so-called 'impact of the West' arrived not all of a sudden, but by slow and gradual degrees, and by peaceful rather than economically ruthless or militarily violent means. Elsewhere in the Arab world, this impact normally arrived with gunboats; with invading and occupying armies; or, as in the notable case of Egypt, with unscrupulous and usurious financial exploitation creating the pretext for military occupation. In all these cases, the popular reaction to the impact was one of rejection and deep social and political resentment, or at best surly and grudging acceptance. When accommodations to the ways of the modern world were finally made, the results produced more problems than solutions. In Lebanon alone, the impact of the modern world arrived with grace, stage by stage, and often upon local invitation; and the accommodations to it also came gradually, and with equal grace.

By the latter decades of the nineteenth century, society in Mount Lebanon, in close association with Beirut, was already developing by leaps and bounds, certainly in comparison with its immediate and broader Arab surroundings. In Mount Lebanon, however, politics remained essentially tribal; and this mountain tribalism was underlined and reinforced, and indeed perpetuated by religious and sectarian differences which provided it with confessional labels and fighting banners. When Mount Lebanon, after the first world war, was expanded to become Greater Lebanon, more tribes brandishing confessional banners entered the Lebanese political arena; and these tribes came from areas which had not shared earlier in the rich social and historical experience of Mount Lebanon and Beirut, so they were not easily absorbed into the Lebanese social system.

Under the mutesarrifate, a succession of determined Ottoman Christian governors, backed by the Ottoman state and by a consortium of European powers, enforced a civic order which provided an administrative framework for further social development in Mount Lebanon. Later, in Greater Lebanon, the French mandate introduced to the country a consitutional order which served the same purpose, and which continued to work for a time after the Lebanese Republic became independent: to all outside appearances, a shining example of liberal democracy and general social advancement in the Arab world. In both cases, however, the fundamental tribalism of Lebanese society, with its confessional labels, continued to lurk underneath the surface, openly reasserting itself whenever it found the opportunity to do so. In the final analysis, tribalism under whatever cover is a poor political foundation on which to build a viable modern society. Greater Lebanon, no less than Mount Lebanon before it, was truly a statue of guilded bronze standing on feet of clay.

9   Phoenicia resurrected

Salim Ali Salam (d. 1938), known in his time as Abu Ali, was a businessman and speculator who was already established by 1908 as a leading political figure among the Sunnite Muslims of Beirut. He had received part of his education at the Greek Catholic Patriarchal College near the family home in the Musaytiba quarter of the city. His sisters had been students at the British Syrian Training College run by the British Protestant missionaries in the same neighbourhood; and he himself sent his sons to study at the Syrian Protestant College in Ras Beirut.

Apart from wearing the Ottoman head-dress – the fez, or tarbush – he was always smartly turned out in the latest European fashion. With his liberal ideas he was a man of the modern world by any standard, no less than any of his Christian peers in the city, many of whom – including the Greek Orthodox archbishop – were his personal friends. A Greek Catholic priest came regularly to his house to teach his children French, while a leading Maronite man of letters was employed to tutor one of his daughters in Arabic. For a number of years, Abu Ali Salam was the head of the Beirut municipality and the president of the Maqasid society – an institution founded by the Muslim notables of the city in the latter decades of the nineteenth century to promote education along modern lines in their community. Subsequently, he was elected as a representative of Beirut in the Ottoman parliament in Istanbul.

Following the Young Turk revolution in Istanbul in 1908, Beirut became the leading centre of a political reform movement for the Arab provinces of the Ottoman empire. The movement pressed for decentralization, at a time when the policy of the Young Turks (the Committee of Union and Progress, or CUP) was to bring the empire under stronger central control, and to Turkify its provinces to the maximum extent possible. When the Young Turks established their dictatorship in Istanbul in 1913, an Arab congress convened in Paris to articulate the Arab national demands for decentralization, and Abu Ali Salam, along with a number of Muslim and Christian friends and political associates from Beirut, went to Paris to participate in its proceedings.

While in Paris, the Beirut delegation called on the French Foreign Office, ostensibly to communicate the general Arab demands. There, Abu Ali was astounded to discover that his Christian friends in the delegation had long been pressing for something entirely different: the tearing away of Beirut, along with Mount Lebanon, from the body of the Ottoman empire, in order to form an independent Lebanese state sponsored by France. As they left the French Foreign Office, Abu Ali admonished the Christian notables for what he considered to be their unseemly and even perfidious behaviour; however, according to his memoirs he received no straightforward answers from them.

Ultimately, Abu Ali's Christian friends gained their objective. When the French forces landed in Beirut in October 1918, to overthrow the short-lived Arab government in the city, his younger sons, having watched the landings, rushed home to report that they had seen their former Greek Catholic tutor among the welcoming Christian throng, cheering and waving a little French flag. When they caught his eye, the priest behaved as if he had never seen them before. Abu Ali spent the remaining years of his life as an unwilling citizen of Greater Lebanon under the

French mandate, leading the Muslim opposition in Beirut. Meanwhile, his former Christian friends and associates in the city took over power in the country as heads of the Christain political establishment. After the end of the French mandate over Lebanon, in October 1943, it was in Abu Ali's house that members of the Lebanese parliament, including his own son Saeb Salam, met to change the Lebanese flag from the French tricolour to the present design: a cedar tree on a horizontal strip of white, bordered by strips of red. The change of flag heralded, at the time, the integration of Muslim elements into the Lebanese ruling establishment. Beyond that, however, much remained to be done. Ultimate power in the Lebanese Republic, for all intents and purposes, remained the preserve of the Christian leaderships.

Since 1920, the Muslims in Beirut and elsewhere had made it abundantly clear that Greater Lebanon, as a national entity separate and distinct from Arab Syria, was meaningless to them, and in the long term unacceptable. The history of Lebanon, as they saw it, was part and parcel of the history of Syria, and ultimately of Arab history in general. While the Christians, for example, regarded Fakhr al-Din Maan as a seventeenth-century Lebanese national hero and the founder of a Lebanese state (which was historically incorrect), the Muslims, as Arab nation-alists, regarded him as an Arab national hero who dared in his time to oppose the alien tyranny of the Ottoman Turks (a view equally incorrect as history).

The Druzes were amenable to attempts by the Christians to promote the idea of Greater Lebanon, picturing the new Lebanese state as the legitimate descendant of the old mountain emirate of which the Druze Maans had been the founders. The Muslims, who had never had a share in the Lebanese emirate, whatever its true history was, were not so amenable. Druzes and Shiites were willing to subscribe to the theory that justified the existence of Lebanon as a historical refuge for the minorities of Syria. This theory, however, did not work politically with the Sunnite Muslims, even though they normally admitted that there was a degree of historical truth in it, as already observed. On the other hand, the Sunnites insisted that Arab rule in Syria under Islam had always been outstandingly tolerant and fair in its treatment of minorities, and there had never been cause for anyone to flee to Mount Lebanon for refuge, unless such a cause was imagined. In cases where persecutions of minorities in Syria could be demonstrated to have historically occurred, the aggressor, it was argued, was not Arab Islam, but the Seljuk, Mamluk or Ottoman Turks: the Sunnite Muslims, in Lebanon as in Syria, were willing to denounce these as foreign tyrants. (More will be said about this confessional quarrel over the nature of the Lebanese past in chapter 11.)

To the Christian ruling establishment in Lebanon, another argument was urgently needed to provide a historical justification for the existence of a Greater Lebanon independent of Syria and of Arabism which all the people of the country, including the Sunnite Muslims of the coastal cities, could accept. In antiquity, the Greeks had used the name Phoenicia to denote the stretch of the Syrian coast between Latakia and Acre. Parts of this coast north of Tripoli and south of Tyre had not been incorporated in 1920 in Greater Lebanon. Nevertheless, it was along the coast of Greater Lebanon that three out of the four greatest of the ancient Phoenician city-states had flourished: Tyre, Sidon and Byblos, the last one locally called Jubayl. The Phoenicians, in their time, had been a great trading people. Those of Tyre, in particular, had established colonies all over the Mediterranean world. They had important settlements in Sicily, and a particularly important colony in Carthage, in present-day Tunisia. In Spain, they founded towns such as Barcelona, and in southern France the town of Marseilles. At one time, the great Hannibal of Carthage had crossed the Alps to conquer Italy. The ancient Greeks had borrowed their alphabet from the Phoenicians, and the Greek alphabet was the direct ancestor of the Latin alphabet of Western Europe.

Conquered by the Persians, then by Alexander the

Great, then by the Romans, the Phoenician cities managed to maintain their commercial prominence throughout antiquity, and in Greek and Roman times formed important centres of Hellenistic civilization. Under the Romans, Beirut rose to special prominence as a centre for the study of Roman law. The whole story, put together, provided an illustrious pre-Arab antiquity for Lebanon around which a superficially appealing Phoenicianist theory of the Lebanese past could be developed.

In the seventh century AD was the Arab conquest, and the Phoenician cities, along with the rest of Syria, became arabized. Yet, according to the proponents of Phoenicianism, these cities never lost their ancient Phoenician peculiarity, which allegedly reasserted itself in discreet and elusive ways time and again. Because resistance to arabization was not possible in the ancient seats of Phoenician culture along the coast, as they fell under strong Arab control, the reassertion of the Phoenician particularism of Lebanon could only maintain for itself a safe base in the mountains. Thus, through the intermediary of the emirates that succeeded one another in these mountains under the Arab and Islamic empires, the Phoenician particularism of Lebanon survived until modern times, when it finally took political form again in the State of Greater Lebanon, and ultimately in the Lebanese Republic. Essentially, therefore, the modern Lebanese nationality, it was argued, was the direct and legitimate descendant of the ancient nationality of the Phoenicians, just as the history of medieval and modern Lebanon was the natural continuation of the history of ancient Phoenicia.

Until the middle decades of the nineteenth century, few people in Lebanon could have known much about the ancient Phoenicians, except for graduates of the Maronite College in Rome who had bothered to read the Greek classics. The vogue of discussing the Phoenicians began in the 1850s, with the initial French exploration of the remains of ancient Phoenicia in Lebanon undertaken by Ernest Renan. The Maronite historian Tannus al-Shidyaq, who came to know Renan personally while he was undertaking his *Mission en Phénicie*,* mentioned the Phoenician past of coastal Lebanon in the opening chapters of his history, without in any way inferring that it had anything to do with the history of Mount Lebanon in medieval and modern times. By the late nineteenth century, however, Christian Lebanese interest in ancient Phoenicia was rapidly gaining ground. Lammens dwelt at some length on the history of the ancient Phoenician cities in his study of Syria, where he treated the subject as ancient Syrian history, in keeping with his thesis (which has already been considered). At the time when his *La Syrie; précis historique* was published in 1921, a journal called *La Revue Phénicienne* was already under publication by a group of Christian Lebanese intellectuals. During the French mandate and thereafter, the further archaeological exploration of the Phoenician past of Lebanon, first by French then mainly by Christian Lebanese archaeologists, was politically geared – officially as well as by private initiative – to strengthening the theory that modern Lebanon was none other than ancient Phoenicia resurrected.

No one, of course, could deny that the ancient Phoenicians had once existed. The Syrian Nationalist Party of Antun Saadeh took a great interest in their history, but claimed their heritage for Syrian nationalism. The Arab nationalists considered them ancient Arabs who had originally arrived in coastal Syria from Arabia. To some extent, they were correct. When the Greek historian Herodotus visited Syria in the fifth century BC, he was told by the Phoenician elders of Tyre that their ancestors had originally arrived as immigrants from the Arabian shores of the Red Sea, and even specified the time of their arrival as being twenty-three centuries earlier.

There has been much argument among scholars as to the origins of the name of the Phoenicians. Some relate it to the Canaanite term denoting the highly valued purple dye which the ancient inhabitants of Tyre and Sidon used to

---

* Ernest Renan published a book by this title (Paris, 1864).

extract from the sea mollusc called the murex – one of the principal articles of the ancient Phoenician trade. In Greek, however, *phoenix*, from which the name Phoenicia derives, was the term used for the date palm; it was also the term used to name the fabulous 'bird of Arabia' which, as it aged, set itself on fire then re-emerged in full youthful vigour from its own ashes. In Arabic, this fabulous bird was known as *tayr al-bulah*: literally, the 'palm bird'. Also, in ancient Arabian mythology, the *faniq* (equivalent to the Greek *phoenix*) – the sacred and inviolate bull – was once worshipped as a divine being; and a village in western Arabia bearing the name Faniqa (exactly Phoenicia), still exists.

To the Christian Lebanese advocates of what we may call Phoenicianism, the Arabian origin claimed for the Phoenicians by Herodotus was a lie. They were encouraged to maintain this view by Western archaeologists and scholars whose speculations on the history of the ancient Near East were frequently contradicted by the direct testimonies of the Greek historian; for this reason, it was common among these Western scholars to dismiss Herodotus, traditionally lauded as the Father of History, as an incorrigible and irresponsible gossip who better deserved to be called the father of lies.

In the Christian Lebanese mythology that developed around the Phoenicians, these people were depicted as the Lebanese of old, and the progenitors of the modern Lebanese who were simply not Arabs, and who had inherited from their Phoenician forebears not only their historically attested mercantile character, but also their intellectual eminence. The Phoenicians, it was claimed, were not only the people from whom the Greeks took their alphabet; they had actually been the original inventors of the alphabet – a claim which no serious scholar today would accept. For this reason, the Phoenicianists argued, the whole of human culture owed the Lebanese a great debt.

Unfortunately for the Phoenicianist theory, the ancient inhabitants of Tyre, Sidon and Byblos, though they used the alphabet, did not leave any literature. Nevertheless, the Phoenicianists claimed that these Phoenicians were actually the originators of a *Liban lumineux* – a luminous Lebanon which, down the ages, has forever radiated thought and enlightenment to the world in the East and the West. By insisting upon praising the glories of their alleged *Liban lumineux*, the proponents of Phoenicianism actually did their idea a great disserve by exposing it to ridicule.

Lebanon since the nineteenth century belonged undisputedly in the intellectual vanguard of the Arab world, giving the Arab nationalists adequate proof that the Lebanese were none other than fellow Arabs who happened to be particularly gifted, perhaps because the circumstances of the modern world made them so. Earlier on, however, the people of Mount Lebanon had been mostly illiterate goatherds and peasants who made no recognizable contributions to world knowledge or culture. There certainly used to be a famous law school in Beirut in Roman times, but what of that? Before the Hellenistic age, the Phoenicians had excelled in seafaring and trade, but in little else. The longest inscription left in the Phoenician alphabet is found on the tomb of one of the kings of Byblos and consists of a series of curses hurled against anyone who disturbed the bones inside. In any case, if anyone had a claim to be a descendant of the ancient Phoenicians, it was the Sunnite Muslims of the coastal towns, who actually considered themselves to be Arabs, rather than the Christians of the mountains, or anyone else.

Phoenicianism in Christian Lebanese circles developed more as a cult than a reasoned political theory, its chief proponents being poets and men of letters writing in Arabic or French.* In reality, the chronicled history of ancient Phoenicia proved impossible to reconstruct, because there are no proper records: only archaeological remains, occasionally with short inscriptions; dubious or obscure

---

* See, for example, Charles Corm, *La Montagne inspirée: trois étapes de la vie du Liban* (Beirut, 1934).

mentions of one Phoenician city or another in ancient Egyptian, Mesopotamian and other records; and some oblique references in classical literature, none being particularly illuminating or detailed.

Whatever was known about Phoenician history, however, did find its way into the history textbooks used in Lebanese schools and created the impression that Lebanon was no new country, but one with 6000 years of national heritage behind it. Tourist pamphlets also emphasized this. When Philip K. Hitti, of Princeton University, undertook the writing of a history of Lebanon, which he published in English in 1957, he devoted a section of his work to the Phoenician past of the country. As a circumspect historian, however, he was careful to call his work not the history of Lebanon but *Lebanon in History*, which could imply that Phoenician history was something that simply happened at one time in Lebanon, without altogether denying that it was an integral part of the history of the country, which is what Hitti appears to have actually believed. The issue was thus left hanging. Arab nationalists naturally scoffed at Phoenicianism, and they had good reason to, although they did not come forward with any reasoned historical arguments against the idea, apart from insisting that the Phoenicians were really the ancient Arabs of Lebanon. They ultimately agreed to have Phoenician history made part of the Lebanese school curriculum, considering that it was a history that, geographically, was Lebanese, provided the Phoenicians were not presented in the accepted history textbooks as non-Arabs.

All this became argument and counter-argument: a matter of tiresome polemics. What of the facts of the issue? In antiquity, when Canaanite was the dominant Semitic language certainly in coastal Syria and western Arabia, Canaanite-speaking communities who used alphabetical writing, and who were particularly adept at seafaring, established a number of city-states along the Syrian coast between, roughly, Latakia and Acre. These city-states were normally independent of one another, and went their various ways. One of them, Tyre, whose inhabitants are known to have claimed a west Arabian origin, came for a time to dominate the commerce of the Mediterranean basin, and had a particularly flourishing North African colony in Carthage. One cannot really tell whether or not these ancient seafaring communities of coastal Syria actually called themselves Phoenicians. The Greeks, however, certainly knew them by that name, and called their coastlands Phoenicia. Apparently, the geographical delineation of Phoenicia was rather vague. In the sixth century AD, the Roman provincial administration of Syria came to distinguish between a coastal Phoenicia (*Phoenicia Marittima*) and a Phoenicia at the Lebanon (*Phoenicia ad Libanum*). The first was administered from Tyre and comprised all the ancient Phoenician coastal cities and their immediate mountain hinterland; the second, surprisingly, was administered from Damascus, and comprised territories of the Syrian interior which included the regions of Baalbek, Homs and Palmyra. By that time, the population of Syria, certainly in *Phoenicia ad Libanum*, was largely Arab. The same was the case with *Phoenicia Marittima*, at least in the mountain hinterland of the coastal cities. Writing of the conquests of Alexander the Great, the Greek historian Arrian considered the inhabitants of the mountain country east of Tyre to have been Arabs even at that early date, which was in the fourth century BC.

From the sixth century BC, as noted in the introduction to this book, the Phoenician cities came to be dominated by a succession of empires: the Persian; the Seleucid; the Roman. The Seleucid empire, with its capital at Antioch, was founded by Seleucus Nicator, one of the three generals who fought over the empire of Alexander the Great after his death in 324 BC, and finally divided its territory between themselves. When the Romans arrived in Syria in the first century BC, the weakening control of the Seleucids over Syria had led to the emergence of a number of local autonomies, among them the Nabatean kingdom in Transjordan; the Jewish kingdom of the Hasmoneans, followed by the Herodians, in Palestine; and the Iturean kingdom in the Bekaa valley, which controlled at least the northern parts of Galilee, and the Lebanon mountains as far west, at least at some points, as the Phoenician coast. The language of Syria at the time had long become basically Aramaic, and the older Canaanite language was already virtually dead. The Itureans, like the Nabateans, for lack of a better term, have sometimes been spoken of as Arameo-Arabs. They represent a stage in the linguistic history of Syria when the Aramaic speech of the population in some regions was already being permeated by Arabic.

Under the Seleucids and the Romans, the cities of ancient Phoenicia became leading centres of the cosmopolitan Hellenistic culture of that age. Greek and Roman colonies of considerable size were established there too, as in other cities of Syria. Under the influence of the Greek colonists, who wielded the stronger cultural influence, the upper classes of the native population of these cities became Hellenized to varying degrees. Those were the Levantines of their times, and among them were the great jurists of the famed Roman law school in Beirut. Hellenistic influence gained hardly any ground in the rural and tribal areas, however, where the Arab element, by the second or third century AD, became increasingly important. In the wake of the Arab conquests of the seventh century, the Hellenistic order in the Syrian cities collapsed as the Greek colonists left. The cities along the coast rapidly fell into decay as the maritime commerce of the Mediterranean at the time came to a dead halt. When this same commerce, starting by slow stages from the ninth century, began to revive, these former cities re-emerged as small Arab seaports, some of which were to grow again in importance with time. By that period, however, their Hellenistic, let alone their Phoenician past was already long forgotten.

Clearly, between ancient Phoenicia and the Lebanon of medieval and modern times, there is no demonstrable historical connection. The historical chasm between the two involves two major changes of language, from Canaanite to Aramaic, then from Aramaic to Arabic, and the accompanying shifts of population which no doubt occurred at the same time. There is also the intervening Hellenistic period to account for, when Phoenicia, certainly by the late Roman period, was no more than a geographical expression loosely used. Not a single institution or tradition of medieval or modern Lebanon can be legitimately traced back to ancient Phoenicia. One must bear in mind, above all else, that the history of ancient Phoenicia was set along the coast, while that of modern Lebanon had its small beginnings since early Islamic times in the mountains, where it remained fixed until the creation of the State of Greater Lebanon in 1920.

So much for history. Yet, the fact remains that most of the Phoenician cities of antiquity did flourish in the coastlands of present-day Lebanon, preserving their ancient Canaanite names in aramaicized or arabicized forms to this day. Judging by what ancient Greek literature has to say about the Phoenicians, the urban Lebanese of today do not appear to be much different in character. Like the ancient Phoenicians, they are free-wheeling and rugged mercantilists; adventurous and footloose, yet staunchly attached to home grounds; free-spending and willing to take on any gamble, yet essentially thrifty; keeping an open mind and adapting to changing circumstances with typical Levantine facility at one level, yet doggedly set in their traditional ways at another; socially playful to the point of irresponsible levity, yet serious, highly alert and efficient, though somewhat unconventional, when it comes to real business, where they have a marked tendency to live by their wits. What makes the modern urban Lebanese so much like the Phoenicians of old is geography, not history. They live in the same cities, along the same Mediterranean shore, and work the same land under the same climate. Geography in some respects can be as important as history.

After the second world war, the Lebanese Republic, as it gained political independence, emerged in a way as a resurrection of ancient Phoenicia, which was in its time a country of merchant city-states. In creating Greater Lebanon, the French in 1920 had attached Beirut to the mountains. After 1943, the mountains became more and more a hinterland to Beirut, which could be easily visualized as a city-state of a modernized Phoenician type at the head of what was essentially a merchant republic.

Among the chief architects of the political structure and economy of this merchant republic was Michel Chiha (d. 1954). Chiha was a Chaldean Christian banker, journalist and intellectual whose family originally came from Iraq. Lebanon, as envisaged by Chiha and by many others of the time, was the natural bridge between the West and the Arab world. The economic destiny of the country, as he saw it, was to become the warehouse and financial and services centre of the Arab world – the Phoenicia of the modern Middle East. In his writings on Lebanon, which were in French,* he made frequent reference to the Phoenicians, and was particularly fond of quoting the Biblical prophet Ezekiel (27: 3, 4, 9, 33) on Tyre, which Chiha liked to consider as the Phoenician prototype of modern Beirut:

> That city which stands at the edge of the sea,
> And does business with people living on every seacoast:
> Your home is in the sea.
> Sailors from every seagoing vessel
> Did business in your shops.
> When your merchandise went overseas,
> You filled the needs of every nation;
> Kings were made rich by the wealth of your goods.

In the writings of Chiha, Phoenicianism, stressed impressionistically rather than historically, finds its most intelligent expression. Chiha, however, was aware that his mercantilist, Phoenician Lebanon rested on shaky foundations. In cosmopolitan Beirut, his political associates in the Christian ruling establishment were refined Levantines, much as he was; in the mountains, however, more archaic

---

* Collections of articles by Michel Chiha are published under the titles *Visage et présence du Liban* (Beirut, 1964); *Politique intérieure* (Beirut, 1964); and *Propos d'économie libanaise* (Beirut, 1965).

social traditions prevailed. In these areas the Christian leaders represented feuding political clans and so were no different from the Druze, Shiite or Sunnite bosses of the various rural and tribal regions. In the coastal cities, including Beirut itself, the Arabism of the Sunnite Muslims, with external support from Damascus and other Arab capitals, was determinedly pitted against the Lebanism of the Christians, and had echoes among the Sunnites, Druzes and Shiites of the hinterland. From the 1930s, the streets of Beirut, every now and then, became the scene of violent clashes between Christian and Muslim gangs, one side brandishing the banner of Lebanism, the other of Arabism.

In 1926, Chiha was the secretary of the committee which drafted the Constitution for the Lebanese Republic. Reportedly, he had personally seen to it that this Constitution did not rule on every detail of the political structure of the republic, leaving the way open for periodical readjustments that would result from give and take among the republic's different confessional groups and political clans. As a young man, Chiha had carried out some free study in Britain, where he developed a great admiration for the resilience of the unwritten British constitution whose forcefulness struck him as deriving entirely from tradition. Such a constitution, Chiha thought, would be ideally suited for Lebanon, because it could accommodate differences without recourse to artificial legal rulings which could please one group, but anger another possibly to the point of violence.

In 1947, Chiha sponsored the establishment of *Cénacle Libanais* – a free forum where differences of political opinion in the country could be ironed out in an atmosphere of rational discussion and channelled to serve the common national interest. Lebanon, he was convinced, was 'a country which tradition must defend against violence'. Yet, what chances of success did the rational cultivation of tradition have in a society where not everybody was equally committed to be rational, and where rationalism in any case was given different political interpretations? Chiha did not live to see the carefully cultivated traditions of his idealized merchant republic of Lebanon – his Phoenicia resurrected – destroyed by the very violence he was so anxious to guard against.

10   Trial and error

Michel Chiha remained correct: there was a potential for violence in Lebanon which could only be contained by political common sense. A rich fund of such common sense in the country could be tapped, provided there was someone at the head of the state to exploit it constructively.

The potential for violence had its strongholds in the mountains, where a full heritage of political rancours and interconfessional suspicions remained entrenched, most notably between the Christians and Druzes of the Shuf mountains. Here, as in other rural regions, latent tribalism rallied around traditional or emerging chiefs who alone were trusted political representatives. Violence, however, had a strong presence in the coastal cities too, where Sunnite Muslims felt highly insecure and continued to nurse feelings of resentment against the Christian ruling establishment, awaiting the opportunity when the tables could be politically turned. In the capital, Beirut, Sunnite Muslims and Christians, by the late 1930s, were already facing one another in organized gangs brandishing the banners of Arabism and Lebanism respectively. The few street clashes that occurred between them at the time may not have been serious, but they did not augur well for the future.

The political common sense needed to bridle this

potential for violence in the country was to be found among individuals in various parts, but the principal base was Beirut. Here, since the nineteenth century, a stong tradition of liberal thinking had developed at a certain social level among Muslims and Christians alike. Here also, common business interests were strong enough to override confessional tensions to some extent. Between the Sunnite and Maronite extremes in Beirut, there was a buffer of moderation – the non-Maronite Christian communities large enough to count politically, namely the Greek Orthodox and the Greek Catholics. Moreover, as the capital of Lebanon, the city was in a position to feel the pulse of the country and offer its services as a clearing house for political differences. While the Sunnite political bosses of Beirut could not afford to alienate their popular following by openly taking positions of political moderation, Sunnite notables who converged on the capital from Tripoli or Sidon were more free to do so. As early as 1926, Muhammad al-Jisr, a prominent Sunnite man of learning from Tripoli, had defied the Sunnite boycott of the Lebanese state by agreeing to serve until 1932 as speaker of parliament. In 1937, another Sunnite from Tripoli, Khayr al-Din al-Ahdab, who had gained prominence in Beirut as an Arab nationalist journalist, again defied the same Sunnite boycott by accepting the premiership of the Lebanese cabinet, whose premises in the capital were established in the old Ottoman Serail, or government house. When his fellow Arab nationalists attacked him for accepting office, he reportedly responded in good humour: 'Should the Arabs one day decide to unite, it would not be my presence in the Serail that would stop them from doing so.'

The Lebanese Republic, at the time, was still under French mandate. In 1939, however, the second world war broke out in Europe; the Germans occupied Paris the following year, and the mandate over Lebanon and Syria was continued by the collaborator Vichy French regime. In 1941, British and Free French forces moved northwards from Palestine to expel the Vichy French from the two countries whose independence the Free French now formally proclaimed. In only a matter of time, it was generally understood, this independence would be made effective, because the British so wanted it; and there was much speculation in Lebanon as to what would happen when independence was achieved.

In certain Christian Lebanese circles, there was real fear that the end of the French mandate would threaten the the survival of Lebanon as an independent country in the Arab world. This Christian 'fear for Lebanese independence from independence', as it was then put, led in 1942 to the formation of a Christian political front called the National Bloc, which insisted that the French mandate over Lebanon, which was bound to come to an end, be replaced by special treaty relationship with France. Christian voices were even raised at the time which demanded that Lebanon be made a national home for the Christians under French protection, just as Palestine was to be made a national home for the Jews, leaving Syria for the Muslims to manage as they pleased. This, for example, was the position openly taken then by Ignatius Mubarak, the Maronite Archbishop of Beirut. On the other hand, there were the many who realized that France was no longer the great power it had once been in the world, and thus could not give the Christians of Lebanon the protection they sought. Moreover, the British and the Americans were determined to bring French dominance over Lebanon and Syria to an end.

In other Christian political circles in close touch with the British and the Americans, great enthusiasm was shown for the implementation of the expected independence of Lebanon, which appeared to promise great political and economic expectations for the country. Christian leaders who were so persuaded had been organized since 1936 as the Constitutional Bloc, which also included some Druze and Shiite notables. This bloc had special strength because it represented important Christian business interests in Beirut, including those of the Chaldean Chiha and Greek Catholic Pharaon families. Michel Chiha and his brother-in-law Henri Pharaon were actually the chief political strategists of that bloc. Among the Sunnites of Lebanon, the enthusiasm for Lebanese independence naturally existed; however, it was articulated in Arab nationalist terms which frightened the Christians, driving large numbers of them to rally in strength around the French-supported National Bloc.

Thoughtful Sunnites were mindful at the time of Christian fears provoked by their talk of pan-Arabism; and some among them, such as the brothers Kazim and Takieddine Solh of Sidon, made a point of attempting to allay these understandable Christian fears. There was all the time in the world, they said, for the Muslims and Christians of Lebanon to debate the issue of Arabism versus Lebanism. Whether the history of the country was a detail of Arab history, or a full history on its own, Phoenician or otherwise, did not really matter that much. Lebanon in fact existed as a country, regardless of the ongoing dispute about the nationality of its people; and its Christians and Muslims were bound to agree that the country, once it became independent, needed to be managed and developed properly. This, rather than the Arabism or Phoenicianism of Lebanon, was the immediate and ultimately the real issue at stake, and serving this end would unite the people of Lebanon rather than perpetuate divisions among them. Details regarding the sharing of power between Christians and Muslims in the Lebanese state could be worked out in a manner which would best serve this aim.

What was actually hammered out between the Christian leaders of the Constitutional Bloc and the Muslim leaders who co-operated with them was the so-called National Pact – an unwritten gentlemen's agreement to supplement the formal Constitution of the country and have equal effectiveness. Of the exact manner in which this National Pact was negotiated and agreed upon, there is no formal record. In 1943, however, when Lebanon finally became independent under a government dominated by the Constitutional Bloc and its Muslim allies, everybody in the country spoke of the accord, whether with approval or cynicism.

What was generally understood, from the very beginning, was that the National Pact involved Muslim consent to the continued existence of Lebanon as an independent and sovereign state in the Arab world, provided it considered itself, so to speak, part of the Arab family. The Maronites in the country could keep the key political, security and military positions as their special preserve: the presidency of the republic; the directorate of public security; the command of the army. Sunday would also be maintained as the official Sabbath day. The Christians of the country needed no less than that to allay their fears of what could otherwise happen to Lebanon. On the other hand, the premiership of the government would be made the preserve of Sunnite Muslims; and other government positions would be distributed equitably among the different Lebanese communities – in the parliament, the cabinet, and in the administration. After 1947, the speakership of parliament came to be reserved for the Shiites. In the original pact, their considerable presence in the country had not been properly taken into account.

In the Lebanese parliament, the representation of Christians and Muslims was fixed at the ratio of six to five – another stipulation of the National Pact intended to keep the minds of Christians at rest. The country, in a succession of electoral laws, was divided into multi-member constituencies, most of them confessionally mixed, and seats in parliament were reserved for members of the different confessions in the mixed constituencies. This was carried out with a view to promoting political integration among the different communities, as Christian deputies for these constituencies had to secure Muslim votes, and Muslims Christian votes, for their election. In each of the mixed constituencies, candidates belonging to different religions and sects could run independently or on the same ticket against other candidates, and the voters could choose between the different tickets as they received them, or make changes if they so pleased, as long as they observed the confessional distribution of the parliamentary seats assigned for their constituency. A more intelligent plan for political integration at the electoral level could hardly have been devised. In the short term, it seemed to work. In the longer term, however, it became increasingly clear that it involved a political vision too subtle for the actual social structure of the country. Within a decade, dissatisfaction was already being expressed.

The question, as it ultimately came to be posed, was the following: should the different communities in Lebanon be represented in government by leaderships that stood for their true confessional or tribal ethos, or should their representation be from elements more given to reason and moderation? In the first instance, the government in the country, at the legislative and executive level, could degenerate into an arena for the settlement of traditional confessional and tribal feuds, and this could only result in political chaos. In the second, the representation of the country in government would not reflect its true social nature; and in some cases, it could run dangerously against the grain. Not that all the Lebanese were unreasonable or immoderate; but there were enough unreasonable and immoderate elements among them to cause trouble if they felt that they were not properly or adequately represented. The Lebanese electoral system, as devised by people of political sophistication, was geared towards securing a majority of moderates in parliament, and it was these moderates who elected the president of the republic and who normally became premiers or cabinet ministers. The more powerful leaders, though they rarely failed to get elected to parliament, were more often than not kept out of the executive, and remained largely active in disgruntled and obstructive opposition.

For real national integration among the Lebanese, political parties that cut across confessional and regional lines were a necessity; and real political parties, such as those that exist in modern democracies, needed to be organized by people who could aspire to the national leadership at the level of head of state. By the terms of the National Pact, only Maronites could head the Lebanese state; therefore, only Maronites were in a position to organize political parties. It remained important for them to persuade members of other communities to follow them in party discipline. This, however, they could not easily do. In 1937, a Maronite paramilitary organization with some mixed Christian following – the Kataeb, or Phalanges Libanaises – had emerged in Beirut under the leadership of Pierre Gemayel (d. 1985). After 1949, attempts were made to transform this paramilitary organization into a real party with a national rather than a confessional following, even to the extent of changing its name to the Social Democratic Party. The effort, however, met with no success. In that same year, the Druze leader Kamal Jumblat (d. 1977) became the first non-Maronite to attempt the organization of a party on the national scale; but his Progressive Socialist Party, though it attracted some Christian and Muslim elements of political opposition, remained essentially a focus for Druzes rallying around the traditional leadership of the house of Jumblat. The Syrian Nationalist Party founded by Antun Saadeh in the 1930s did cut across confessional lines, but it was a pan-Syrian rather than strictly Lebanese party. Nowhere was its following strong enough to provide it with access to power. The Lebanese Communist Party, which had existed since the early days of the French mandate, also had a following from among different religious groups, but it was too small to really count politically.

In 1958, Camille Chamoun (d. 1987), then president of the republic, clashed with the Arab national unity movement led by President Nasser of Egypt (1954–71), and so became a hero to most of the Christian Lebanese. After leaving office, he organized the National Liberal Party (Parti National Liberal, or PNL), which was essentially a grouping of his Christian supporters under his personal leadership.

In the absence of real political parties with national followings among the masses, political life in the Lebanese Republic became the preserve of shifting alliances among politicians who formed parliamentary or extra-parliamentary fronts or blocs. In each constituency, candidates for elections belonging to different religious groups formed rival 'lists', each dominated by a local political boss. In the fronts and blocs, as in the electoral lists, political alliances were normally temporary, reflecting interests of the moment among the politicians concerned. In parliament and the government, the discipline of the blocs and fronts was loose, and politicians changed sides whenever it suited them. The electorate was only remembered at election time. This naturally led to a high degree of political alienation of people from government, and impeded the development of national allegiance to the state.

To curb the power of traditional Muslim or Druze leaders where such leaders happened to be particularly strong, the Lebanese Christian political establishment created rivals to them from among politicians of the second rank who had no natural popular following. To strengthen these naturally weak politicians against the more powerful traditional leaders, government favours to the public were largely channelled through their intermediary. Thus, their power came to depend entirely upon government support. It was such people who became the 'moderate' or 'loyal' (Arabic, *muwali*) Muslim and Druze politicians, on whose allegiance the Christian heads of state felt they could count. The practice, however, proved counter-productive, because it threw the most powerful Muslim and Druze leaders throughout the country into the ranks of the opposition (Arabic, *mu'aradah*) – not the 'loyal' opposition of normal democracies, but one which resorted whenever possible to political obstructiveness.

To boost their threatened traditional power, in the rural areas as in the cities, these leaders of the Muslim and Druze opposition played unscrupulously on the ever-present confessional or tribal rancours and suspicions among their followers. They also readily accepted, and often solicited, external political support from Arab and foreign parties who were eager to interfere in internal Lebanese affairs for reasons of their own. As social tensions began to develop in the country in the wake of its uneven social and economic development, these same traditional leaders, whose power rested on the most archaic forms of loyalty, came to be regarded, paradoxically, as leaders of the Left, against the Right which was seen to be represented by the Christian ruling establishment. Whenever matters came to a head, the Christian establishment discovered, to its alarm, that the 'moderate' and 'loyal' Muslim and Druze politicians it had so assiduously cultivated were, in the majority of cases, poor allies to count upon. At the moment when most needed, they yielded to popular pressures from their respective communities and turned to join the opposition, or kept to their homes.

For the uneven social and economic development of the country, which produced the tensions exploited by Muslim and Druze opposition, both the ruling establishment and the opposition leaders were equally to blame. Successive regimes and governments left the development of the country to unbridled capitalist initiative. On the occasions when planning was implemented, private interests applied pressures to make the plans ineffective. In the rural and tribal areas, the traditional leaders had no interest in seeing their constituencies develop, fearing this would rob them of the mainstay of their power: the blind tribal or quasi-tribal allegiance of their followers. Development could make the blind see; and this, from the point of view of tribal leaderships, was politically undesirable. Moreover, while their constituencies remained undeveloped, partly because of government neglect, and partly through their own obstruction, such leaders could always lay the full blame on the government and present themselves as the protectors of the people. In the game of confessional politics, this permitted such leaders to portray what was in effect a government inefficiency for which they themselves were partly responsible as a discrimination by the Christians in power against non-Christians. But many Christian rural constituencies suffered as much from governmental neglect as Muslim or Druze ones.

On the surface, however, the Lebanese Republic after it gained independence appeared to bustle with development.

Because of its free economic system, the wealth of the Arab Middle East converged there, exactly as Michel Chiha had predicted in the days of the French mandate. Its economy, which was mainly one of services, had an educated, trained and highly experienced infrastructure without parallel in any other Arab country; and Lebanese know-how everywhere became proverbial. Beirut, by the 1960s, had four universities, two of them of long standing, attracting Arab students from all directions. Its free press stood in a class of its own in the Arab world, and Lebanese newspapers and magazines were widely read from the shores of the Arabian Sea to those of the Atlantic. Lebanon, meanwhile, was making some notable progress in the industrial sector, and its industry along with its fine agricultural products had ready Arab markets. Beirut, by day and night, became the playground for rich Arabs, and the mountain towns and villages around the capital, which had long been renowned as summer resorts, rapidly developed as centres for Arab aestivation.

Much of the economy of Lebanon tended to centre around Beirut and its immediate neighbourhood; yet Beirut came to radiate prosperity to such an extent that hardly any part of the country was left entirely untouched by its influence. Most important of all, despite its many political faults, Lebanon was a democracy where individual freedom in all walks of life was guaranteed and respected, for the citizens of the country as well as for visitors and foreign residents. In its Arab surroundings, it was seen as a true oasis of freedom by Arabs and non-Arabs alike.

The success story of the Lebanese Republic in the 1950s and 1960s was made capital of by the advocates of Lebanism. They would explain that Lebanon simply had to be there for the general good: not for the Lebanese alone, but also for all Arabs, and for the world at large. Lebanon, they pointed out, was the showcase of the Arab world; the natural intermediary between the Arabs and the West, not only in business, but in all other respects. The Lebanese were a people who lived in two worlds, which placed them in the ideal position to interpret one to the other: to articulate the Arab heritage and Arab causes in a manner that the West could understand; and to provide a screening mechanism for Western social and cultural influences reaching the Arab world. They alone could explain to the Arabs what was actually happening in the outside world, and explain to the outside world what the problems and aspirations of the Arabs were.

Within the Arab world, Lebanon was in a unique position. To Pierre Gemayel, the founder and leader of the Kataeb party, it was the one country where a Christian could be fully Christian, and a Muslim fully Muslim, in the enjoyment of the same religious and civic freedom which was complete and unconditional for both. Others, along the same line of thinking, depicted Lebanese society as a mosaic of different communities and sects in an ideal state of balance, each of them freely recognizing the existence and rights of the other. Where else could such tolerance be found? Yet others saw Lebanon as the one country in the world where the East and the West could meet on an equal footing, with the understanding that the East in the country was locally represented by the Muslims, and the West by the Christians. Charles Malik (d. 1987), a Greek Orthodox Christian and professor of philosophy at the American University of Beirut, who was serving in 1959–60 as president of the General Assembly of the United Nations, depicted the Lebanese as a people who had access to the holiest of holies of the West and of the East at the same time, which put them in a unique position to understand both cultures at their deepest levels.* This certainly was true of the highly developed intellectual circles around the American University of Beirut, and in the broader area of Ras Beirut where a tradition of broad, liberal thinking had come to prevail among the religiously mixed population. But how much further did it go?

The National Pact certainly provided Lebanon with an ideal framework for a working democracy. What was

* Said in an address to an American audience at Colonial Williamsburg, Virginia.

needed for it to function was a society with a broad civic
base genuinely committed to its principles. However, it was
exactly this that was lacking. Writing his memoirs in the
1960s,* the Druze man of letters Said Takieddine, having
spent most of his active life abroad, noted what appeared to
him a strange incongruity in the Lebanese character.
Outside their country, he remarked, the Lebanese are often
people of the world, as urbane and sophisticated as any
people can be. Back in their mountain villages, even those
among them who had achieved the highest distinctions
abroad immediately shed all sophistication and reverted to
type, becoming thoroughly and shamelessly immersed in
the pettiest mountain feuds. Takieddine, who came from
the town of Baaqlin in the Shuf, spoke only of the Lebanese
of the mountains; but the same applied to the Lebanese
people in general, with the exception of only a select group
of marginal outsiders. With the outbreak of the Lebanese
civil war in 1975, even many of those shed their civility
and reverted to a rash and wanton tribalism.

All things considered, was the Lebanese Republic something worth preserving? In their more lucid moments, even
the staunchest opponents of the Lebanese political system
were prepared to admit that it was, with some essential
reforms. Yet, what were these reforms to be? The Christian
ruling establishment was convinced that the Lebanese
political system, by providing for confessional representation
in government at all levels, was ideally suited for Lebanese
society, where confessionalism was a fact of life which had
to be taken into account. The National Pact, therefore, was
not something to be tampered with. The Christian leaderships, however, were the chief beneficiaries of the system
as it stood. For this reason, their defence of it could not be
taken to be purely a matter of principle. There were many
Muslims and Druzes who agreed with the Christians that
Lebanon, given its special social nature, could only be run
on the basis of the National Pact, provided its fundamental
principles were properly understood and applied. On the

* Said Takieddine, *Ana wa'l-tannin* (Beirut, 1961).

other hand, there were Muslim and Druze leaders who made common cause with the ideological parties, such as the communists and the Syrian nationalists of the PPS, and insisted that the real problem in Lebanon lay in confessionalism, which had to be officially abolished in favour of a secular political party system. Confessionalism, of course, being of the very nature of Lebanese society, could not be abolished by law. Thrown out by the door, it could always come in again by the window. Nor could a political party system cutting across the confessions be created to replace it by law. It could only come about by gradual stages, once Lebanese society became better integrated. Moreover, the clamours for the secularization of the Lebanese political system were themselves highly confessional, especially when they were articulated by traditional leaderships which fed on confessional group feelings among members of their respective sects. In nearly all cases, the anticipated achievement was not actual secularization, but the dismantling of the Maronite political dominance over the country which the confessional system was seen to perpetuate.

There remained the more fundamental question: should Lebanon be secularized only at the political level, or should the secularization of the country also reach the social level? The Druzes, as represented by Kamal Jumblat's Progressive Socialist Party, did not object to the total secularization of the country, although their main insistence was on political secularization – if for nothing else, to clip the wings of the Maronites. With the Muslims, however, among whom the Sunnites at the beginning were the most vocal, it was another matter. To them, the complete secularization of the country was out of the question. Why this was so needs some explanation.

In the Lebanese Republic, civil, commercial and criminal law was the same for all, and its administration remained in the hands of the state courts. On the other hand, matters of personal status involving marriage, divorce and inheritance were left to the religious courts of the different sects which were officially recognized as part of the

Lebanese judiciary. Among the Muslims, the Sunnite and Shiite religious courts, where matters of personal status were concerned, applied their different interpretations of the Islamic canon law, called the sharia (Arabic *al-shari'ah*). For the Christians and the Druzes, who had no equivalent of the Islamic sharia, the Lebanese parliament, in consultation with Christian and Druze religious leaders, ultimately enacted a special code of personal status law to apply to all the Christian sects, and another to apply to the Druzes. Thus, starting in the 1960s, the Christian religious courts on the one hand, and the Druze on the other, came to apply different laws on questions of personal status which were legislated by the civil body of the state. The Muslims, for their part, would not accept such civil intervention in matters relating to the only part of the sacred sharia which they could still apply. In Lebanon, as in most Arab and Islamic countries, Muslims had long come to accept the rule of civil law in all matters except those relating to the structure and regulation of the family. In this respect, the Turkish Republic, which had been fully secularized since the 1920s, was the only exception. From the Muslim point of view, removing the family from the rule of the sharia could not be permitted. Even the idea of giving Muslims the free choice between civil or religious courts to conduct their family affairs was considered totally unacceptable.

While matters regarding personal status remained outside the realm of the common civil legislation, each citizen in Lebanon had to belong by law to one of the recognized religious communities, and the religion and sect of every person had to be clearly indicated not only in the government registers, but also on the individual identity card. This meant that every Lebanese citizen, regardless of personal wishes, was officially recognized as having two identitities, one national, the other confessional. What was surpising, in the circumstances, was not the continued division of Lebanese society along confessional lines, but the degree to which national integration in Lebanon, particularly in Beirut, was actually achieved at certain social levels by individual initiative – in the face of the obstacles set up by the established confessional system and the archaic political and clerical interests that secured its perpetuation.

By the 1970s, confessionalism in the country was already eroding to a considerable extent, owing to intermarriage between members of different religions and sects, making increasing use of the civil marriage facilities provided by neighbouring countries such as Turkey or Cyprus; to strong personal and family friendships which paid no regard to confessional differences; to secular education; and to common social, business and cultural associations of various kinds. Formally, however, this developing social trend towards secularism, which tended to be restricted to the urban classes, gained no political recognition. The truly secular among the Lebanese, realizing that secularism was a matter of social attitude whose growth was conditional on social development, did not make much of an issue about it. Those who did, in most cases, were parties deriving their power from the very confessionalism they publicly condemned, and to whom the call for political secularism, or for total secularism, was no more than a useful political ploy.

Thus, at the level of politics, the call for secularism, rather than being sincere, came to be acted out as just another confidence game between the parties concerned, much as the game of devious Lebanism versus devious Arabism described in the second chapter of this book. From the one side, the Muslim and Druze parties pressed for the abolition of confessionalism in favour of secularism at the political level, with the full knowledge that such an abolition would not be possible unless confessionalism was also abolished at the social level. From the other side, the Christian political leaderships, realizing that the Muslim and Druze call for political secularism was actually aimed at disestablishing the Christian political control of the state, responded by insisting that true secularism in Lebanon could not be achieved unless confessionalism was abolished at the social as well as at the political level. They fully knew, of course, that the Muslims were not prepared to entertain this suggestion even as an intellectual exercise. Otherwise, the Christians insisted, the Lebanese system must be left as it stood, which was ultimately what they wanted. On both sides, the positions taken on the issue were hypocritical. This certainly did not mean that there were none among the Lebanese who sincerely wanted to live under a secular system of government and a civil law touching all walks of life and common to all. What it did indicate was that the truly secular-minded among the Lebanese had nothing to do with the issue, unless they happened to be unknowingly serving one political side or the other as dupes.

Thus, in Lebanon, an essentially confessional bid for political secularism came to be countered by an equally confessional bid for total secularism, the political motives behind each of the two bids being highly cynical and devious, known to all but the most innocent and gullible. From the Christian side came the ostensibly sincere plea, often articulated by Pierre Gemayel and others, that the Lebanese Republic under the National Pact was actually a secular state. In every other Arab country, so the Christian Lebanese argument went, Islam was pronounced by a special article of the constitution to be the state religion, or at least the religion of the chief of state. Only Lebanon had no state religion – neither in the terms of its Constitution, nor in the terms of the National Pact. Yet, in Lebanon, Muslims rightly saw themselves as being grossly under-privileged. They certainly had a share in government and administration; just as certainly, they had no direct say in ultimate decision making, which remained the preserve of the Maronites.

The problem was, however, that the decisions the Muslim Lebanese always pressed for were of a dimension that frightened the Christians. When they were not responding with excessive zeal to external calls for pan-Arab unity, as happened between 1958 and 1961 when Syria and Egypt were politically merged under President Nasser as the United Arab Republic, they were pressing the Lebanese state to throw all caution to the winds in the full and unconditional espousal of pan-Arab causes, such as that of the Palestinian revolution after 1967, regardless of any sacrifice to Lebanese national interest that could compromise the very sovereignty of the state, and even its territorial security and integrity.

From the Christian Lebanese point of view, such political behaviour on the part of the Muslims of the country appeared irresponsible and blatantly unpatriotic. For this reason, the Christians maintained that their Muslim compatriots could not be trusted with what was admitted to be, in theory, their rightful share in national decision making at the highest level. From the Muslim point of view, it was the Christians – specifically the Maronites – who were not only unpatriotic but, worse still, callous 'isolationists' (Arabic, *in'izaliyyun*), because they seemed so determined to be insensitive to pan-Arab aspirations, forcing Lebanon to stand out in the Arab world as a sore thumb every time a vital Arab issue was at stake.

Moreover, the Muslims repeatedly pointed out that there were demographic realities in the country to reckon with, which justified their demand for a greater share in power and made the issue a pressing one. Even if one granted that the Christians had originally formed a bare majority of the population of Lebanon in 1920, or even as late as 1943, hardly anyone doubted that the balance of numbers in the country had long been tipping increasingly in favour of the Muslims. A fair census, the Muslims insisted, could establish the facts on this sensitive point; but the Christians would not hear of a census. The last one actually taken in Lebanon had been in 1932, under the French mandate, and there was a general suspicion, even among many Christians, that it had been a rigged one, at least to some extent. From that time on, only official population figures, which were generally known to be heavily doctored, had been released by the Lebanese census department, to the head of which only Christians were appointed, and whose records were kept in strict secrecy.

Of course, a census in Lebanon was badly needed for

purposes of proper development planning, if for nothing else; and such a census, in theory, could have been undertaken without classifying the population by religion and sect. The very idea of a census, however, was unacceptable to the Christians in power, even if it did not make the population count on a confessional basis. Any form of census, it was feared, could indirectly reveal demographic facts that were not in the Christian interest. On the other hand, the Muslims did not press for a census in the interest of development planning, but simply to demonstrate the extent to which they had become the majority in the country, thereby throwing the Christians more on the defensive than they already were.

Here again, what was involved was a political game rather than an honest transaction; and this game, as all the others, was played out at the expense of the real national interest, and regardless of the dangers involved to all concerned. On both sides, there were the professionals and accomplished amateurs who played the game, and the masses that cheered or booed as the occasion called for; and from time to time these masses descended into the arena to join forces with the players. The plain fact was that most of the Lebanese, no less than their leaders, were more concerned with the game than with the national interest, and their wild clamours encouraged the leaders to play the game hard, and way beyond the limits of safety. To begin with, the game was played according to rules; but when the leading players began to break the rules and play foul, their supporters saw to it that they paid no penalties. By the early 1970s, the Lebanese political game was already degenerating into a general brawl in which external as well as internal parties freely participated. The worst fears of Michel Chiha were about to be realized: tradition, in Lebanon, was rapidly ceasing to be effective as the means to protect the country from the violence that would destroy it.

11 The war over Lebanese history

To celebrate the third centennial of the birth of Fakhr al-Din Maan, regarded by generations of Lebanese as the father of modern Lebanon, in 1974 the government erected an equestrian bronze statue of the great Druze emir in Baaklin, his native town in the Shuf, in the front yard of the local government house. The following year, the Lebanese civil war broke out in Beirut and spread to other parts of the country, ultimately reaching the Shuf in 1983. The outcome of the fierce hostilities in this region was the total eviction of the local Christian population from all but one town. The Druzes were naturally jubilant in their victory. For the first time in three centuries, they had succeeded in regaining full control of their historical home grounds.

The triumph of the Druzes in the Shuf war was hardly complete when the statue of Fakhr al-Din in the town of Baaklin was unceremoniously brought down with a charge of dynamite. In nearby Mukhtara, however, a portrait of the same emir continued to occupy its place of honour in the main hall of the ancestral palace of Walid Jumblat, the paramount leader of the Druzes and the victor of the Shuf war. The symbolism involved was significant. Fakhr al-Din was one figure in the history of Lebanon who was deemed worthy of special honour and unanimous respect by all people in the country, regardless of whether or not he was actually the founder of a Lebanese state. Whatever the true nature of his rule, he remained a man of exceptional enlightenment and religious tolerance, which recommended him for acceptance by the Muslims as well as the Christians as a pre-eminent national hero. From the Druze point of view, however, Fakhr al-Din was essentially a figure of Druze history, and in his time a controversial one, whose person and career had been unduly glorified by Christian historians to serve Christian political purposes. To the Druzes, the bronze figure which was brought down from its pedestal represented Fakhr al-Din in his undeserved Christian apotheosis, and it had been set up in his native town by the Christian Lebanese ruling establishment to stand as a false witness to what this same establishment had made of the history of Lebanon. The portrait hanging in the palace of Mukhtara, on the other hand, was that of the true historical Fakhr al-Din, as recognized by his own Druze community. For decades, the Druzes had insisted that the true history of Lebanon was not that advanced by the Christians, and that the Druze role in it had been deliberately misconstrued by Christian political trickery and historiographical sleight of hand. Now was their chance to drive the point home.

Walid Jumblat, in fact, minced no words about this question. Since 1983, he has repeatedly declared that the rewriting of the Lebanese history textbook was a necessary precondition for any lasting political settlement in Lebanon, if not the primary one. Before succeeding his father to the Druze leadership in 1977, Jumblat, a graduate of the American University of Beirut, had taught history for some time in a secondary school, and the issue in his mind was clear: the continuing civil war in Lebanon was, in a fundamental way, a war to determine the correct history of the country. If Lebanon was ever to stand on its feet again, the Lebanese must be taught their history accurately, and all the Christian-fabricated myths formerly raised must be dropped. Jumblat conceded that the ultimate definition of what constituted proper Lebanese history was a matter which could finally be left for trustworthy specialists to decide. Meanwhile, in the schools of the Shuf now fully under his control, a new version of this history was to be taught, radically different from the official one: a version which many non-Druzes considered somewhat bizarre, but which the Druzes nonetheless regarded as closer to reality than what was actually being taught about Lebanon elsewhere in the country.

In the same schools of the Shuf where this new version of the history of Lebanon came to be taught, other changes in the curriculum were made, in keeping with the political ethos of the Druze community. Students in these schools no longer honoured the Lebanese banner and national anthem, nor did they defer in any way to the state as a matter of principle. From the Druze stand, the Lebanese Republic as it actually existed was no different from the official version of Lebanese history: it was a creature of the Christian political establishment, geared to serve its devious ends. The situation was not the same in the Sunnite schools run by the Maqasid Society in Beirut, where a point was made of upholding with full reverence all the established symbols and traditions of the Lebanese state. This remained an important factor at a time when Lebanon as a country was rapidly disintegrating and needed the loyalty of every citizen in order to preserve its existence with hope for better times. In these Sunnite schools of Beirut, unlike the Druze ones of the Shuf, the history of Lebanon continued to be taught strictly according to the official government curriculum. Yet, it was in these same Maqasid schools, four decades earlier, that the war against the official version of Lebanese history was first declared.

In those days, two teachers at the Maqasid College, Zaki Nakkash and Omar Farrukh, decided that what they considered to be the continuing Christian falsification of the history of Lebanon could not be allowed to proceed unchallenged any further. Nakkash and Farrukh were not only critical of the manner in which Lebanese history was officially presented and taught; they actually regarded the very concept of a historical Lebanon as anathema: a Christian invention which was highly suspect, deliberately intended to serve Christian interests in the country, and ultimately Western imperialist interests in Syria and the rest of the Arab world. In the view of Nakkash and Farrukh, Lebanon was historically part of Syria; strictly, the country could claim no special history of its own. Moreover, the history of Syria as a whole, let alone Lebanon, was ultimately Arab history, and must be treated as such, rather than artificially divorced from its Arab national context, as in the politically mischievous work of Henri Lammens.

It was on this basis that Nakkash and Farrukh, in 1935, brought the controversy over the history of Lebanon into the open by the publication of a history textbook for elementary schools which they co-authored, entitled *Tarikh Suriyah wa Lubnan* (History of Syria and Lebanon). In this book, Lebanon was denuded of all special historicity outside the Syrian Arab context.

The Christian establishment in Lebanon, allegedly in league with the French High Commission in Beirut, was quick to react to this challenge and immediately commissioned the production of another textbook of elementary school history in which the special historicity of a Lebanon separate and distinct from its Syrian and Arab surroundings was strongly underlined. The task was entrusted to two Christian scholars of the front rank: Asad Rustum, a Greek Orthodox Christian who then held the chair of Near Eastern history at the American University of Beirut; and Fuad Afram al-Bustani, the scion of a Maronite scholarly dynasty of long standing, who taught Arabic literature at the Jesuit Saint-Joseph University. The joint effort of these two scholars resulted, in 1937, in the publication of *Mujaz Tarikh Lubnan* (Précis of the history of Lebanon) – a work which emphasized the special historical character of Lebanon to an extent which no Muslim was willing to accept, and which even many Christians regarded as going far beyond the limits of reason. The work was originally intended for use in government schools, but the determined opposition of the Muslim community successfully prevented its official adoption.

Subsequently, other textbooks of Lebanese history for elementary and secondary schools were published and generally adopted. Each new attempt slurred over the more sensitive issues regarding the historical nature of the country. The controversy, however, did not end there, but was further compounded in time by Marxian and other ideological interpretations of the Lebanese past. The Muslims, on the whole, were willing to accommodate such ideological interpretations, provided they did not help consecrate a special national character for the country. On the other hand, Nakkash, Farrukh and others of their school continued to maintain a tireless watch over all Christian activity in the field of historical writing on Lebanon, lest what occurred in 1937 should ever happen again, and the Christians somehow manage to establish their concept of the historicity of Lebanon as the official one at a time when Muslim vigilance happened to be slack.

In pressing for the recognition of a special national history for Lebanon, the Christians were prepared to be opposed by the Sunnite Muslims; but they were initially convinced that they could count on a high degree of Druze support. In all the interpretations of Lebanese history which they advanced, they carefully emphasized the importance of the Druze role in the medieval and modern history of the country, sometimes to the point of over-emphasis. The Druzes were naturally flattered but they remained wary of the motives behind the Christian attention. As they saw it, the history of Lebanon had never been a concerted march of progress by Maronites and Druzes toward the achievement of common national aims. Starting with Ottoman times, it was more than anything else a record of Maronite usurpations of Druze rights. Moreover, Druzes who were knowledgeable in the oral traditions of their community could point out exactly how their Christian compatriots had falsified the history of the country under the Maan and Shihab emirs, by gross exaggeration or outright invention, making of it a story of

Lebanese national hope and fulfilment in which Christians and Druzes equally shared.

Unlike the Sunnite Muslims, most Druzes did not deny Lebanon a special history. Their attitude towards the subject, however, was frequently cynical. The Christians, as far as they were concerned, were welcome to have the history of Lebanon exactly as they wanted it; all the better if they chose to delude themselves into believing that the Druzes, down the centuries, had shared their Lebanese national aspirations. To expect the Druzes to join them in the delusion was an entirely different matter. Moreover, the Druzes were convinced that what they knew concerning the country's past by tradition or instinctive cognizance was the real truth, and was bound to gain general acceptance sooner or later as the correct history of Lebanon.

The Christians, by and large, never despaired of winning the Druzes over to their own historical understanding of Lebanon in due course. They also believed that among the Muslims of the country, the Shiites could ultimately be persuaded to accept their view of the history of Lebanon without much difficulty. The Shiites were not in fact opposed to conceding that Lebanon had a special historicity. On the other hand, while the Druze political role in the medieval and modern history of the country had always been one of central importance, that of the Shiites had been at best a marginal one. In Ottoman times, the community had been the victim of Maronite expansionism in the northern regions, and of Druze expansionism in the south. Among the Shiites of Jabal Amil, in South Lebanon, there was in fact a rich lore which celebrated the valour of the local chiefs and heroes who had risen to defend their territory against repeated invasion from the Shuf in the days of the Shihabs; and this lore was not of a kind that endeared the memory of the Lebanese emirate to Shiite hearts. Apart from this, the local Shiites proudly remembered a time when a great tradition of Shiite religious learning had flourished in a number of Jabal Amil villages. This period was prior to the days of Ahmad Jazzar, the formidable Ottoman Pasha of Acre whose forces were sent to ravage the Shiite parts of South Lebanon, where they dispersed the more eminent among the local scholars and ransacked their libraries. Shiite religious learning, however, was only meaningful to Shiites; and while the achievements of the Jabal Amil scholars in the field were held in high esteem for a long time throughout the Shiite Muslim world, and most of all in Iran, they naturally had no impact on the Lebanese scene outside strictly Shiite circles. No effort of imagination could convincingly depict them as part of a general Lebanese heritage.

To the Druzes, who were a small Syrian Islamic sect mainly concentrated in Lebanon, Lebanese history was naturally important, and this explained why they constantly bickered with the Christians – and more particularly with the Maronites – over it. With the Shiites, however, it was a different matter. Unlike Druzism, Twelver Shiism represented one of the main religious and political departures in Islam. Far from being restricted to Lebanon, it claimed large numbers of adherents in many parts of the Islamic world. From the Shiite point of view, Lebanese history in the final analysis did not matter much. What if the Christians, or the Maronites, had falsified it to suit their purposes, as the Druzes claimed?

According to Shiite doctrine, the whole of Islamic history since the death of the Prophet, as commonly understood, was a sham, except for the brief reign of the rightful Imam Ali as caliph, and the martyrdom of his son Husayn at the battle of Karbala, as he made a last bid to redeem the legitimacy of the Islamic state and reset its history on the correct course. In the annals of Islam, as seen by the Shiites, the battle of Karabala, in AD 680, was the turning point beyond which everything in Islam, as represented first by the Umayyad and Abbasid caliphs, then by successive dynasties of sultans, was illegitimate and unjust. Compared with this enormous historical iniquity, of what significance were the rights or wrongs of the small regional history of Lebanon?

The Shiites of Lebanon, no less than the Druzes,

identified themselves as Arabs; and both communities also considered the Christians who lived among them to be Arabs, regardless of how diverse communities among these Christians chose to identify themselves. From the Shiite as from the Druze point of view, the history of any Arab country or community, in the final analysis, was Arab history. Here again, however, there was a subtle difference between the two approaches. To the Druzes, to be Arab was to belong to the Arab people or race and take pride in the Arab heritage. Like the Twelver Shiites, the Druzes, being of Ismaili Shiite origin, did not accept the first three of the Orthodox caliphs as rightful Imams; nor did they accept the religious legitimacy of the Umayyad or Abbasid caliphs as Imams. They were fully prepared, however, to regard all these caliphs as figures of Arab history, and accord them honour in this respect where honour was due. From the Druze point of view, the Fatimid caliphs, in their day, were true and infallible Imams whose succession was divinely pre-ordained in accordance with the cosmic plan. No less than the other caliphs, however, these Fatimids, quite apart from their special religious standing, could also be seen by the Druzes as figures of Arab history. In Druze religious doctrine, what really counted was eschatology rather than history. The ultimate truth was one thing, and should be kept in the heart of the believer and vindicated with the arrival of the millennium; the historical truth was another, and should be appreciated for whatever it was worth in worldly terms.

In Twelver Shiite doctrine, on the other hand, eschatology was inseparable from history. The arrival of the millennium, with the return of the Twelfth Imam, would not only vindicate the correct Islamic faith; it would also re-establish the legitimate Islamic state at the political level, and so reset the whole of history on the right course. As seen by the Twelver Shiites, Arab history since the death of the Prophet, and more particularly since the martyrdom of Husayn, had shared with Islamic history the same blemish. As it stood, and until the true cause of Islam was finally vindicated, it was only acceptable as a record of events, ultimately no more meaningful than the events of the history of Lebanon.

In fact, in Shiite opinion, while one could dismiss the main events of Lebanese history without judgement, because this history did not bear on fundamental Islamic issues, one could not do the same with the history of the Arabs to the extent that it was Islamic. Even if one were to forget the first three Orthodox caliphs, whose legitimacy the Shiites denied, how could one remain silent about the Umayyads, who tricked Ali into agreeing to have his right to the caliphate put before arbitration; usurped power after his death; then shed the hallowed blood of his son Husayn at Karbala? About the Abbasids, who betrayed the rightful Imams of the house of Ali time and again; persecuted them and their kin; and kept the last among them as miserable prisoners in their capital? Or about the Fatimids, who deluded the simple into believing that they were rightful Ismaili Imams of Islam, when they were, to Twelver Shiites as to Sunnites, no better than common impostors?

The Twelver Shiite attitude to Arab history as Islamic history was in principle unforgiving. Not all the Shiites of Lebanon, however, were theologians, and many among them were willing to accept the facts of Arab history as the Druzes or the Christians who identified themselves as Arabs did. Moreover, even religiously-minded Shiites, conscious of the minority status of their community among Arab Muslims, tended to remain quiet concerning their special historical world view. Centuries of repression had taught them not to try to explain to other Muslims what their particular interpretation of Islam really was; and even had they tried, they would have not found many receptive listeners. For religious sympathy, Arab Shiites had to look outside the predominantly Sunnite world of Arabism and turn to Iran. To the Sunnites, Islam, in principle, was one thing to all Muslims. The Shiites agreed, on the basis that Islam was what they themselves understood it to be; yet they kept their special doctrines as far as possible to themselves.

As seen by the common run of the Sunnites, Arab history

was inseparable from the history of the Sunnite Islamic state. Writing in 1948, Sati al-Husri, a leading advocate of Arab nationalism and a prominent political figure in Iraq, made this observation: the Muslim Arabs, unlike the Christian Arabs, had first conceived of their history in terms of the caliphate, following it in periods, phase by phase and dynasty by dynasty, from the Orthodox caliphs, to the Umayyads, to the Abbasids, and finally to the Ottomans. 'For this reason,' he noted, 'there was no vision of history in their minds worthy of being called Arab national history.' To the early Arab nationalists among the Muslims, Husri further noted, Arab nationalism essentially involved the reclamation of the Islamic caliphate, then held by the Turkish Ottomans, for a caliph of the Arab race. For this reason, he concluded, true Arab nationalism was first articulated by Christian Arab intellectuals who, not being Muslim, were better prepared to appreciate true Arabism without confounding it with Islam. To these Christians,

> The Arab nation was among the greatest nations in history. It had a civilization prior to Islam, and a much more developed one after Islam. Christians had participated in the development of Arab civilization before and after Islam; and this civilization was not a purely religious one, as the ignorant imagine, but exhibited numerous traits which had no connection with religion whatsoever.*

This, to Husri, was the proper nationalist view of Arab history, as distinct from the confused Islamic (strictly, the Sunnite Islamic) view; and Husri, as a Sunnite Muslim Arab, deferred to the Christian Arabs as the first to promote the idea.

The nationalist vision of Arab history, first promoted in Christian circles then generally adopted – most enthusi-astically, by Sunnite Muslims – was far more confused

---

* See Sati al-Husri, *Muhadarat fi nushu' al-fikrah al-qawmiyyah* (Cairo, 1951), pp. 122–4.

than Husri took it to be. The undeniable fact remained that the Arabs owed their stature in world history mainly to Islam. Moreover, the only political unity of which the Arabs had any historical experience was the one which had been imposed on them by Islam. Otherwise their history had always been one of baffling diversity, strongly marked by tribal and regional particularism.

Had Arab nationalism recognized Arab history for what it actually was, the concept would have developed on a firmer and more factual basis, producing a more realistic vision of what could make of the Arabs a modern nation, and what their future could be. But the task of unravelling Arab history before and after Islam in its diverse areas was not an easy undertaking. Moreover, what Arab nationalists were determined to discover and emphasize in the Arab past were elements of unity rather than diversity; and whatever elements of unity there were, if a true Arab unity it was, could not be found except in the early centuries of Islam. This was the period between the seventh and ninth centuries of the Christian era when the history of the Arabs at the imperial level only – certainly not at the parochial one – happened to be running the same course as the history of Islam.

Thus, the first three centuries of Islamic history were stripped of their non-Arab dimensions by the Arab nationalists and called Arab history. Islam, apart from being a religion, was interpreted as a movement of Arab national unification. The Islamic conquests which were undertaken by the Arabs in the name of Islam were depicted as Arab conquests. This, viewed in one perspective, was true. The earlier Islamic conquests, though undertaken in the name of Islam, did result in the actualization of Arab political dominance in areas which had long been predominantly Arab in population – notably Syria and Iraq. It was highly arguable, however, whether or not the Islamic empire of the Umayyad and Abbasid caliphs, which came to extend from the borders of Central Asia and the Indian Ocean to the Atlantic, was in fact an Arab empire. Certainly, the caliphate which stood at the head of this empire, though held by Arab dynasties, was an Islamic rather than an Arab institution, representing an Islamic rather than Arab sovereignty. More important, the imperial civilization which reached its apogee under the Abbasid caliphs of Baghdad was an Islamic rather than Arab civilization, in which non-Arabs as well as Arabs participated. This civilization, in fact, had many of its leading centres outside the Arab world.

Still, the illusion could be maintained that the history of the earlier centuries of Islam was actually Arab history; and what helped promote this illusion was the fact that Arabic, being the language of Islam as a religion and a state, naturally became the language of Islam as a cosmopolitan civilization, and continued to be so for many centuries. What remained to be explained, however, was what happened historically to the Arabs after the sovereignty over the world of Islam slipped from Arab to non-Arab hands. While Arab nationalism could appropriate Islamic history for the Arabs for the period when the Arab role in Islam was dominant, or at least clearly visible, it could not do so for the periods when the Arab role – certainly at the political level – was hardly discernible, if at all. To circumvent this problem without subjecting their theory of Arab history to radical revision, Arab nationalists had to disown the history of Islam from some point. The one chosen was the year 1258, when the Mongols sacked Baghdad and brought what remained of the nominal sovereignty of the Abbasid caliphate in their historical capital to an end. What followed, it was explained, was a period when the Arabs were in eclipse – an age of 'degeneration' or 'regression' (Arabic, *'asr inhitat*) when the Arabs fell under alien rule and were reduced to political and cultural torpor.

Thus, in Arab nationalist historical theory, Arab history came to be depicted as passing through four different phases:

1   A pre-Islamic phase when the history of the Arabs was still parochial, although their potential for subsequent greatness was already discernible.

2   A phase of unity, power and glory, which began with
    the rise and expansion of Islam under Arab leadership,
    and ended with the extinction of the Abbasid caliphate
    of Baghdad.
3   An age of degeneration when the Arabs fell under
    Turkish or Persian rule and were politically and
    culturally dormant.
4   An age of national reawakening (called '*asr al-nahdah*)
    which began in the nineteenth century and continued
    into the twentieth, pointing the way to the future.

Even during the centuries when the Arabs were in
eclipse, so the theory went, there were sporadic stirrings
here or there which indicated that the Arab national
consciousness, though dimmed and confused by general
regression, was never completely extinguished. Among the
more important of these stirrings were those that occurred
in Mount Lebanon, where a tradition of Arab autonomy
was maintained in the darkest of times. This explained, to
a great extent, why the Arab national reawakening, in the
nineteenth century, started from Lebanon. Thus, far from
ignored in Arab nationalist historical theory, Lebanon was
actually given a place of honour.

The Arab nationalist vision of Arab history did indeed
make a point of accommodating a special historicity for
Lebanon within the broader Arab context. Among the
Christian Lebanese, there remained many who were
prepared to settle for that much and no more. However, the
accepted nationalist interpretation of the Arab past was
fundamentally incorrect as history, and there were many
Muslims who recognized this from the very beginning. Not
all Sunnites were prepared to deny the Islamic legitimacy
of Mamluk and Ottoman rule over the Arab lands simply
to put their Christian Arab compatriots at ease. From the
strict Sunnite Muslim point of view, the Mamluk and
Ottoman sultanates were legitimate successors of the Arab
caliphate which had actually led Islam to further glories.
The Shiite Muslims, like the Christians and the Druzes,
were fully prepared to denounce the Mamluks and the

Ottomans as alien tyrants and oppressors. On the other hand, they were reluctant to endorse without reserve a theory of Arab history which implicitly recognized the Islamic legitimacy of Umayyad and Abbasid rule.

Until the 1970s, the Muslim Arab reserve against the historical claims of Arab nationalism – Sunnite as well as Shiite – remained an undercurrent in the Arab world. In Lebanon, the war over the exact nature of Lebanese history continued to be fought mainly under the banners of Lebanism and Arabism. With the outbreak of the Lebanese civil war, however, Islamic fundamentalism in Lebanon as elsewhere ceased to be a mere undercurrent and came to the surface, receiving a strong boost by the 1980s with the triumph of the Shiite Islamic revolution in Iran.

The Shiite Muslim Arabs had always tended to regard Arab history as having little meaning by itself, outside the context of historical Islam. The new generation of fundamentalists among the Sunnites were in full agreement with this interpretation. As these Sunnite fundamentalists now began to see it, the whole idea of Arabism was a modern Christian Arab invention deliberately aimed at breaking up the unity of Muslim ranks in the Arab world. Moreover, as an underhanded ploy devised for this sinister purpose, it was far more dangerous than the idea of Lebanism, which was no more than a frank and open expression of the justified or unjustified fears of a Christian minority inhabiting a tiny corner of the vast Islamic sphere. In many parts of the Arab world, Sunnite and Shiite Muslim fundamentalists felt an urgent need to close ranks against the claims of Arabism, where the imminent danger to Islam by internal subversion was seen to reside.

In Lebanon, this closing of fundamentalist ranks among the Muslims produced a complete reshuffle of positions. Certainly among the Sunnites, fundamentalism was restricted to small groups of activists. Among the Shiites also, the truly committed among the fundamentalists were reckoned to be no more than a small minority. In both cases, however, the fundamentalists were organized and often well armed, and enjoyed strong external political support from Iran.

While their public platform was seriously disturbing to the common run of Christians, the fundamentalists appeared as a direct danger most of all to their own Muslim communities, whose accepted way of life they threatened to disrupt. Thus, many Muslims in the country, and most notably the Sunnites of Beirut, became increasingly conscious of an urgent need to join forces with the Christians, under whatever conditions, in a common Lebanese stand to stem the fundamentalist tide. The Druzes also were gravely disturbed by the Muslim fundamentalist surge, which threatened sooner or later to reopen the unsettled question of their acceptability as an Islamic community. To the Druzes, Arabism had offered an ideal way out of the predicament they had historically faced. In the predominantly Muslim Arab world, where the Islamic validity of their special religious doctrines could not easily be recognized, they could most readily find a place for themselves as Arabs among Arabs. In this respect, their attitude was no different from that of the Christian Arabs in Lebanon and elsewhere who favoured Arabism for the same reason. Moreover, Druzes and Christians in Lebanon had lived together in the same towns and villages for centuries, so that the Druze way of life, at the traditional no less than at the evolved level, was not much different in many respects from that of the Christians. On this count also, the Druzes looked upon Islamic fundamentalism with unconcealed abhorrence.

Paradoxically, while most Muslims, along with the Druzes and the common run of the Christians, were alarmed by the forceful appearance of Islamic fundamentalism on the Lebanese scene, the more extreme Christian advocates of Lebanism viewed the increasing activism of the Muslim fundamentalists with a satisfaction which they rarely bothered to hide. To them, it provided the ultimate confirmation of what they had always said concerning Islam: that Muslims, politically, could not be trusted, and that their co-existence with Christians on equal terms in the same country was not possible without special political guarantees for the Christians. More important, the Christians in Lebanon who were most open in their castigation of political Islam were the ones who agreed most with the Muslim fundamentalists in their negative outlook towards Arabism and Arab history. To the Christian as to the Muslim extremists, what the Arab nationalists called Arab history was no more than a doctored version of the history of Islam, and a poorly doctored one at that – a view which, in fact, was objectively correct. From this view, now strongly and openly endorsed by Islamic fundamentalism among the Shiites and Sunnites alike, the Christian extremists were quick to draw the corollary: Arabism, in Lebanon as elsewhere in the Arab world, had never been anything more than a Muslim pretence or a Christian delusion.

If there had never been such a thing as historical Arabism, had there ever been such a thing as historical Lebanism, or was Lebanism also a pretence or a delusion? Could it be that both sides in the war over Lebanese history were wrong, and that the historical truth lay elsewhere? Or were both sides right, but viewing the same historical truth from different angles? And in either case, is there such a thing as an absolute historical truth regarding the matter in question? As the issue was debated in the country to the accompaniment of fighting and massive destruction, there were those who further wondered: were prizes intended for everybody at the end of the game? Would there be winners and losers; or was it an endless game which no side could win or lose?

12 A house of many mansions

For any people to develop and maintain a sense of political community, it is necessary that they share a common vision of their past. In communities having a natural solidarity, fictionalized history often suffices for this purpose. This remains true of tribes alleging descent from mythical ancestors and honouring the memory of legendary heroes, as well as of some highly advanced nations which popularly claim for themselves more national history than is their due, or distort what history they actually have in the manner most flattering to the national ego, with the assistance or to the dismay of their historians.

For a historical fiction to serve a political purpose, however, it must be generally accepted. While this acceptance may be common in societies which have a high degree of homogeneity at more than one level, and where differences at other levels are of a minimum, it is more difficult to achieve in societies which are heterogeneous in structure, and which happen to exist mainly because circumstances somehow brought their different component elements together. In a society having a heterogeneous structure, historical fictions that flatter one group may turn out to be unflattering and sometimes highly objection-able to others, and only a fiction which is equally complimentary to all the parties concerned can stand a chance of gaining common acceptance. Even then, the political success of the fiction remains conditional, varying with the unpredictable fluctuations of the society balanced precariously between stability and instability.

In short, historical self-deception is a luxury which only societies confident of their unity and solidarity can afford. Such societies, having an ample fund of common sentiment and shared interests to rely on, can easily escape with cherishing fictional or fictionalized versions of their past, the more flattering the better, leaving proper history for the historians. Divided societies, on the other hand, cannot afford such fanciful indulgence. To gain the degree of solidarity that is needed to maintain viability, their best chance lies in getting to know and understand the full truth of their past, and to accommodate to its realities. Factual history, in cases of this kind, has often to be forcibly extracted from the privacy of the historian's study, and thrown undressed and dishevelled into the open, for all to see it as it is and learn to accept and live with it as best they can.

Lebanon today is a political society condemned to know and understand the real facts of its history if it seeks to survive. How the thorny complexities of the present conflict in Lebanon will ultimately be resolved is not a matter for historians to determine. Certainly, however, no political settlement in the country can be lasting unless it takes questions of history into account. Before the people of Lebanon can hope to develop the degree of social solidarity that can enable them to stand together as a coherent and viable political community, they have to know precisely what they are, and how they relate to the world around them. This means that they have to learn exactly why and how they came to be Lebanese, given the original historical and other differences between them. Otherwise, regardless of how the present quarrel in Lebanon is patched up, they will continue to be so many tribes (the current euphemism is 'spiritual families'): each tribe forever suspicious and distrustful of the others; each tribe always alert, extending feelers to the outside world in different directions, probing for possible sources of external support in preparation for yet another round of open conflict.

What applies to Lebanon in this respect also applies to the whole Arab world. What Arab nationalism, which is a phenomenon of the last hundred years, continues to propose and promote as Arab national history is no less fictionalized than the history of Lebanon. It has succeeded in deluding the general run of the Arabs into believing that the political unity they had once experienced under Islam was in fact an Arab national unity which they have subsequently lost, or of which they have been deliberately robbed; and this makes it difficult for them to properly accommodate to the political realities of their present. The only difference is that the confusion between Arabism and Islam, which began with the earliest days of Arab nationalism, did succeed in convincing most Arabs that the political and cultural history of Islam, to the extent that it bore on the Arab past, was in fact Arab national history. This presented no problem to the Muslim Arabs, but it did present a serious problem to the non-Muslims, who could not as easily relate to the fiction. Today, however, Islamic fundamentalism reclaims the Islamic history of the Arab world for Islam, and Arab nationalism, certainly with respect to the dubious historical rationale behind it, finds itself in serious trouble. This Islamic reclamation of what has long passed for Arab national history leaves the Christian Arabs at a loss as to how to proceed, and confirms the old suspicions among them about the authenticity and sincerity of claims of Arabism where such suspicions exist. In the case of Lebanon, this further underlines the differences among the Lebanese, and makes the search for the true historical identity of their country all the more complex.

To gain the needed historical knowledge and understanding of themselves at the required level of accuracy, where are the Lebanese to begin? For a start, a general cleaning up of the cobwebs in their various communal attics would help. All prejudice and counter-prejudice regarding the past of Lebanon and of the Arabs would have to be thrown out. In the preceding chapters, some critical assessment was made of the different theories of the Lebanese past advanced by the Christian Lebanese political establishment to promote the idea of a historical Lebanese nationality. None of these theories have so far proved generally marketable. The Muslims and Druzes in Lebanon could easily spot the flaws in them and surmise the distinctly Christian political motives behind them. Also, the Muslim and Druze attitudes regarding the history of Lebanon have been surveyed and subjected to summary analysis. Apart from correctly emphasizing the basic Arabism of Lebanon, which the Christian theories of Lebanese history deliberately underemphasize or ignore, these Muslim and Druze attitudes remain elemental and poorly formulated, particularly as they fail to define exactly what the historical Arabism of Lebanon involves. As they stand, they can barely be considered anything more than surly reactions to the fundamental Christian attitude on the matter. In either case, what is actually in question is a hard and fast political position rather than an open-minded and genuine search for the reasoned historical understanding that is required. This leaves the question of the Lebanese past in the realm of polemics, rather than in the realm of history where all questions regarding the past of societies legitimately belong.

For the rethinking of Lebanese history to be successful, it has to start from a clean slate. There are some important facts of the present to be taken into account. Regardless of whether or not Lebanon did have a special history before a particular time, the country has certainly been in existence within its internationally recognized borders since 1920, and has shown itself to be remarkably durable. The years of civil war since 1975 have torn Lebanon internally to shreds, reduced large parts of the country to rubble, and caused massive movements of population between different regions; but the civil war has failed as yet to destroy the fundamental political and administrative structure of the Lebanese Republic or to put an end to its existence as a sovereign territorial state by removing it from the map.

So far, the Christians of the country, whatever the rights or wrongs of their case, have proved irreducible by force. The Muslims – Sunnite or Shiite – and the Druzes have proved equally irreducible. The two sides remain in strong disagreement on how the Lebanese Republic ought to be generally interpreted and run; but both sides, certainly at the level of the hard core, appear to have become equally convinced that there can be no viable alternative to Lebanon as territorially constituted. The war lords on either side fiercely hold on to the communal cantons they have come to head as virtually independent despots, and none among them show much intention of yielding any of their acquired powers for the general good. Yet, these same war lords, to maintain some public credibility, feel compelled to declare themselves in principle, every so often, for the continued existence and fundamental territorial integrity of the country, even as they persist in acting to the contrary. In their public statements, all of them normally claim that their ultimate aim is to secure the reconstitution of a viable Lebanon.

There is also the changed Arab attitude towards Lebanon to consider in rethinking the country's history. While some Arab parties at one time did express varying degrees of reserve about the peculiar political standing of Lebanon in the Arab world, none do so at present, and not too much remains of the earlier Arab investments in Lebanese political discord. At the present stage of the Lebanese conflict, no Arab party openly declares itself for one Lebanese side against the other – normally, the Muslim against the Christian – as some had done at the earlier stages. In fact, all of them have finally begun to express deep concern about the continuing plight of Lebanon, and seem genuinely to press for a Lebanese political settlement which would be fair to Christians and Muslims alike.

In the Arab world today, the Lebanese identity is generally accepted for the reality it has become; no one any longer denounces it as an extravagant claim. Also, in many Arab circles, the general Arab culpability for what happened to Lebanon has finally come to be openly admitted and condemned. Certainly at the level of Arab political responsibility, a mood of rational understanding and political realism with regard to Lebanon is now noticeable. Arabs who have a sincere concern for the welfare of Lebanon fear that this mood may not survive the Lebanese conflict; but it is certainly there for the moment.

From these facts of the present, three important conclusions may be drawn which bear on the question of the historical reinterpretation of Lebanon.

1 The bitter experience of the civil war has amply demonstrated that neither side in Lebanon can easily force its opinion on the other. This means that the problems of Lebanon – including those concerning Lebanese history – can only be resolved by rational give-and-take among the Lebanese people in the light of the relevant realities.

2 There are clear indications that the country, despite all appearances to the contrary, has somehow arrived at a stage of fundamental political consensus involving the non-combatant majority among the different Lebanese communities, and perhaps others as well. Its continued existence as a sovereign and independent state within its present borders, should it come to be somehow secured, would now be possible regardless of whether or not there was such a thing as Lebanon before 1920. This means that one need not invent a special history for Lebanon before that date unless the country happens to have one.

3 The Arab world, whatever its initial position on the question of Lebanon, has come to accept the Lebanese Republic as it actually exists, and to understand and appreciate the delicate structure of Lebanese society, certainly for the time being, as at no time before. This means that the admission of the historical Arabism of Lebanon, to the extent that it is a fact, no longer need be taken to involve any danger to the continued sovereignty and integrity of the country; nor need it threaten the status of any particular group among the Lebanese, granting that it could have involved such a danger in the past. One may argue that the Arabs have finally become solicitous of the

continued sovereignty and integrity of Lebanon because they have come to realize that the undoing of Lebanon can easily spill out to the rest of the Arab world and result in the undoing of other Arab countries and regimes. If this is the case, it would provide the ultimate guaranty that the present expressed Arab concern for the welfare of Lebanon is genuine for as long as it may last, for the very reason that it has complex ulterior motives involving a general Arab self-interest.

In the opening chapter of this book, it was pointed out that the reluctance of the Christian political establishment in Lebanon to make the needed concession to the reality of Arabism lay at the very root of the country's original problem. Because they did not claim for themselves a historical nationality separate and distinct from the common Arab nationality, other Arab countries which came into being after the first world war, at about the same time as Lebanon, did not have much difficulty accepting themselves and recognizing one another as legitimate Arab states. Because the Christian Lebanese hesitated or declined to do the same, and at the same time claimed for the different communities which happened to form the population of Lebanon a special historical nationality separate and distinct from the common Arabism, they kept the legitimacy of the Lebanese state in question not only for other Arabs, but also for large and important sectors of the Lebanese population.

Today, however, the situation is different. A distinct sense of territorial identity has in fact come to exist among the Lebanese, as among the peoples of other Arab countries – to all effects, a sense of special state nationality which in most cases is strong enough not to need historical justification. At the same time, throughout the Arab world, there is a consciousness of common Arab identity – at its weakest, a latent sense of Arab community – which can only be politically disregarded at some cost. To this extent, Arabism remains an important political reality which all Arabs and people dealing with the Arab world have to take into account. And Arabism, again, need not be historically justified. It simply has to be understood for what it is: a primordial bond which unites the Arabs at some levels without overriding all the differences between them, but which certainly has the power to make them feel deeply guilty when they wilfully or unwilfully ignore its subtle imperatives.

The question of religion is central to the rethinking of Lebanese history. It has already been remarked that one of the main weaknesses of Arab nationalism as an idea was the fact that it originally confused and continues to confuse the history of the Arabs with the history of Islam. To make the proper distinction between these two related yet different strains of history is not easy – if for no other reason, because the Arabs, historically, only had a common history when they happened to fall together under the rule of Islam, and to the extent that they did actually fall under the same Islamic sovereignty at different periods. Moreover, because the overwhelming majority of the Arabs happen to be Muslim, Islam naturally underlines the sense of common ethnicity among most Arabs, as it underlines the sense of ethnicity among other Islamic peoples, such as the Iranians or the Turks. Unlike other Islamic peoples, however, the Arabs are not all Muslim. Historically, Judaism and Christianity flourished among the Arabs long before the coming of Islam; and throughout Islamic times, important communities of Jewish and Christian Arabs continued to thrive in different parts of the Arab world, albeit under certain social and legal restrictions.

In the present century, the Zionist movement was successful in eroding and ultimately eradicating Jewish Arabism, even to the extent of virtually effacing its memory following the emergence of the Jewish State of Israel in Palestine in 1948. The Christian Arabs, however, remain important to this day. One community among them – the Maronites in Lebanon – stands at the head of one of the modern Arab states. Moreover, the Muslim Arabs do not all follow the same brand of Islam, as do the Iranians who are predominantly Shiite, or the Turks who are overwhelmingly Sunnite. To be fully Arab in ethnic identity, though not necessarily in actual political commitment to Arabism, one need not be a Sunnite, Shiite or Kharijite Muslim any more than one need be a Muslim at all.

When ordinary Christian Arabs find their Muslim compatriots identifying themselves as Muslims and as Arabs in the same breath, they naturally feel excluded and repelled – in extreme cases, to the point of dissociating themselves from Arabism. Yet, these same Christian Arabs almost invariably find themselves unvolitionally rising to the defence of Islam at the slightest external provocation. When they fail to do so, or when in extreme frustration they succumb to the temptation of attacking Islam in the presence of outsiders, they normally end up feeling that they have betrayed a cause which they in some way deeply share.

Despite frequent pretences to the contrary, the Islamic world, even beyond the precincts of Arabism, is in some respects less alien to Christian Arabs than the Western Christian world with which they share their religion, and in many instances much of their acquired culture. This applies to the Maronites of Lebanon as much as it applies to others. Ordinary Christian Arabs, regardless of their day-to-day frustrations with Islam, instinctively feel they have an inalienable right to their say in Islamic affairs; and the more confident a Christian community is of its political standing, the more strongly it partakes of this feeling. At the last Islamic summit conference held in Kuwait in 1987, Amin Gemayel, the Maronite president of the Lebanese Republic, made a point of attending and participating in this distinctly pan-Islamic political function in person as the representative and legitimate spokesman for Lebanon. At earlier conferences of the kind, it was the Muslim premiers of Lebanon who used to attend, ostensibly as the representatives of the Muslims of the country rather than of the Lebanese state as a whole. No Christian in Lebanon went on record as being opposed to the decision of the Maronite president to set the precedent of attending

Islamic summit conferences; and regardless of the particular political motives that made him take this decision at the time, or how it was viewed by the Muslim Lebanese, or among the Muslim heads of state who found a Christian colleague for the first time claiming a rightful place in their midst, the event was of considerable symbolical significance. It implied that the Christians of Lebanon, no matter how staunchly Christian they may feel, still consider themselves to be intrinsically part of the world of Islam, no less than the Muslims of the country.

To understand the Christian Arab position on this point, one must bear in mind that Islam is not only a religion, but also a world society whose history bears on all the communities and peoples that participated in it down the centuries – Muslim and non-Muslim alike. Moreover, the Christian Arabs share with Islam its Arabic language, and therefore much of its heritage in that language, as well as fully sharing in the ethnicity of the Arabs as the first of the Islamic peoples. For this reason, they have always felt far more closely integrated with Islamic society than other Christian peoples of the Islamic world.

Islam as a religion has always drawn hard lines to distinguish in law between Muslims and non-Muslims living under its rule, and there were many times in their history when the Christian Arabs smarted under this discrimination no less than others. Yet, Islam remains directly meaningful to them as a great march of history and historical civilization to which the Arabs – Christian as well as Muslim – owe their stature in the annals of the world. This Christian vision of the Islamic past of the Arabs first found expression in the Christian Arabic literature of the nineteenth century, most of which was of what would be called today Lebanese authorship. At about the turn of the century, it provided the inspiration for the romantic historical novels on Islam written by Jurji Zaydan, the Greek Orthodox Christian from Beirut who founded the well-known Egyptian publishing firm called Dar al-Hilal. Zaydan also made a point of writing a history of Islamic civilization (*Tarikh al-tamaddun al-Islami*).

The same Christian Arab sentiment for Islam also stands out, for example, in the published works of two prominent Christian Lebanese scholars of Islamic law and jurisprudence, the Maronite Emile Tyan, and the Greek Catholic Edmond Rabbath. The Christian Arab poets who have sung and continue to sing the past glories of Arabism along with those of Islam are beyond count, and the Maronites hold a particularly prominent place among them.

This being the case, would it be possible to gain full comprehension of the subtleties of the Christian sector of Lebanon, let alone its Muslim side, independently of the historical context of Islam? Before emerging as a state in the present century, Lebanon, strictly, was neither Syrian nor Arab historical territory. Since the seventh century of the Christian era, it had been officially part and parcel of the world of Islam. Throughout this time, and except for the period of the Crusades during the eleventh and twelfth centuries, all legal authority on the territory of present-day Lebanon ultimately derived from an Islamic sovereignty: that of the Umayyad, Abbasid or Fatimid caliphs; then that of the Seljuk, Ayyubid, Mamluk or Ottoman sultans. The same applied to all other parts of the eastern Arab world except the Yemen and Oman, where the Zaydi Shiite Imams in one case, and the Ibadi Kharijite Imams in the other, claimed the paramount Islamic sovereignty for themselves; more often than not they were successful in actualizing this claimed sovereignty over their respective countries in part or in full. One other exception was the first Wahhabi state which emerged in central Arabia in the eighteenth century. It rejected the Islamic legitimacy of Ottoman rule as a matter of principle in favour of another local Islamic arrangement based on a special puritan reinterpretation of the Islamic faith. Iraq between the sixteenth and seventeeth centuries was only an exception to the general rule, in the sense that Islamic sovereignty over this particular Arab territory was a matter of dispute at the time between the Sunnite Islamic state of Istanbul and the Shiite Islamic state in Persia. The same applied to some parts of eastern Arabia, most notably to the islands of

Bahrain which fell under Persian rule continuously from 1602 until 1783.

To Patriarch Istifan Duwayhi, writing the general chronicle entitled *Tarikh al-azmina* which embodied the annals of the Maronites and those of Mount Lebanon and the rest of Syria down to his time, the Islamic state in its different phases provided, not surprisingly, the principal frame of reference. The period of this scholarship was the latter decades of the seventeenth century, when the Ottoman state still stood near the peak of its power. As indicated in an earlier chapter, Duwayhi first called his chroncile *Tarikh al-Muslimin*: literally, 'The history of the Muslims'. The choice of this first title on the part of the learned Maronite patriarch for his principal historical work is significant. More significant is the fact that Duwayhi also thought it appropriate to introduce the history of his own Christian community into this particular chronicle – its political and social and even its ecclesiastical history – as an aggregate of parochial detail ultimately relating to the general annals of Islam.

Essentially, however, the history of Islam is a history of empire and civilization which provides no more than the broader framework for the understanding of the history of the Arab world in medieval and modern times. What it says must not always be taken at face value. It speaks of institutions which were not always consistently operative, and of sovereignties which were seldom as effective as their theoretical claim. To comprehend the nature of these historical Islamic institutions and sovereignties is highly important, but in most cases falls far short of telling the entire story. For most of the time, the history of the Arabs under Islam had little more than a tangential bearing on the mainstream of Islamic history.

Even during the relatively brief period when the Arabs actually stood at the head of the Islamic empire, Arab history was not restricted to the history of the caliphate as the sovereign institution in Islam, but equally involved a whole complex of regional, sectarian and tribal rebellions against the established Islamic order. Once the Arab ascendancy in Islam ceased to exist, the history of the Arabs became, to all effects, so many different regional experiences, each to be understood for what it was, much as was the case before Islam. In different parts of the Arab world, different autonomies emerged and disintegrated under different internal and external circumstances. In some cases, the emergence of such regional autonomies produced local flowerings of Arabic culture which enriched the Arab as well as the general Islamic heritage. This, for example, was the case with the Arab principality which arose in northern Syria in the tenth century AD under the Hamdanids of Aleppo. It was also the case with some of the principalities that flourished in the Yemen between the tenth and fifteenth centuries. There were many instances, however, when the regional Arab autonomies rose and fell with monotonous regularity, without leaving anything of value behind by which they can be remembered.

In parts of the Arab world which happen to have the geographical constitution of natural countries, such as the Yemen or Oman, the rise and fall of local autonomies, generally taking place within set territorial limits, could easily pass for an understandable continuum of local history. In other parts, however, such real or apparent historical continuity was rare, as the territory of one autonomy did not necessarily conform in extent to the territory of the autonomy that preceded it, or the one that followed. This was very much as it was with geographical Syria – the Bilad al-Sham of the Arabs – which includes the territory of present-day Lebanon. Here, however, as in some other parts of the Arab world, the local history was not restricted to the usual humdrum stories about the rise and fall of regional autonomies which in many cases failed to outlive the meteoric careers of the political adventurers who were their founders. It also involved a far more coherent type of history: that of specific religious communities which were highly organized at more than one level, and which had a distinct advantage over their neighbours in regional compactness and group solidarity.

This was most eminently the case with the Maronites and Druzes of Mount Lebanon.

With the Maronites and the Druzes, we come to the heart of the matter: the question of the historical origins of modern Lebanon. What we have here are two sects, both equally Arab in ethnicity, one Christian, the other Islamic, set apart from the other Christian and Muslim sects of historical Syria by the readily demonstrable continuity of their respective histories. In each case, the solidarity of the sect, though essentially tribal or quasi-tribal in nature, derives additional strength from its religious organization. Among the Maronites, the institution of the patriarchate is approximately as old as Islam, although its history can barely be reconstructed any earlier than the eleventh century. Among the Druzes, the councils of initiates which maintain the discipline of the community at the religious level date back at least to the fifteenth century, and there are indications that they existed in some form before then. In both cases, the religious organization of the community has provided it down the centuries not only with a constant frame of reference, but also with a receptacle for its historical experience. When historians today speak of the medieval and early modern history of Lebanon, what they actually have in mind is for the most part Maronite and Druze history.

The Maronites and the Druzes are not the only sects in the Arab world that can boast of a political as well as a religious history dating back many centuries. The Ibadis of Oman and the Zaydis of the Yemen can certainly make the same boast. The Wahhabis, who appeared on the Arabian scene much later, can also claim a political as well as a religious history. Starting from the seventeenth century, the originally different historical careers of the Maronites and Druzes in Mount Lebanon began to intertwine at the political level into one story: the story of the quasi-autonomy enjoyed by the two communities in Mount Lebanon under the Maan and Shihab emirs. Here again, the political developments involved were not unique, but fitted into a general pattern which involved similar political developments in other parts of the eastern Arab world at the same time, and in other historical periods.

At this juncture another matter may be considered. Had the regime of the Maan and Shihab emirs in Mount Lebanon disappeared before the nineteenth century, its historical relevance to the emergence of modern Lebanon would have hardly existed. As it happened, however, this regime in Mount Lebanon continued long enough into the nineteenth century to witness the beginning of the direct Western political and military impact on the Ottoman world – an impact that ultimately resulted in the destruction of the Ottoman empire and the emergence of the modern Middle Eastern states from its ruins. When the regime of the Lebanese emirs finally collapsed, the Western powers were already active on the scene, and all of them took an interest in preserving some special political status for Mount Lebanon, where the strong Christian presence, and the quarrels that now erupted between the Maronites and the Druzes, provided them with ready avenues for political intervention in the affairs of Ottoman Syria. Thus, they saw to it that the emirate in the mountain was replaced by other administrative arrangements on the same territory in order to retain its special political character under their collective guaranty. This privileged status for Mount Lebanon was successfully maintained until the moment when the destruction of the Ottoman empire finally arrived with the first world war. Subsequently, Mount Lebanon became the political nucleus around which the State of Greater Lebanon was formed.

In this respect also, the Lebanese case is not unique but fits into the broader pattern of modern Arab history. The Western powers in the Arab world, starting with the nineteenth century, did not restrict their political angling to Mount Lebanon. They pressed and probed wherever they could; and in every case, they sought to gain their ends by offering guarantees for the perpetuation of some threatened local autonomy or quasi-autonomy, or by taking advantage of political or tribal differences and quarrels wherever they happened to find them. In Mount Lebanon, the general

Western interest in preserving the special political status was spearheaded by France. In other parts of the eastern Arab world, the initiative was British. This remained the only difference. Otherwise, in all cases where the Arab autonomies or quasi-autonomies coming under Western protection were perpetuated long enough, they ultimately emerged as independent Arab states, or served as political nucleuses for the emergence of such states.

To understand the political past of Lebanon as Arab history, one must discount the erroneous Arab nationalist view of this history as a united national march that went wrong at some point, and correctly assess it as the parochial history that it normally was: an account of so many different Arab regional experiences of one kind or another, fitting more or less into a general pattern. No Arab country today need feel any guilt about accepting its actual existence as a wilful or unwilful departure from an Arab national historical norm. It is only when the Arabs succeed in ridding themselves of the highly idealized Arab nationalist vision of their past that they will be able to live together in the modern Arab world as a coherent political community whose various members – including Lebanon – relate to one another constructively and without reserve.

In the case of Lebanon, however, there is more than the political side to the story. Because the different communities which came to form the population of Lebanon in 1920 remain in serious disagreement over issues which are fundamentally political, they continue to think of the past that relates to Lebanon mainly in political terms. This often blinds them to other facts of their past which largely account for their present standing in the social and cultural vanguard of the modern Arab world. Politically, the past of Lebanon mostly involves a Maronite-Druze story in which other Lebanese communities played only marginal roles, if any. The story of the social and cultural development of Lebanese society, on the other hand, is one which can be eminently meaningful to all the people of the country.

Admittedly, it was the French, in political collusion with

the Maronites, who created Lebanon as a political entity in 1920 and put its different social ingredients together for the first time. France, however, did not create these ingredients, which were already in existence in different compartments of the country long before. One may further maintain that the general Western interest in Beirut and Mount Lebanon, starting from the last century, was a prime contributor to the development of certain sectors of the present Lebanese population, and that this external rather than internal initiative largely accounts for the advanced standing which Lebanon came to enjoy in the modern Arab world at the social and cultural levels. However, no outside agency could have created the apparently indigenous resourcefulness and ingenuity of the people of Lebanon, their exceptional adaptability, and their attested potential for development.

Among the Lebanese people, the Christians were the first to begin adapting to the ways of the modern world, and the Shiites among the Muslims were the last. In all cases, however, the process of adaptation and development created social and economic tensions between the different Lebanese communities, and also within each community, which invariably resulted in political conflict and outbreaks of violence. This, at least, is the way the social development of modern Lebanon since the last century is viewed by one Shiite Lebanese intellectual of the younger generation, Talal Husseini. Speaking of the present, Husseini depicts the continuing political conflict in Lebanon as a surface phenomenon which is bound to vanish once all the different confessional elements in Lebanese society, including his own community, become equally adapted to the modern world. Behind the violence of the civil war, he sees cultural rather than political, social or economic disparities, producing the existing political and social confusion as they instinctively seek be be rectified. Writing on 3 December 1981 for the Beirut daily *Al-Nahar*, he remarked:

> The overwhelming majority among the Lebanese have a strong hunger for civilization . . . What civilization they have

achieved has not all been vain pretence. Some of it has been real ... The competitiveness among them in the pursuit of civilization is perhaps the prime justification for the [present] war. Yet, herein also ... lies the most serious defect of civilization among the Lebanese ... The essence of the idea of civilization entails that it should commonly apply to all those with an equal claim to belonging to the city, without regard to any difference of origin. Nevertheless, it is not correct for us to consider that those [in Lebanon] who have been ahead of others in acquiring civilization and its means – who are by majority Christian – are the party guilty for the fact that civilization has not come to include all the resident population. Nor is it correct to assume that this civilization, in its first impact, could have been generally applied ... Being Western in its essence, it appealed more readily to the Christian community, because of the symbolic communion [between it and the West] in the same religious heritage ... In any case, [what Lebanon has had] is a civilization; and the desire for its proper acquisition, and its general application at the fundamental level, is a matter on which the destiny of the Lebanese depends, considering that their success in transforming their country from Lebanon the Refuge, to the Lebanon of the One Civilization, is their only chance of survival.*

Here is one emerging view of Lebanon, essentially histori-cal, which looks beyond the details of political history and conceives of Lebanese society during the last two centuries as the unique experience of one people of the modern Arab world with Western civilization – an experience which must succeed and transcend all community differences among the Lebanese people if Lebanon is to survive. In a way, it is a view which involves prizes for everybody. In its light, as in the light of other views of the same kind which the present sufferings of the Lebanese people may help proliferate, the past of Lebanon ceases to be a question of

---

* Also published in a collection of essays by the same author entitled *Al-Awham wa'l-umur wa'l-ashya'* (Beirut, 1983), pp. 41–2.

political rights and wrongs, of outstanding tribal or quasi-tribal scores to be settled, and acquires more meaning with respect to the present – and even more, with respect to the future.

In the final analysis, history is not merely a search for knowledge. It is also a search for understanding; and the house of understanding has many mansions. As the mere story of the past, history can only have an antiquarian value, and as such can be left to the scholars. To be socially meaningful and useful, it has to be given all the relevant dimensions. Should the Lebanese attics one day be properly swept, there would be no end to the ways in which the history of Lebanon could be reinterpreted – for the good of Lebanon, and also for the welfare of the Arab world.

Select Bibliography

Abu-Husayn, Abdul-Rahim. *Provincial Leaderships in Syria, 1575–1650.* Beirut, American University of Beirut, 1985.

Ajami, Fouad. *The Vanished Imam: Musa al–Sadr and the Shia of Lebanon.* London, I.B. Tauris, 1986.

Bakhit, Muhammad Adnan. *The Ottoman Province of Damascus in the Sixteenth Century.* Beirut, Librairie du Liban, 1982.

Beydoun, Ahmad. *Identité confessionnelle et temps social chez les historiens libanais contemporains.* Beirut, Lebanese University, 1984.

Binder, Leonard, ed. *Politics in Lebanon.* New York, Wiley, 1966.

Buheiri, Marwan. *The Formation and Perception of the Modern Arab World: Studies by Marwan Buheiri.* Lawrence I. Conrad, Tarif Khalidi and Basim Musallam eds. Princeton, Darwin Press, 1988.

Chevallier, Dominique. *La Société du Mont-Liban à l'époque de la révolution industrielle en Europe.* Paris, Geuthner, 1971.

Fawaz, Leila Tarazi. *Merchants and Migrants in Nineteenth-Century Beirut.* Cambridge, Mass., Harvard University Press, 1983.

Gordon, David C. *Lebanon: the Fragmented Nation.* London, Croom Helm, 1980.

Havemann, Axel. *Rurale Bewegunen in Libanongebirge des 19 Jahrhunderts: ein Beitrag zur Problematik Sozialer Veranderungen.* Berlin, Klaus Schwarz Verlag, 1983.

Haddad, Robert, M. *Syrian Christians in Muslim Society: an Interpretation.* Westport, Conn., Greenwood Press, 1970.

Hourani, Albert. *Syria and Lebanon: a Political Essay*. London, Oxford University Press, 1946.

——. *Minorities in the Arab World*. London, Oxford University Press, 1947.

——. *A Vision of History*. Beirut, Khayats, 1961.

——. *Arabic Thought in the Liberal Age, 1798–1939*. Revised edn, Cambridge, Cambridge University Press, 1983.

——. *Europe and the Middle East*. London, Macmillan, 1980.

——. *The Emergence of the Modern Middle East*. London, Macmillan, 1981.

Hudson, Michael C. *The Precarious Republic: Political Modernization in Lebanon*. New York, Random House, 1968.

Johnson, Michael. *Class and Client in Beirut: the Sunni Muslim Community and the Lebanese State, 1840–1895*. London, Ithaca Press, 1986.

Khoury, Philip S. *Syria and the French Mandate: the Politics of Arab Nationalism, 1920–1945*. London, I.B. Tauris, 1987.

Khuri, Fuad I. *From Village to Suburb: Order and Change in Greater Beirut*. Chicago, Chicago University Press, 1975.

Longrigg, Stephen Hemsley. *Syria and Lebanon under French Mandate*. London, Oxford University Press, 1958.

Moosa, Matti. *The Maronites in History*. Syracuse, NY, Syracuse University Press, 1986.

Norton, Augustus Richard. *Amal and the Shia Struggle for the Soul of Lebanon*. Austin, University of Texas Press, 1987.

Owen, Roger, ed. *Essays on the Crisis in Lebanon*. London, Ithaca Press, 1976.

Polk, William. *The Opening of South Lebanon, 1788–1840*. Cambridge, Mass., Harvard University Press, 1963.

Rabinovich, Itamar. *The War for Lebanon, 1970–1987*. Ithaca, NY, Cornell University Press, 1984.

Rafeq, Abdul-Karim. *The Province of Damascus, 1723–1783*. Beirut, Khayats, 1966.

Rondot, Pierre. *Les Chrétiens d'Orient*. Paris, Peyronnet, n.d.

Salibi, Kamal S. *Crossroads to Civil War: Lebanon 1958–1976*. Delmar, NY, Caravan Books, 1976.

——. *Maronite Historians of Medieval Lebanon*. Beirut, American University of Beirut, 1959.

——. *The Modern History of Lebanon*. London, Weidenfeld and Nicolson, 1965.

——. *Syria Under Islam: Empire on Trial, 634–1097 A.D.* Delmar, NY, Caravan Books, 1977.

——. *Muntalaq tarikh Lubnan, 634–1516*. Beirut, Caravan Books, 1979.

Spagnolo, John. *France and Ottoman Lebanon: 1861–1914*. London, Ithaca Press, 1977.

Tibawi, A.L. *A Modern History of Syria including Lebanon and Palestine*. London, Macmillan, 1969.

Yamak, Labib Zuwiyya. *The Syrian Social Nationalist Party: an Ideological Analysis*. Cambridge, Mass., Harvard University Press, 1966.

Zamir, Meir. *The Formation of Modern Lebanon*. London, Croom Helm, 1985.

Index

238